ICONiC

www.penguin.co.uk

Also by Zandra Rhodes

THE ART OF ZANDRA RHODES
ZANDRA RHODES: A LIFELONG LOVE
AFFAIR WITH TEXTILES
ZANDRA RHODES: 50 FABULOUS YEARS IN FASHION

ICONiC

MY LIFE IN FASHION IN 50 OBJECTS

Zandra Rhodes

WITH ELLA ALEXANDER

bantam

TRANSWORLD PUBLISHERS

Penguin Random House, One Embassy Gardens,
8 Viaduct Gardens, London SW11 7BW
www.penguin.co.uk

Transworld is part of the Penguin Random House group of companies
whose addresses can be found at global.penguinrandomhouse.com

First published in Great Britain in 2024 by Bantam
an imprint of Transworld Publishers

A CIP catalogue record for this book
is available from the British Library.

ISBN 9780857505217

Typeset in 12/15.5 pt Minion Pro by Jouve (UK), Milton Keynes
Printed and bound in Great Britain by Clays Ltd, Elcograf S.p.A.

The authorized representative in the EEA is Penguin Random House Ireland,
Morrison Chambers, 32 Nassau Street, Dublin D02 YH68.

Penguin Random House is committed to a sustainable future
for our business, our readers and our planet. This book is made
from Forest Stewardship Council® certified paper.

I dedicate this book to my mother Beatrice, who shaped and guided my life from the very beginning, to Salah who entered my life so unexpectedly and enabled me to fulfil my dreams, and, finally, to my sister Beverley, who has patiently always been my supportive, amazing sister.

Contents

1980s

1990s

My name is Zandra Rhodes and I am a self-confessed hoarder. My home overflows with curiosities that I have collected throughout the course of my life. From art to found objects, each tells a story about my journey. They remind me of friends, family members and the experiences that have shaped me, both good and bad. I never throw anything away; these mementoes inspire me and become more beloved over time. To look around my colourful penthouse at the artworks, photos and rarities that fill it is to see my life's history. They evoke memories and emotions, some long buried, others more recent. What follows is my life as told through 50 objects.

Self-portrait, 1997

1

Fly Spray

I SUPPOSE WHAT MUST COME first in any story of my life is an account of my mother. She was and remains one of the most important people I have ever known. She died of lung cancer when I was twenty-seven and, even in death, she was magnificent. Her essence was imprinted on me from the start. I know this is true of all mothers and their children, but I was coated in her flamboyance and originality just through her choice of name for me: Zandra with a Z. Throughout my life, people have struggled with it. I remember having to stand up at school when we had to say our names alphabetically for the register and every teacher I ever had would tell me I'd made it up. I'd have to tell them time and again that, no, it was my real name. I found it terribly embarrassing. Why did she spell it with a Z? My mother's only explanation was that she wanted to call me Xandra, but my grandmother – a straight-talking Cockney – said no one would know how to pronounce it, so I became Zandra with a Z instead. My great-grandmother was called Zilpah, so there is a tradition of unusual names in my family. Zilpah is actually the Hebrew word for 'frailty', and we've researched our family tree to see if we have Jewish ancestry but can't find any evidence of it.

My first memory of Mummy is unforgettable – I remember her holding me up to the stars watching the doodlebugs flying over-head en route to London. Even the way she gave birth to me was dramatic: her waters broke during an air raid, so she and my father left the house and walked down the hill to the hospital to have me. Of course, when you're remembering things so early in life, your mind can't be trusted. Photos and other people's mem-ories often become your own, but one thing I know to be true is that I was born on 19 September 1940 in Chatham, Kent, during the Second World War.

As a royal naval dockyard town, Chatham was often a target for enemy bombers. The story goes that I inconveniently decided to enter the world on an evening when bombs were coming down thick and fast. My parents were safely installed at our house at 288 Chatham Hill when my mother went into labour. She waited until her contractions were unbearable before asking my father to call a taxi but, of course, no one wanted to brave the streets during an air raid, so they were forced to walk two miles down Chatham Hill to the local hospital. The noise of the doodlebugs was deafening, the pitch of the whistling bombs increasing as they approached the ground. No one forgets those sounds, I imagine. They had to duck to avoid the shrapnel shells that kept exploding in the sky around them, and one plane flew so low my father can even remember seeing the pilot. Anyone who saw them from their taped-up windows must have thought they were mad – a breathless couple moving as quickly as they could amid falling bombs, one desperately trying not to give birth.

By the time they got to the hospital, my mother had lost both her shoes, which shows you how fast they were trying to run. I can't imagine that experience scared her much: she was so reso-lute. I was born a few hours later. Whenever either parent recounted this story during my childhood it was with great humour and jolliness, in which I was jokingly reprimanded for my poor timing, rather than as a terrifying near-death experience. That sort of stoic attitude was typical of the time – how else would anyone have functioned if they'd processed the trauma they'd all lived through?

My mother's father, my grandfather Harry Twigg, died before I was born. He was from Stepney Green in East London, a true Cockney. Until recently, I had it in my mind that he was a colonel in the army, but my sister told me that he was actually much lower in the ranks – a sergeant. It's funny the lies we tell ourselves to make our worlds feel more exciting. I don't know how he met my grandmother, Beatrice Elam, but she was from Haggerston in East London, so they didn't grow up far from each other. I do know that they got married in South Africa because he was fighting in the Boer War out there. He was stationed in various places with the army, which was how they ended up in Chatham, a naval and army town. He was a Freemason and when he died, they said he owed them a lot of money.

Nanny worked hard to repay that debt, working in a newsagent's with my Auntie Amy in Gillingham. I adored my grandmother, she was a direct, no-nonsense person and a strong woman, both in terms of her convictions and her sense of self. I remember her getting cross with a few noisy boys playing up on the bus and banging their heads together in her sensible, matter-of-fact way. When I was nine or ten, I used to get dressed in my best clothes every Sunday morning to visit her at her house and we'd sit together while she showed me how to knit.

Mummy, Beatrice Twigg, was born in Hendon, Middlesex, on 23 January 1910. She had an older brother, Harry, who went into the navy, and a twin sister, Amy, who must have had a terrible time growing up in her sister's shadow as Mummy was always the strong-minded, flamboyant one. Amy was quieter, more ordinary. They didn't look alike and they weren't very close; they were the definition of chalk and cheese. That fact that Mummy lived through two wars must have been quite character-forming and doubtless contributed to her work ethic and stoicism. She grew up watching women go to work as part of the war effort, rather than stay in the home. She was a great fighter and I wonder whether growing up in the First World War influenced her in that regard.

Mummy loved fashion and would draw beautiful fashion illustrations that I've sadly lost. She had a great hunger for style and was always rather flamboyant; it was just how she was. In the mid-1930s, she managed to save up for a ticket to Paris in the hope of getting a job with one of the big fashion brands. Back then, you took a train to Paris and it was a very glamorous way to travel. I think Mummy would have taken the night ferry, an international boat train that started at London's Victoria station and finished at the Gare du Nord in Paris. The idea was that you slept during the journey, but what with the noise caused by the pumps that adjusted the level of the sea at Dover docks, it must have been difficult. The idea of her making that major journey from Chatham to Paris on her own at a time when women had so little freedom is just extraordinary.

Without knowing a word of French, she got a job as a pattern-cutter at the House of Worth, the oldest couture brand in the world. I'm not sure she knew how to cut patterns either, but she managed to work round it. When she started, she cleverly asked to be shown the House of Worth way of pattern-cutting, which suggested she knew how to cut ordinary patterns but she wanted to make sure she knew their way of doing it. Mummy was no fool. She returned just before the Second World War broke out and had me a year later. I wish I'd asked her more about her time at the House of Worth, but when you're young, you never think someone's going to die: you're so preoccupied with school, college and then getting a job. It's only when someone's gone that you realize there's so much you hadn't asked and wish you had.

Mummy didn't look like anyone else. She would collect me from school dressed to the nines in the most extraordinary clothes, which I hated because other people noticed her. I always thought everyone else's mothers were much older, but it was the way Mummy dressed that made her seem much younger than she was. She had a pair of green lizard-skin towering wedges that weren't dissimilar to the kind Terry de Havilland went on to design in the sixties. She wore a green astrakhan coat with a Persian lamb collar, and often a hat. She was so ahead of her time. Despite being so stylish, it never took her long to get ready – the whole process was as quick as lightning. She knew what she liked and how she wanted to look, so she didn't spend ages getting dressed. I just wanted her to look like everyone else and asked her many times to change the way she dressed, but she took no notice. She had this wonderful curl at the top of her head which she regularly sprayed silver, an avant-garde and unusual thing to do in the forties and fifties. You could say that perhaps my mother's early experimentation with unusual hair tones influenced my own hair colouring later in life. Much of her influence was subconscious: I wasn't always aware of how deeply imprinted on me she was, but the way she lived her life undoubtedly shaped my own.

Once she mistook the fly spray for hair spray, which made her head sting like mad. We were heading to London and she sprayed that lock of hair silver, as she always did. She didn't realize until we were on the bus on the way to Chatham station and her head began to sting. We ran into a pharmacist in town who told her

My mother in the 1950s

that, unless she wanted to wash her hair then and there, which she didn't because we'd be late, she'd have to live with it for the rest of the day.

Mummy was always in a hurry – there was never enough time

for all the things she wanted to do in a day – which led to all sorts of accidents. Another time, a pencil had found its way into the lining of her pocket and when she was running for the bus, it skewered her legs. Things happened to her that didn't happen to anyone else, which always made life exciting.

Not only did Mummy not look like other people, she didn't think like them either. She used to see people in a Daliesque way, as alarm clocks or as cucumbers, prunes and custard. When she was really tired, she had out-of-body experiences, seeing herself sitting in another part of the room, a form of disassociation that frightened her. I can't say I've had that experience, but I do find myself talking to her from time to time. I find it amazing to understand now how much I've inherited from her.

Although we lived in Chatham, London was still a big part of our lives. We would catch the train at 6 a.m. to arrive in London at 7 a.m., then go to a Lyons Corner House for breakfast. It was a famous chain and there was one right next to Charing Cross station. It was a noisy place, soundtracked by the clinking of cups and clanking of cutlery. Waitresses would rush around wearing starched caps with a big red 'L' in the middle. There were all sorts of people there who had clearly been up all night, and my mum would point out the prostitutes who were often asleep at the table. I was nine or ten. She would do the same when we went to Selfridges at Christmas, pointing out the prostitutes walking down the street. 'Look, girls, there's another of those ladies!' I'm not sure many mothers would draw attention to ladies of the night – who does that? My mother was always keen to show us the things she knew and the way the world operated. She had a very rounded view of it.

As part of my mother's work as a senior fashion lecturer at the Medway College of Art, my sister and I would sometimes feature in her students' fashion shows. I must have been about six and my sister three. I loved wearing those bold and dramatic clothes at the college or at home, but hated wearing them in front of the local children who would laugh at me. I didn't have many friends when I was young, probably because I worked very hard at school. I would always hand my homework in on time, which didn't make me very popular. My mother was there in the background telling me that if I worked hard I'd get somewhere.

'Ignore them,' she'd say, of the children who made unkind comments about my appearance. 'Sticks and stones will break your bones, but names will never hurt you.'

Mummy was the one who made the money and paid for everything in our family, which can't have been easy for my father back in the forties and fifties when gender roles were still so traditional. She didn't make decisions in a dominant way, but she was certainly the one who made them. I find it fascinating when people talk about their mothers as their best friends. I was in awe of my mother: we were not friends. I am an extension of her ambition. I have always been tortured by being unable to do something really, really well, to be not just good but the best. I suppose this must have come from my mother, but not because she openly applied pressure to me. She didn't exert any discipline on me or my sister: we just instinctively respected her enormously.

When Mummy wasn't working at the college, she'd be making wedding dresses for private clients at home. She also made bespoke outfits for anyone attending court presentations and ran her own fashion label dedicated to this niche, named 'Beatrice Rhodes Court Dressmaker'. My sister and I would sit by her and watch her sew. She was always surrounded by fashion magazines like *L'Officiel* and *Vogue*. My sister and I used to fight for the chance to go shopping with her.

She taught evening classes so wasn't home until nine or ten at night. Our main meal was lunch, at home, and the only time my mother cooked was at weekends, which was unusual for women at the time, who were largely stay-at-home mothers. We weren't children who had a key, my mother didn't want that, so we had a housekeeper we called Auntie Kath. She cooked the lunch we came home for. When I got in after school, I'd make myself something like beans on toast for my supper.

Before going on a date with one of my first boyfriends when I was about seventeen, I boldly said, 'Mummy, I'm going to a dance and I'll be back late.' She replied, 'Oh, don't worry, I know you'd never do anything wrong, and you can tell if it's wrong because you wouldn't do it in front of me.' You can imagine what a rod of iron that holds you with, the sense of guilt that comes when someone has given you their complete trust. To say to someone, 'You are completely free, you have my total trust because I know you would never put a step wrong,' means that, in a way, they hold you for ever. I felt terribly guilty the first time I slept with a man because I wasn't married, a sin in the eyes of my mother. I was twenty-one, and art college had done a good job of corrupting me, but her expectations and trust still weighed heavy. I found it difficult to look at her when I next went home.

In 1968, four years after I left the Royal College of Art, Mummy suspected she had lung cancer and tricked the doctor into telling her by saying that the nurse had already done so. 'She shouldn't have informed you,' the doctor replied, but my mother said, 'Look, you've told me what I wanted to know. Now tell me how long I have to live.' Then she drove herself up to London, sat in front of me and said, 'I'm dying of lung cancer, I have six months to live and I want you to make this the best six months of my life.' I burst into tears. It was impossible to me that anyone so strong and powerful could be so ill. She held me, but also said, 'That's how it is.' Quite brutal, really, when I think about it.

She wore the fact that she was going to die like a suit of armour and continued teaching up until three months before her death. One day, a student started telling her all her problems and my mother said, quite flippantly, 'You must pull yourself together. I'm dying of lung cancer – we must all face our problems.' I sometimes think of that poor person – my mother's words would have been enough to knock the wind out of anyone's sails. She talked about death with an air of defiance. That said, it wasn't easy for her. When I spoke to my aunt after Mummy died, she said my mother sometimes broke down and held her hand. She would admit that she was frightened to die, which seems incredible to me – I don't think I ever saw her cry.

For her final six months, she lived with my sister and her husband, who looked after her. My father couldn't have managed it. He didn't even know how to cook. I saw her whenever I could. She looked terrible when she was dying, which she'd have hated – the indignity of not looking as flamboyant and imperious as she had throughout her life. At the end, she'd be lying there in bed and I never knew whether that would be the last time I'd see her. One day, about half an hour after I'd left her to go back to work, she died. It was very difficult, but I'm one of those people who shuts things away. Despite my appearance, I'm not a heart-on-my-sleeve type. I'm not very outwardly expressive with emotion. Everything I feel goes into my work. I suppose that's the case for most designers.

Until she died, I'd always thought I was a weak person in comparison with my mother, but then I realized I was as strong as her. In dying, she passed all her strength to me. Nearly sixty years later, when I was diagnosed with terminal cancer in March 2020, I responded in a similar way. When the doctor told me I had six months to live, I said, 'I have far too much work to do before then. I can't possibly die yet.' It didn't worry me. I just knew I had to get my life in order and, thankfully, I'm still here to tell the tale. My survival is down to my mother's fighting spirit.

At the time, though, I thought I could never live without my mother because she had always given me strength when I felt tremendously low. Whether it was at school or at the Royal College, and I knew people were laughing at me or talking about me behind my back, she'd tell me to be strong.

'These people are insignificant to you and your work,' she'd say, convincing me to pull myself together. It was, of course, my mother who influenced me into art, signing me up for weekend classes. I had to work hard to be good at other subjects, but art was different. I didn't have to think about it, I could just do it.

I hope I have lived up to my mother's expectations, and I like to think that my sister and I are the fulfilment of her ambitions. My sister has four children and is a wonderful mother and grand-mother; I am a successful fashion designer who has led a very different but fabulous life. I talk to people who knew my mother just to hear their stories about her. She was very proud of the fact that, as a fashion tutor, she could take a student with no clear opportunities and teach them how to sew and make something of themselves. Throughout my life, I have met people in the unlikeliest places whom she taught, and they tell me she was the great influence of their life too. She was a whirl of energy and style who managed to steer people in the right direction without their knowledge. She was the power behind me, and as I've grown older, I find it frightening and exhilarating to realize how much like her I'm becoming. In that sense, she is more alive than ever.

2

Racer Bike

MY FATHER, ALBERT JAMES RHODES, and I didn't have much of a relationship. Looking back, I suspect that was because my mother unwittingly brought me up to feel ashamed of him. Reigning over our family by sheer dint of her charisma and strength of character, she never ran him down, but I always felt that my father was uncouth and should have bettered himself. Children can be snobs, so I may well have formed that opinion all on my own.

My parents met ballroom dancing in Chatham just before the Second World War, not long after my mother had returned from working as a pattern-cutter and fitter at Worth in Paris. They made an attractive pair. Dad looked like a cross between Clark Gable and Errol Flynn, all high cheekbones, deep-set dark eyes and a square jaw, and of course my mother was wonderfully glamorous and dressed more extravagantly than anyone else in outfits she made herself. Both were excellent dancers: at one point they were crowned Kent champions for their ballroom dancing and this – along with cycling – was one of the few things that bound them together.

In most other respects my parents were a real mismatch, but they were both enthusiastic members of a cycling club called the Medway Wheelers of which, at one stage, my mother was the only female member. At weekends, they would go for long rides together, but my father would also go out every morning on his own before work, often cycling up to sixty miles. I keenly remember that he loved to cycle more than anything. He was always fixing his racer bike, a lightweight model with dropped handlebars and one of those saddles that would cut your behind in two. Lost in his own world, he would spend hours tinkering with it; those hours are among my clearest memories of him.

With so little in common, my parents should probably never have married but, in those days, you just got on with it. They were from very different backgrounds. I don't know if you could call my mother's family middle class, given that my maternal grandfather Harry was a Cockney, but they were a little higher up in the social hierarchy than my father's side, and my mother's father was strongly against the relationship. He made it very clear he didn't want his daughter marrying someone he perceived to be beneath her. In comparison to my mother, my father was a scruffy, gruff sort of person, a bit like Alf Garnett from *Till Death Us Do Part*. He served in the air force in Egypt, but for most of my childhood he worked as a lorry driver in Chatham naval dockyard. As such, he was always in his dungarees, which I found embarrassing, as I did his table manners and the way he spoke with his mouth full.

While my sister and I would fight over who got to spend time with my mother, we did not have the same conversations about my father. He was never keen on our having friends over and would moan that it would mean less food for the rest of us. That seemed ridiculous to me. We weren't rich, but we certainly weren't poor either, and no one would have missed the two slices of bread and butter that a friend of mine would eat for tea on the rare occasion they were allowed to visit. Looking back now, and knowing that my mother was the main breadwinner in our household, I can see that my father would have felt emasculated and undermined. It was perhaps for this reason that he was so stringent with anything he perceived as extravagant, such as jam. 'Zandra, you can have either butter or jam, but not both,' he would say.

'But Mummy pays for it,' I'd reply, which made him clamp down even harder.

It's perhaps unsurprising that I never felt close to my father or had any deep interactions with him. In fact, on one occasion I remember having a row with him when I told him through clenched teeth that I'd never have chosen him as my dad. He chased me around with a carving knife while my mother screamed at me to get out of the house. I struggled to understand why she had chosen him as her partner, until she told me she'd felt obliged to marry him after he'd shared the story of his dark upbringing.

Although my father never talked about his childhood, my mother told me in secrecy when I was young that my paternal grandmother, Rose, had been a prostitute, and that she had been murdered in the street. This was said to have happened when my father was a young boy, and he was taken in by his father's sister and her husband, both big drinkers. It was a shocking family tale that was never discussed privately, let alone in public. More recently, thanks to the rigorous research of my sister's grand-daughter Harriet, I have discovered the truth surrounding my grandmother to be quite different.

Rather than being a prostitute, it transpires that my grand-mother had affairs with various male lodgers while my paternal grandfather, Charles – a military man from Lancashire – was away with the navy. These affairs produced three more children, one of whom died as a baby. Presumably having found out about his wife's infidelities, my grandfather ended the marriage in 1919. Divorce was unheard of back then, but even more surprising is that he was granted sole custody of my father. Even today, it is unusual for a father to be granted custody, so you can only imagine how rare it was a century ago. Leaving my father to be raised by his sister and her husband, my grandfather went off to restart his life and later remarried.

My grandmother, however, was indeed murdered, although I have recently learnt that she lost her life at the hands of one of her lovers, a Welsh coal miner and married man named Harry Thompson. Apparently, when Harry found out that my grandmother's romantic affections were . . . spread out, he grew jealous and brutally attacked her. She was forty-one years old. Newspaper articles from the time report that he nearly decapitated her with a razor in front of one of her young daughters. Thompson immediately handed himself in to the police and was hanged for his crime on 8 February 1926. The two girls, my father's half-sisters, were placed in a children's home.

I never wanted to know any of this and have no desire to discuss it any further. The facts remain that my grandmother was murdered and my grandfather abandoned my father with an aunt and uncle who drank heavily. They were often inebriated, and my father often dragged them home from the pub. As a result, he never drank and neither do I. I'm sure my father was shaped by what happened to him, but we never got on until much later in life.

Despite their differences, he and my mother remained together until her death in 1964. I believe she once tried to leave him – she packed a suitcase and took my sister and me to Ramsgate to stay with a friend in her boarding house. I have a memory of seeing my father standing miserably in the garden in his dungarees as we left. We went back, but as I was only about ten, I never thought to ask why. Reflecting on this now, I suspect my mother felt trapped in the relationship, but didn't feel she could leave him. Divorce would have been unthinkable to her.

After my mother died, my father eventually married a widow called Mary, who thought he was fabulous, and he became happier, although I still never saw much of him. My sister Beverley says he softened and was a loving, kind grandfather to her children. Apparently, he was very proud of me and would shout about my achievements to whoever would listen. Perhaps he had learnt to leave in the past what happened to him as a child and to enjoy what he had.

3

Jacqueline Doll

THE FIRST PIECE OF CLOTHING I ever made was for my Jacqueline doll, which I was given when I was eight back in 1948 and still have. It was a Christmas gift from my parents and I adored her. She's stuffed with something – it could be mohair or felt, I'm not sure – and her head is made of papier-mâché. She used to be very pretty, with curly hair that was pinned to the sides of her head and pale blue eyes that were lightly shaded with brown, which made them stand out. Jacqueline also had rosy cheeks and her mouth was painted red. You could say she was quite heavily made up for a toy, but I didn't notice that at the time. I didn't play games with her, really. I was more interested in her clothes. My mother knitted her an oatmeal cardigan with a burgundy, yellow and green striped trim and little flowers embroidered on the shoulders. It's been attacked by moths in the many years since, but you can still make out the love and skill that went into its creation.

My mother taught me to sew and I made different dresses for my doll to wear. I was around ten when I made the first, which was a multi-coloured style, hand-stitched with striped bias binding. I was always very careful with my toys, but particularly with Jacqueline. It was important to me that she was well dressed and nicely presented, and I liked playing with the colour and pattern combinations. When I was sifting through my belongings for the purposes of this book, it was Jacqueline – now a somewhat raggedy shadow of her former self – that evoked the strongest memories of my childhood.

Both my parents took part in the war effort. My father was sent to Egypt with the air force, and my mother worked as an ambulance driver. As a result, I was often left in the care of my maternal grandmother, Nanny Twigg, and Auntie Amy. I loved my granny – she looked exactly how grannies always used to, grey hair in a net, pleated skirt, cardigan and polished shoes distorted with the outlines of her bunions.

I always sat on the counter of the newsagent's that she ran – at

My Jacqueline doll

first propped up in a box with a cushion, and then when I was old enough I'd perch with my legs dangling over the edge. This eventually went wrong after I was bitten in the face by a dog at a friend's house, which hurt rather a lot. The unfortunate result was that when anyone I didn't know came too close to my face, I would bite them and not let go. My mother had to take me to an analyst. Then I had to sit in a windowless room with a woman. God knows what she said, but even after I learnt not to bite people, I still wasn't allowed to sit on the counter.

War was normal to us because it was all we knew. I have an early memory of drawing chalk butterflies on an air-raid shelter when I was three or four. I was only five when news broke that the war was over, so I don't have clear recollections of rationing, although I suppose I must have been dressed in rationed clothes and have eaten dull, rationed food. I was also far too young to understand the scale of the genocide that had happened during the Holocaust, or how many of the country's men had been killed fighting. Certainly none of it was explained to me. Indeed I don't remember talking about the conflict much at all. Back then, people were very careful about what was said or displayed in front of children – it was easier to control what little ones were exposed to because we didn't have a television, let alone the internet. We had a radio but that was pretty much it for external influences. That said, my childhood was still strange in the sense that we lived amid the wartime rubble, both metaphorically and physically, for years afterwards. I was in no way aware of the strangeness of any of this at the time: children accept whatever they're exposed to as normal.

There were lots of bomb sites and clapped-out houses that were gradually cleared and rebuilt. Our school teachers would talk about how they'd lost their husbands and fiancés in the war in a way that felt very ordinary. After it was over, there wasn't much discussion of what had happened – I suppose everyone was very keen to move forward and repress their memories.

During that post-war period, our family fared a lot better than most. Beverley had arrived in 1943 and we still lived in the same house – a 1930s three-bedroom terrace – which fortunately hadn't been bombed. It sat on top of a hill, the second in a block of four identical houses, each of which had a small front garden, which you entered through a little gate. I remember sitting on that gate watching the tanks return in convoy from the war.

My parents had chosen our house for the parquet flooring, which was perfect for practising their ballroom dancing. It was in a nice area, unlike some other parts of Chatham that had been badly damaged by the conflict, leaving slum-like homes. We had a bathroom, a precious commodity; a lot of people still had outside toilets. We had an electric bar heater in the bathroom, which was set so high it only heated your head. In the winter, even the insides of the windows would ice over and so, at breakfast, we'd turn on the kitchen gas stove and sit with our feet in the oven.

We were always well turned out – my parents made sure we had clean shoes and clothes, which wasn't the case for a lot of people we saw in the town. So many were left down and out, without homes, marred by poverty and haunted by the loss of loved ones. Hitler's damage extended far beyond those who fought on the battlefields.

It was a strange backdrop to grow up in, but I remained mostly unaware of the destruction caused. The area was still semi-rural, 'the almost countryside'. Our house was a short bicycle ride from woods crammed with bluebells and celandines. I got to know it all very well, the hedgerows, the trees, the river, the way the ground sloped and rose again. Our back garden overlooked the rolling North Downs, a farm and a white chalk pit. That view was one of the first things I ever drew. My sister and I would play board games together, but I was a boring child, always absorbed in painting or drawing. Probably my interest in art came from Mummy, who always spent any free time sketching. Beverley sometimes joined me when I found new scenes to capture with a pencil or paintbrush. She was much more outgoing than I was – she'd go out with friends from a young age, and when we were teenagers she got a job and a boyfriend. I was much more reserved. All I wanted was to draw and do my homework. Beverley was much better at being a sociable young person than I ever was. She went on to marry the man she'd dated as a teenager, her lifelong partner David, with whom she had four children. She's now a grandmother of seven. We weren't hugely close as children but became much closer as we grew older. I truly believe we are the exact different halves of Mummy: I have the big fashion career and Beverley is the dynamic, caring mother-and-grandmother figure. She always makes time for everyone and has just as much energy as I do; she just channels it in a different way. We speak on the phone nearly every day, and she is tremendously important to me. If you'd told me when I was a child we'd be that close, I'd have laughed. A three-year age gap when you're children feels like decades, but the older you get, the smaller it becomes until it's barely there at all.

My parents raised Beverley and me to be busy. Doing nothing was not allowed – there was never any lazing around or lying in at weekends. We'd walk to the North Downs as a four, where we'd pass a long row of colourful wooden Romany caravans. I was fascinated by the way they were decorated, the intricate, elaborate hand carvings and the vibrant paintwork. They seemed so remarkable and I loved drawing them. My mother clocked my interest in art early on, and I was sent to art classes on a Saturday morning. Her gentle steering was never obvious to me. I'm sure I would have kicked back if I'd felt I was doing something she really wanted me to do. We'd go on bike rides together or, if it was rain-ing, we'd sew or listen to the radio. We might have a tea party for my doll Jacqueline and Beverley's Geraldine.

Holidays involved trips to nearby Seasalter or Leysdown-on-Sea on the Isle of Sheppey where, in the summer, we rented a caravan. Daddy drove us there in our funny old Morris Eight. I would be wearing a knitted bathing costume – they droop when they're wet – and Beverley and I would run out to the sea together. Even on holiday, we'd get up early, sometimes at 4 a.m., to collect mushrooms. We were a funny bunch, the Rhodes family.

One of the things that marked me out as a boring child was how much I loved school. I started at Byron Road Primary in Gilling-ham, Kent, when I was four and I liked it from the start. I remember nearly nothing substantiative about primary school except that I was quite good at most things, which of course made me like being there. It's very easy to enjoy doing something you're naturally gifted at. I sat in the front row and didn't like the back because people played around. I was, in short, a swot. The land-slide of information, of images and facts, was exciting to me. I loved learning to read and write. I liked, and still do, the way that words look graphically, how they appear as little designs of their own. I was naturally left-handed but taught myself to write with my right hand so I could use italic script. I often incorporate words into my designs, like calligraphy.

The only subject I struggled with was maths. I couldn't under-stand it at all. Right from the start, I had no problem with working hard. There was no point in working unless I was top of the class so I just kept grafting. I didn't want to do anything else. When I eventually became a teenager, Mummy would say, 'You should go out sometimes, Zandra,' but I refused. What kind of teenager behaves like that? I wanted to be the best at every subject, bar maths, which I accepted would always be outside my realm of understanding.

My work ethic and bullish desire to be top was bolstered after I failed the eleven-plus, which determined whether you were smart enough to go to the good grammar schools or the somewhat less well-served secondary moderns, now called comprehensives. This exam still, incredibly, exists in Kent and other parts of the UK today. I never regarded my failure as a negative. Mummy told me not to worry, that I was a bright child who would still do well if I continued to work hard, which I did. It was almost an act of defiance to prove to the world that I was highly capable even if one silly exam result suggested otherwise. I did two years at a secondary modern, then passed the thirteen-plus to attend Chatham Technical School for Girls Fort Pitt. It had sprawling buildings, one of which was used as a medical school set up by Florence Nightingale and also as a hospital during the Crimean War. Because of that, several rooms were tiled from floor to ceiling, some entirely in green and others in white. The playing fields overlooked the River Medway.

I was in my element there. I was challenged academically, and my hard work was rewarded with good grades. My best friend Lynda, who was every bit as conscientious as I was, would join me at the front of the class and we'd compete to see who could achieve the best grades. We're still friends today. Art continued to be my favourite subject. I had to work hard at everything else, but art came naturally. My hands knew what to do to create an image, and it felt tremendously freeing to find something I loved so much. My teachers would use my work as an example to the rest of the class. It was a skill that also helped in biology: I could write an essay on photosynthesis and do cutaway drawings of plants. It made things difficult for Beverley, who followed me at the school a few years later. She was constantly compared to me

and challenged as to why her work wasn't done to the same obses-
sive standards. It must have been incredibly annoying to have
such a meticulous, over-achieving older sister.

I don't remember ever getting into trouble, but one teacher
took a dislike to me from the very beginning. As mentioned,
people have often struggled with my name. This teacher was
going through the register and pronounced it Sandra rather than
Zandra. I gently corrected her (I'd already had a lot of practice in
doing so), and said, 'No, it's Zandra with a Z.' The teacher, Miss
Barr, took umbrage and told me, 'That can't possibly be true.' A
few weeks later, the same teacher read out my misspelt homework to the class, emphasizing phonetically my errors. Everyone
was rolling around laughing, so I laughed too. I mean, what else
are you going to do – cry? She turned round and barked, 'So you
think this is funny? In that case, you can go and tell the joke to
the headmistress.' I cried all the way. She didn't like me because I
was different. Thankfully the headmistress was very kind to me,
helped me with my spelling and sent me on my way.

I decided then that my name was important to who I am. It's
part of what makes me an individual. I practised my signature
over and over again. I became Zandra, with the emphasis on the
Z. Actually, I didn't want to be ordinary. I would have to be per-
sistent in the pursuit of my individuality.

Of course, my intense approach to my studies came at a cost of
any real social life. Dating seemed an unnecessary distraction
from my homework, but when I was around seventeen, I met my
first boyfriend. The only extracurricular activity I indulged in
beyond art was ballroom dancing, which I did midweek at a
dance school at the top of Star Hill in Rochester. One Wednesday
evening, I was hovering at the side of the room when I was asked
to dance by a smartly dressed boy called Geoffrey. He was older
than me, maybe twenty-five or thirty, and wore a bow tie with a

black suit. He seemed more mature than boys my age, in whom I had no interest whatsoever: they all seemed so noisy and uncouth. I wasn't in love with Geoffrey – it wasn't a butterflies-in-the-stomach sort of thing, but I enjoyed having him as a boyfriend. He was a nice middle-class boy, which was very important. I had no desire to repeat my mother's mistake and date someone who wasn't from the same background or above. I wanted to find my equal. Again, it was imperative that Geoffrey fitted in around my work, so I saw him at the weekends and even then he never occupied both days – my focus was on being the best at school. We often sat and watched television at his home with his parents: the set was a status symbol as not everyone had one back then. Sometimes, he'd come and keep me company while I sketched outside. We went to the cinema a few times although I can't say I remember what we watched, and not because we were up to no good: it wasn't like that. We had a few vague sexual encounters in his car on drives out to the country, but not often. It was all very chaste and innocent until I went to the Royal College of Art. That was when my awakening in every sense truly began.

4

Flower Fairies Books

I WAS BROUGHT UP READING Cicely Mary Barker's *Flower Fairies* books. I adored the vivid illustrations of children dressed as fairies, each accompanied with a poem that captured the flowers' individual characteristics. Barker's watercolour pictures were inspired by the detail and realism of the Pre-Raphaelite Brotherhood, who were in turn influenced by the natural world. Her books helped me see nature as magical, and if you can see the beauty, colour and sparkle of the natural world, you'll always have something to sustain you even on your worst days.

Nature has always inspired my work, not just sweeping landscapes and recognizable landmarks, but small, everyday natural beauties. Flowers, for example, are a recurring theme throughout my collections, although I prefer to interpret them as bold, almost Matisse-like forms. During Covid, when we were all cooped up at home, I started painting the cacti, the camellias and other plants dotted around my house and terrace, which focused me. Nature is very forward-thinking; it's forever moving ahead, regardless of what humans are doing. It doesn't care about the minutiae of our lives or even pandemics. It just keeps resiliently, blithely pushing ahead, despite humanity's best efforts to destroy it. I find that both calming and admirable. Nature is a tough old nut.

The *Flower Fairies* books were one of the first ways in which I learnt to appreciate the natural world and see it for what it is. Mummy used them to teach Beverley and me about flowers. The semi-country surrounding Chatham was slowly disappearing in the forties and early fifties, but it was still our kingdom. At weekends, my sister and I would hold Mummy's hands, climb over the back garden wall and stomp through the green to find evidence of the flower fairies. Strangely enough, we never found any tiny winged impeccably dressed humans fluttering amid the fields, but we did discover a great many of the flowers that Barker's books spoke of. I loved drawing them, faithfully trying to maintain the same level of accuracy and detail as the author. It was another way Mummy shaped me, I suppose, to spark and nurture my imagination in a dismal post-war environment.

In a funny way, the *Flower Fairies* books also encouraged me to look at clothes. It would have been impossible for me not to notice what the fairies wore and how they reflected the personality of the flower: a tunic-style, floor-length dress in dusty pink for the Wild Rose Fairy, a 1960s-style blue mini with a ditsy print for the Forget-Me-Not Fairy and the Daisy Fairy with her skirt made from white petals, tinged with pink. They had fabulous accessories too, especially during the cooler months. The Horse Chestnut Fairy and his glossy, spiked, cloche-like hat made from a conker shell; the shocking yellow pointed pixie boots worn by the Winter Jasmine Fairy. When I was still at primary school – I must have been about ten – I was cast as a poppy in the end-of-year play. Mummy set about making the most exquisite costume for me, an exact copy of what the Poppy Fairy wore in the book. The red skirt was divided into individual petals, each made of scarlet crêpe paper, and she dyed a segment of the material at the waist to replicate the flower's bold, dark centre. The other mothers must have hated her – it was so beautiful and well beyond the skills of anyone who hadn't worked at a couture house like Worth, as Mummy had.

To me, it wasn't a big deal: I was often dressed in things that made me stand out. I remember walking across our local park wearing a wonderful straw bonnet with flowers when other children started laughing and throwing stones at me. I still liked my bonnet. Somehow I knew that not looking the same as everyone else was a positive. Around thirty years ago, I was sent a letter by a girl from my childhood. She said, 'I used to get the school bus with you and I am so sorry that my friends and I always laughed at you.' I just replied saying, 'Well, that's nice, but I never noticed anybody laughing.' Thick skin protects you. It's luck if you have it as it allows you to do anything.

The *Flower Fairies* books have, without a doubt, influenced my work. Decades on, I looked to them for inspiration for my spring/ summer 1982 and spring/summer 1985 collections, where I imagined a world in which the fairies had grown up and needed romantic, ethereal evening outfits to fly about in: sheer chiffon dresses in soft white, pale pink and blue, subtly covered with floral, striped and geometric prints and silver embroidery, fantastical crinoline dresses and separates, in which I used origami techniques to create 3D flower embellishment.

Jumping ahead a few decades, long after I had met my life partner Salah Hassanein and was living between London and the US, I returned to those books. I was living with Salah in Del Mar, a beach town in San Diego, and every weekend I'd walk along the state beach at Torrey Pines, either with him or, when he got too sick, with friends. We'd take the stairs up to Torrey Pines State Natural Reserve for a hike. It's a rugged oceanfront park with beautiful rock-faces, a peregrine falcon nest in the cliffs and, of course, the rare, bushy pine trees it's named after. At least three hundred varieties of wildflower live there, most of which are native only to California, including its own very fabulously sunny brand of poppy, which comes in bright yellow and orange. In 2012, Beverley was visiting me and we embarked on a morning hike up to the reserve, following the dusty pathway up the cliffs. I started pointing out the local flora, as our mother had done a very long time ago in Chatham. We decided to create a

Poppy Fairy in the style of Cicely Mary Barker

book, *The Flower Fairies of California.* I'm doing the illustrations and she's writing the poems. We're yet to finish, but I have a big folder in my studio dedicated to it, and, at some point, I'll get the drawing done. In a sense, it feels like a circular route back to where I started in the disappearing countryside of the Medway towns.

5

Canterbury Pilgrims Appliqué

FOR AS LONG AS I can remember, I was aware that my Auntie Ena had supernatural powers. She was a medium and a psychic, but I didn't realize she was so famous until much later, when my high-profile American clients asked to meet her. She and Uncle Harry, my mother's brother, would visit us in Chatham and Ena would say, 'There's a presence here.'

It was unnerving and Mummy used to get very cross with her. 'We don't need to hear about all that, Ena,' she'd say, ever the realist. 'The real world is quite enough to contend with without the involvement of bored spirits.'

I must have absorbed my mother's disbelief because I never engaged with Auntie Ena's premonitions. Neither Beverley nor I ever pursued her 'gifts' or asked her to demonstrate her skills, which she claimed enabled her to connect with spirits, or 'misty people', as she called them. She also believed she could predict the future through voices she heard over her left shoulder. She was adamant that she foresaw the death of her father, and the safe return of Uncle Harry from the Second World War. Indeed, she always claimed to have predicted the start of the war, although I would say that the outbreak of the conflict was fairly obvious if you read a newspaper.

Ena was a small woman of around five foot two. She had deep-set dark eyes, wavy brown hair cut relatively short, and an intense look about her. Her clothes were very ordinary: she'd always be in a prim pleated skirt, blouse and sturdy black shoes with a low block heel. I never noticed her ethereal or mystical qualities because to me she was just our auntie about whom my mother would moan ahead of any visit. 'You know, girls, that it's all rubbish,' she'd say. 'The only world worth connecting with is the one we currently live in. Anything else is just nonsense.'

My auntie had first met Uncle Harry aged thirteen when my grandparents had moved with Mummy, Auntie Amy and Uncle Harry from London to Gillingham in Kent. They were neighbours, and Harry always said he knew he wanted to be with Ena from the moment he saw her across the street. They grew closer after her father died a year later and got married when she was just seventeen.

Ena couldn't remember a time when she wasn't psychic – even when she was two or three. She said she would fly upstairs and downstairs after her body had been put to bed. She would see and hear what the grown-ups were doing and thought there was nothing unusual about it until the 'misty people' told her that her father had a week to live. Apparently, the following Friday – a week from the night the voices had warned her – he slipped and fell down the stairs of their house, fracturing his skull and injuring his spine, dying instantly. After that, I think Auntie Ena realized her visions were out of the ordinary. It must have been very strange to know that she saw and heard the world differently from everyone else.

Uncle Harry was sceptical about his wife's powers at first but came round to accepting them after they had a séance in which apparently Ena spoke to my late grandfather, Harry's father. Later she became a spiritualist minister, and the first woman to speak at Southwark Cathedral in January 1970 as part of a panel discussing 'The World and Eternity', whatever that meant.

I'm completely incurious about the supernatural world and have refused Auntie Ena's advice on multiple occasions. It frightens me, and I simply don't want to know. Not long before she died in 1984, I was on a work trip in America and my secretary phoned from London and said that Auntie Ena had asked me to call her urgently. Overseas calls were rare back then as they were extremely expensive, yet Auntie Ena was concerned enough to want me to phone her.

'I had to contact you, Zandra. The spirits are telling me you're in grave danger,' she said, over the crackly phone line. She seemed so panicked that I broke my own rules and asked for more information.

'What is it, Auntie Ena? Will I die in a plane crash? Am I with the wrong boyfriend or making bad financial decisions?' I asked.

She paused, then said huffily, 'One cannot command specifics from the Other Side. I am only relaying that your mother is worried about you.' Well, that seemed terribly vague to me, so I thanked her for her concern and we hung up. I never did find out what particular peril awaited me.

When I told Beverley about Auntie Ena's dramatic call, she said, 'What's new? Mummy was always worried about you.'

I have zero interest in finding out about my life ahead of time. If I have to live through years of horror, I'd rather live through them and come out at the other end without causing myself more stress worrying about it before it happens. I see no point in scaring myself. The only thing that truly frightens me is running out of new ideas. The more successful you are, the less time you have to hunt for new inspiration. There seems to be less and less opportunity to reach into the wilderness, exploring new thoughts and embarking on new experiences that might spark the development of something new. I find it very difficult. Sometimes I don't see any ideas anywhere and I just have to keep working until they appear. When that happens and I feel lost, I call my friends and we talk it through – I certainly don't need a spirit guide to help me on my way. Often, my friends are a portal to my creativity.

Beverley has a picture by my mother of the pilgrims en route from London to Canterbury on her upstairs landing at her home in Amersham. It was made with appliquéd felt and it depicts the travellers filled with anticipation for the unknown adventures that lay ahead of them. It's very restful to look at. Auntie Ena loved it and wanted it for her séance room, presumably because it said something to her about our journey to fulfilment and enlightenment. Whenever I'm visiting Beverley and see it on her

My mother's Canterbury Pilgrims appliqué

landing, it reminds me of Auntie Ena and her supposed constant trips back and forth to the Other Side. I suppose we're all on a journey of sorts, but I don't believe in thinking too deeply about spirituality. I think we should all live each day as it comes and make the most of the time we have.

6

Sketchbooks

I NEVER GO ANYWHERE WITHOUT my sketchbooks, a habit I acquired when I was a little girl. As my obsession with drawing grew, I sketched everything I found interesting – my mother sewing, local churches, the fields at the bottom of our garden, allotments and flowers. I felt then as I do now that if you draw something it remains in your mind's eye longer than a photograph does – there's something about putting ink or paint to paper that sears an image into your brain.

By the time I turned sixteen, I knew I wanted a job that enabled me to draw and was considering becoming a children's book illustrator. I had no interest in fashion, or at least I thought I didn't. Despite poring through Mummy's *L'Officiel*s and *Vogue*s and my clear interest in sewing, I didn't have a real leaning towards clothing. I was still at the stage of wanting to do the opposite of my mother, who was at that point head of fashion at Medway College of Art, our local art school. I definitely didn't want her to teach me. I think she knew that, so never suggested fashion. It's funny to me now how much she shaped and influenced me without my noticing. Her belief in me pushed me in the direction I ultimately took.

It was obvious to both of us that I should apply to do a course at Medway, so she took me to the college to present my bulging sketchbooks to the college principal. To my delight, he told me that my work was so advanced I could bypass a year of the two-year intermediate foundation course, which offered an introduction in a variety of artistic forms. From there, you chose the medium you liked best and specialized in that course. I was giddy at the thought of being able to focus all my time on art.

I joined Medway College of Art in 1957, when I was seventeen. My mother was highly regarded there, and I didn't want anyone to think I was being given an unfair advantage so I avoided her and didn't tell anyone we were related. I'd even get different buses from her, so that we wouldn't arrive at the same time. If she was bothered by the pains I took to distance myself from her, she never showed it.

Unsurprisingly, I loved dedicating all my days to art – I was, I'm sure, an annoyingly precocious student but easy to teach because I was so committed to my subject. Nothing was more interesting, calming or satisfying to me than drawing and painting. On the first day, the teacher asked, 'What are the different types of Greek columns?' and I automatically said, 'Doric, Ionic and Corinthian.' It must have been so irritating for my classmates to have such a swot in their midst. As part of the intermediate course, I began experimenting with paper printing processes, such as lino-cutting and lithography, which introduced me to print-making in earnest. It felt both technical and artistic, a real challenge of practicality and creativity. I was told I'd do more of it on the National Diploma in Design, which was a two-year course, taught by a woman called Barbara Brown.

I can't underscore enough the impact Barbara Brown had on my career. Already a successful textile designer at Heal's, Barbara would travel down from London two days a week to teach at Medway. I didn't know it then, but her work had been treated with the same suspicion that mine would be in the years to come. She made large, abstract designs based on machines and architecture that were often seen as too bold for mainstream manufacturers, who just wanted pretty florals. Later on in the sixties, long after I'd left for London, she created optical illusions using mathematical formulae to suggest motion. She used colour to powerful effect, which I definitely soaked up. Like me, she was determined to design prints as she wanted to, so she refused to give up. It was only Heal's, who commissioned her patterns every year, that truly recognized her innovative work. She was the first person I had come across who really looked like a designer.

If my mother was glamorous in an obvious sense, Barbara was stylish in a more artistic way. She looked like a bohemian designer and was decked out head-to-toe in black. There was a Victorian appeal to her clothes: austere, buttoned-up shirts and dresses, pleated dark skirts and lace-up ankle boots. She had a thick fringe and her dark brown hair was always piled high in a bun. She wore an old smock for working in the dye room. I copied her style almost completely, doing my hair in the same way and wearing a similarly Victorian-inspired black dress with torn lace trim accessorized with jet jewellery – I must have looked like a hippie version of an Emily Brontë character. We were both usually covered with paint or dye from whatever we'd been working on that day, a real sight for sore eyes. Even today, I can never seem to get the paint from underneath my nails.

Barbara was the first person to take me inside the world of textile design, which changed my life for ever. Beyond that, she gave me and the other three students in my class a foundation in what it takes to be a designer in any medium. On the first day of the course, she gave us a lecture that became integral to my work. 'Drawing is the basis of any design job,' she said, standing at the front of the funny little annex where we worked. 'If you can draw, everything else will work. What I want to teach all of you over the next two years is the art of seeing. You can't just draw any old thing because it becomes a doodle. You have to really, really look at things carefully. You have to understand what's happening and why and, crucially, to understand the emotion of it. The art of seeing and trying different mediums to depict what you see is what makes a truly great artist. You can't just copy others either. You have to find your own way.' She was right, of course. To be a good designer, you must be able to draw, to look and see deeply. Nothing makes you absorb space, a scene or a person like having to draw it. Also essential, if you want to make any sort of impact, is to develop a unique signature something that sets you apart.

Like most good teachers, Barbara was strict and demanded a lot of us. We were set endless assignments: some were based on

Life drawing class at Medway College of Art, 1959

the history of design, others on certain design styles, which we would then have to hone. She told us to take our sketchbooks wherever we went because you never knew when you might see something that begged you to draw it. Just having it with you, she said, will encourage you to think and see like an artist. She required us to draw in the wind, rain or sleet, which I had no issue with. I understood that ideas don't arrive fully formed out of thin air, but rather through talent and hard work. Every time I drew, I felt a profound sense of coming home. It was like discovering my own language. She would inspect our homework each week, and if we hadn't done it, she'd refuse to talk to us. It was a brutal approach to teaching, but if you put in the time, Barbara would reward you with *her* time, encouragement and belief.

She drove a few of us in her ramshackle Mini up to Manchester to visit the textile manufacturers there to show us what commercial prints looked like and how they were made.

'I don't want any sneering,' she warned us, en route. 'The point is to see why they're doing it and how.' It was torrentially raining that day, and we walked bedraggled between the different manufacturers better to understand the process of making textiles for money. Florals were very popular at that time, a bit like the prints you see everyone wearing today, clichés of flowers. Many are based on old textiles that were beautiful when they were first made because they were beautifully drawn. Sadly, some are now so badly drawn that they make something as visually appealing as a flower look awful, a terrible crime.

Back in Medway, we were taught how to draw botanicals with almost scientific accuracy, landscapes in different mediums with gouache or watercolour paint, and buildings to scale. We experimented with a broad range of techniques – lithography, paint, technical drawing, sketching and, of course, textile design, which quickly became my favourite. I loved the challenge of it – designing patterns, then finding ways of incorporating them into the designs of existing items, like furniture, bedding and clothing. Attention needed to be paid to the measurements of the prints and how they'd work towards an end product within the design, creating elevated everyday art forms. The process required a meticulous eye for detail to which I was very happy to commit myself. I started designing prints that weren't standard all-over designs, but rather one- or two-way works with painterly qualities. They had to be greater than the flat pattern on fabric. They could be, I thought, artworks in their own right.

Finally, I had found the thing I was meant to do. Barbara showed me how to create my own colours, which set my imagination off in a thousand different directions. There was so much one could say and do with colour. I made extensive notes on the dyes and formulae that formed each shade, then played with the combinations to create new bright and vivid tones. I became even more obsessed with drawing – I spent nearly all my spare time creating. I drank up every piece of homework set by Barbara, and genres I struggled with, portraiture for example, I practised and practised over and over until I reached a level I was happy with.

'You can't rely on talent,' said Barbara. 'You've got to work at it.'

The course was based in a shed-like space away from the main college building, which we all loved because we could make as much noise and mess as we wanted. It was a mucky but gorgeous playground, a place to experiment, create and work hard. There was a small print table and a tall iron stove in the corner that provided the least amount of heating. By this point, I'd ended things with Geoffrey (it was never going to be a lasting thing) and had started dating one of my fellow students, David Green. I don't remember much about him, except that he had dark hair and was nice-looking, although not traditionally handsome. He was a hard worker too, and we used to draw, print and paint together.

At the end of the first year, Barbara asked us to gather round her paint-splattered table. 'If you want to pursue a career in design, the only place to train is the Royal College of Art,' she said, looking at us individually but letting her eyes land for longer on me. 'The entrance criteria are tough, and you'll be put through the wringer to gain a place, but if you're interested I'll be happy to work on your submissions.' I knew that Barbara had studied there, so naturally it was the only place in the world where I wanted to continue my education. David was also keen, so we set about making our sketchbooks as full as they could be. I would get up early and walk round Chatham, sometimes getting the bus to Rochester to find things to draw, paint or print. During the holidays, I'd sit in my granny's garden and paint the trees. To say I was committed to the task at hand seems an understatement. I went bonkers with it all.

Securing a place on the Textiles MA at the Royal College involved sitting a pressurized entrance exam spread out over three days. I travelled up on the train each gruelling day. 'All you can do is your best, Zandra,' Mummy would say every morning. 'And the best you have done.' I don't remember what I drew during that exam, but I remember feeling terrified – each student was required to design prints that could be transformed into tex-tiles while being observed by a group of tutors. There was then a lengthy interview, which I have largely blocked out on account of how stressful the whole thing was, and a portfolio review – that part I enjoyed. I have always been comfortable when talking about the ideas behind my work, and the techniques I've used. There were only eight places on the course and, rumour had it, thirty applications for each.

The day I received the news that I had successfully got into the Royal College was the best day of my life so far. The letter arrived at home a few months after my interview and exam, when I was out drawing in Rochester. Mummy presented me with the envelope when I arrived home. I never received any post, so we all knew what it would be. The RCA-headed letter read:

Dear Miss Rhodes,

Following your application, I am delighted to be able to offer you a place on the Textiles Master of Arts degree at the Royal College of Art, commencing on 22nd September 1961. To accept this offer, please reply to this letter at the address listed above within the next 28 days. Congratulations.

Yours sincerely,
John Drummond
Professor of Textiles

I fully understood the importance of the occasion. This was a huge door opening, and I felt an enormous sense of achievement and undiluted excitement. I'd done it! I'd also, it transpired, won a scholarship, which paid my fees. My mother gave me the sort of hug that leaves you feeling breathless. I wonder now if there was anything bittersweet for her in seeing her child live out dreams that perhaps she'd had before the war broke out and she married my father. If there was anything mixed with the joy she showed me that day, I wasn't aware of it. Even my dad was pleased. I couldn't wait to tell Barbara, who had been so instrumental in ensuring my future. She was pleased, she told me, but not at all surprised.

7

Medals

IT TOOK ME A WHILE to find my feet and confidence when I started at the Royal College of Art. During my first week, I asked a fellow student, a tall brunette called Julie, what she thought of a design I was working on. I forget the exact nature of the piece, but I had reached a point with it where I needed to take it further and didn't know how. So I asked her opinion. She looked at me straight on, and said, with almost admirable indifference, 'Honestly, I don't give a fuck what you do.' I felt as if I'd been knifed. At Medway College of Art, I had been listened to, and everyone had been interested in what everyone was doing. No one had ever sworn at me, and I certainly never used words like 'fuck'. I was woefully naive about everything – work, love and art. I thought, as most eighteen-year-olds do, that I knew everything but, of course, I knew very little. I had been a celebrated star pupil and now I was a country nobody with a lot to prove.

I didn't enjoy my first term at all. The Royal College was run like most art colleges in that you had a tutor but you weren't actually taught or required to do specific things. There was no real structure. You chose what you worked on, which was both daunting and freeing. No one told you what to do, and students smoked in class. We had lectures, but we were guided rather than instructed. We were trusted to get on with things to the best of our ability and were assessed at the end of the summer term.

The year was divided into lectures on calligraphy, horizontal stripes, vertical stripes, spots and a substantial focus on floral designs. Textiles were still very much led by botanicals back then, and Richard Chopping taught those classes. Richard, or Dickie as he was known, had already started designing the illustrations for Ian Fleming's James Bond book covers, so was already a name. I found the lack of structure, with the free-thinking independent approach to learning, very difficult. I have always been task-oriented and was unnerved by having to create my own schedules and set my own goals. At Medway, I had been set assignments; I was told where to be at certain times and – like the teacher's pet I was – I found it easy to do my work on time, and always endeavoured to deliver my best work.

I am a contrary mix of chaotic and fastidious – my mind and studio are often a mess, but I like structure and a certain amount of order. I imagine it has something to do with a desire for control – if you're in control, you feel less stressed, or I do. Too much structure can leave one feeling trapped, but too little makes me feel overwhelmed. I need my mind to feel free in order to come up with new ideas. Unclear guidelines are my idea of hell, so it took me a while to get used to my new life in London.

My home was a third-floor bedsit in Bolton Gardens, Kensington, which cost around four pounds a week, a lot of money in those days. My mother paid for it, presumably by taking on extra sewing work on top of her tutoring at Medway, because my scholarship only covered my tuition fees. It must have been a huge strain on her financially, but of course she never mentioned it and I never questioned it. Children seldom think about the sacrifices their parents make for them. My mother would have done anything to help me live out my artistic potential. The flat belonged to a buxom German lady, who, I think, arrived during the war. I had a long, narrow room that stretched on for about seven metres, with a single bed. At the end of the room, there was a big window overlooking the trees of Bolton Gardens, which was rather lovely. I shared the kitchen and bathroom with my landlady. I lived there throughout the three years I was at the Royal College.

There were a lot of exciting people at the Royal College at that time. In sculpture, there was Roland Piché; in painting and printmaking there were Patrick Caulfield, Derek Boshier, Norman Ackroyd and R. B. Kitaj. Peter Blake had graduated a few years before I started and was already becoming a poster boy for swinging London. Film director Ridley Scott finished his graphic design course the year I started, and used to pop in every now and again. The golden boy was David Hockney, who was two years above me and was spoken about by both tutors and students, quite rightly, as if he was a god. A lowly first-year, I didn't talk to God personally. By 1961, David had already started to make it. He had an agent, which was a huge deal to all of us just beginning our adventures in art. He looked just as he does now. He had already identified his uniform: bleached-blond hair, which was very unusual for men back then, wide-rimmed glasses and crumpled rugby shirt – a bohemian dandy in paint-covered slacks. He was instantly recognizable. I loved his work, the punchy use of colour and his mastery of line. I only really got to know him when I started spending time in LA in the seventies. What I like about David is that he's just a long-playing record about his work – it's all he talks about. He's Mr Focused, a fellow workaholic, who is deeply committed to his métier. I always find it fascinating when someone talks with such enthusiasm about what they do. Back in 1961, though, I wouldn't have dreamt of talking to him – the British social class system may have been slowly eroding, but everyone knows that the social order and power dynamics of schools and colleges are far trickier to upend.

My Medway boyfriend David had also managed to secure a place at the Royal College, but it wasn't long before we split up. I don't remember exactly why I decided to end things, or the specifics of that final conversation, but I suspect it might have been to do with a fellow textiles classmate called Alex McIntyre. I think it's possible that Alex was also part of the reason I started to feel more at ease at the Royal College. I don't recall the first time I properly saw him, this man who would become one of the most important people in my life, only that we were always the two who were left working in the paint room long after everyone else had gone home. The college was accessible 24/7 then, and we may as well have slept there for all the hours we spent there. Most students clocked off late afternoon, but I would remain there until 10 p.m., sometimes later. I'd always arrive early at 7.30 a.m. after being let in by the cleaners. It wasn't a love-at-first-sight thing as far as I can recall, but there was a connection. We were both very hard-working and deeply enthusiastic about our work. I loved how talented he was, a highly skilled screen printer who was obsessed by detail. He was a slip of a man with a soft Mancunian accent, a mess of wavy, light brown hair, and a strong, masculine face with clear eyes. Alex was always quite natty; he wasn't madly flamboyant but loved beautiful-coloured jersey shirts that made him look well turned out. He wore his talent and his handsomeness lightly.

Alex told me he'd first seen me on the open day at Manchester College of Art that my Medway tutor Barbara Brown had arranged, and then at the entrance exam for the Royal College. I'd never met anyone from up north before, and he was completely different from anyone I'd ever come across. He was a driven and quietly self-assured northerner with a strong accent, a man sustained by art and a love of spinach tarts. In a class coated in ambition, over-confidence and nicotine, Alex was a grounding, calming force. He said he loved how enthusiastic I was about the world, which I still think is a lovely compliment. I just liked being around him.

My memory prevents me from detailing the precise moment we got together, but all I know is that we did and after that point we were pretty inseparable. We understood how important work was to the other and would sit in companionable silence beavering away. He worked at the college bar too, so sometimes I'd join him there after I finished work. It wasn't wild, but we danced to Beatles records and loved each other. In the early stages of our relationship, Alex suggested we go up north to meet his parents, who lived in Oldham, Lancashire, not far from Manchester. 'If we're going to do this, you need to know where I'm from and what my parents are like,' he said. His parents had an unhappy marriage, so I suppose we had that in common.

That week-long visit up north made a huge impression on me, and I look back on it with real fondness. It was so wild and different from southern England. We went for wonderful walks around the moors, up hills, and over fences. I was never very good at steep inclines, but it was all so beautiful that I happily trudged on regardless. There were no mobile phones, let alone any with cameras, so we just drank it all up in the moment rather than stopping to take pictures. We'd end up in a pub at the end of the day and just talk for hours about what we wanted to do with our lives, the patter of two young people bound by chemistry and a shared mindset. Alex probably still does the same walks, but my health is such since I had chemotherapy that I wouldn't be able to now. My breathing isn't as good. He really did introduce me to the wonders of the north and, despite the explosively acrimonious way things eventually ended between us, I'm very grateful for that.

London was really starting to take off, but I was so absorbed by my work that I didn't take in much outside college. The paint rooms, my work and Alex became my whole world. We didn't need anything else. The building was on Exhibition Road, next to the Royal Albert Hall, so when the Rolling Stones performed there, we looked out of the window from the professor's office to see them going into the building. I was aware that it was a lively time to be in the capital, but I didn't party in the same way as many of my classmates. I would either be at college or working at home in my skinny long room near Gloucester Road.

My tutor Dickie Chopping became a friend. I loved Dickie – he was a wonderful teacher with such an exacting eye. He loved the natural world and would bring in fresh flowers and plants from Kensington Flower Market for his students to draw. Alex and I would drive in Alex's Mini to visit Dickie and his partner, the artist Denis Wirth-Miller, at their quay house at Wivenhoe, Essex, where we were fed and nourished with exquisite vegetables, pies and tarts. There were piles upon piles of books, which gave the cottage a rakish, intellectual air. Dickie and Denis were both of the artistic disposition and had a tumultuous relationship. Their quarrels were exacerbated by a certain Francis Bacon, who was often a guest at their house. I remember on one occasion in 1963, Denis and Dickie charging at each other with carving knives. I have no idea what they were fighting about, but I imagine a certain amount of drink was involved. Francis would be the malevolent pixie in the middle of it all, stirring and darkening situations. He would play them off against each other because he was evil. I can't offer much more detail – it all happened so long ago – but there was something searingly nasty about Francis. He had a strange but strong energy that defeated so many people. As in his art, he made everyone ugly.

Whether it was thanks to Alex or perhaps the influence of Dickie, whom I respected and admired, I finally started getting into my stride with work after my somewhat rocky start. My breakthrough came in my second year, in 1962, when I started exploring other departments. Although I knew I loved printed textiles, I still wasn't really sure where I belonged, or what kind of artist I wanted to be. There wasn't huge crossover between the different departments at that time, but I found myself drawn to fashion. Just as I felt comfortable when I first started design-ing fabric prints back at Medway, I immediately felt at home. The department was run by a formidably stylish woman called Janey Ironside, who was on a mission for her subject to be taken as seriously as an academic discipline. Janey had cropped dark hair and always wore dark clothes, her face punctuated with red lipstick. Her students included the shoe designer Moya Bowler and the fashion designers Bill Gibb and Ossie Clark, who was two years below me. At that time, the fashion students would host catwalk shows at the end of term to showcase their designs, and I would loiter in the studios watching the models being fitted into the clothes. Grace Coddington, who went on to become the legendary creative director at American *Vogue*, was among them. She looked amazing even then – so lithe and gamine.

My time in the fashion studios prompted a change in direction that had probably been bubbling under the surface since I was a little girl, quietly influenced by my mother. I liked the idea of producing things of use, and few things are more useful than clothes. I also started to design dress prints, huge colourful Matisse-like creations that dominated the fabric. Although my own appearance was relatively muted at that point (I had an unhealthy obsession with eyeliner and black false eyelashes), I was working closely with colour and still devising my own shades. I decided to bring everything together – colour, print and fashion – and turned my back on furnishing fabrics to focus instead on clothing materials. I had finally found my artistic language, and it existed within this hinterland between fashion and textiles. I realized that this was what I'd been trying to do all along, but I was using the wrong backdrop.

Few things feel as profoundly wonderful as landing on the thing you're meant to be doing. If you're lucky enough to find yourself in that position, grab it and put everything into it. I didn't have to think twice about whether it was the right decision. I knew innately that I was where I should be, which made the fight to move into a different discipline easier. Cross-pollination across departments was uncommon at that time – there was a general feeling that it was best to stay in one's lane – so I simply had to push my way in. No one told me explicitly that I couldn't move into fashion, but I was aware that it wasn't standard practice. I worked between the print and fashion departments, ignoring the stares from my peers until they got used to me being there.

I looked at the artist Sonia Delaunay, who combined textiles, fashion and art, and the abstract, vivid panel prints of Italian fashion designer Emilio Pucci, whose designs were then a mainstay in the pages of British *Vogue*. I wanted to create clothes that had confidence and power. My prints would be designed flat but would never be used statically: I wanted them to be cut and combined in different ways. The textiles would take precedence, controlling the design process. I began treating myself as a canvas; the prints would be self-assured, but I didn't want people to have to hold up their arms for the print to be seen at its best. To make sure my designs still had utility, I pinned painted paper to myself, observing how they looked in relation to the body. I then rearranged the textile accordingly. This remains a method I use today.

I still didn't know how to make a garment, so I turned to my mother, who did the practical part of making the textiles into dresses. I then wore them with a pair of second-hand Roger Vivier platforms and jewellery bought from Woolworths. My textiles were used by fashion students, one of whom was the out-spoken but hugely fun Ossie Clark. Alex had studied with Ossie at Manchester College of Art, so he and his girlfriend Celia Birt-well had become friends of ours. I collaborated with Ossie, producing a yellow silk textile covered with flowers like flags that appeared as shorts and a top in his final show.

I felt I was in a competitive atmosphere but it wasn't cutthroat. Back then, we were all united by a drive to progress our careers and pool talents to create the best possible product. Some of that camaraderie changed further down the line, but perhaps that's inevitable when money gets involved.

If the soundtrack to college was the Beatles and the Rolling Stones, the resounding image was Andy Warhol's soup cans. Pop Art had arrived in London from America, where it had begun in lowly advertising and comics. Art born of mass culture felt entirely new; it was no longer stuffy high culture. Warhol and Roy Lichtenstein were producing vivid works that challenged what art could be, making us look at ordinary items in a new way. It was as if an ice bucket had been thrown over the artistic landscape on a hot day – it was a shock and a delight.

Commercial art was becoming the new fine art, and it trans-lated well into textiles. I felt as if I was studying my métier at exactly the right time. My work was hugely influenced by Pop Art, and my sketchbooks bulged with vibrant homages. In my final year in 1964, we were asked to choose our 'Major Task', essentially for our final diploma show. My chief inspiration came via David Hockney's huge 1961 painting *A Grand Procession of Dignitaries in the Semi-Egyptian Style*, which depicted three elusive figures walking one in front of another down an incline. The tableau was inspired by the Greek poet Constantine Cavafy's 'Waiting for the Barbarians' and each of the men were painted to look like cutouts. What stood out to me were the medals that the second figure had pinned to his cloak, as well as along the top border of the painting. I don't know what it was about them specifically that struck me – it could have been the distinctive shape or their potential to be filled with saturated colour – but I decided that medals would form the theme of my final project.

I visited the Imperial War Museum, and the Wellington Collection at Apsley House near Hyde Park, and set about researching the various shapes and sizes of medals. I sketched the examples I saw, noting the bright grosgrain ribbons that they hung from. Influenced by military portraiture, I also toyed with stars and bows, incorporating them into my final design. Colour came next, and I decided the seriousness and pomp of the medals should be juxtaposed with Pop tones that infused a playful, positive energy. I have always loved garish shades – the colours often criticized for being too much or too bright – because they bring such richness and vibrancy to a design. I can appreciate elegant Scandinavian muted design, but it doesn't interest me. I have no desire to make things complement each other: life should be interesting, not tasteful. I felt proud of the results – it was the embodiment of what I wanted to achieve by infusing art with dress textiles. The final hand-printed textile cloths were hung on the walls, and my sketchbooks were presented on an accompanying table to explain my process.

My 'Medals' print for Heal's, 1964

To my utter delight, the Medal Series was bought by Heal's and produced as a furnishing fabric called Top Brass. It wasn't a clothing manufacturer, but it was a start and the boost I needed that affirmed my prints were at least of merit. Those medals were a strong visual representation of my style that even back then was bold, big and uncompromising. I was starting as I meant to go on.

What made the Heal's coup even more appreciated was a slight setback I'd had the month before in June. The college liked what I was doing, and one of my tutors told me that the great Emilio Pucci himself was making an in-store appearance at Woolland, a luxury department store that used to sit between Harrods and Harvey Nichols. Given our respective love of wild, abrasive prints, the tutor thought I'd be well suited to working at Pucci and suggested I go along to tout my wares. Strangely, I didn't feel apprehensive – I was proud of my work, and thought it was worth a punt. I went along wearing a grey suit – a copy of an Emmanuelle Khanh style that my mother had made, a mini skirt and matching jacket – with my white Roger Vivier shoes.

Mr Pucci was due to arrive at 2 p.m., when he would meet customers by his concession. I got there early and laid out my designs on the office floor. The great man arrived, looking every inch the consummate Italian aristocrat with immaculate, slicked-back hair, a deep tan and a sharp, navy blue suit. He was imbued with a quiet, restrained luxury that seemed entirely at odds with his energetic, swirling designs. I made a mental note that I would always be a poster girl for my own work. He walked straight over to me – after all I was hard to miss with my work splayed all over the carpeted floor. I introduced myself: 'Hello, Mr Pucci, I'm a huge fan of your prints and I wondered if you'd care to look at my designs?' He paused, looked at my colourful, highly saturated textiles and said, quite simply, 'I think you should design in black and white.' He turned on his heel and focused his gaze on the queue of people waiting to meet him. That was it, my dreams of working in Florence with Pucci dashed. It was quite the burn, but can you imagine if I'd listened to him? A life without colour isn't one I'd care to inhabit. We weren't all meant to fit in.

The most important things I learnt at the Royal College were how to design independently and what to discard. Any fool can learn technique if they work hard enough, but what's really valuable is knowing what's useful and what to get rid of, what doesn't work for you and what doesn't fit. I learnt that I didn't want to be a traditional textile designer designing mediocre furniture fabrics. My prints didn't fit that mould. I didn't fit that mould. I wanted to design dress fabrics that would challenge and inspire a strong feeling, good or bad. I wasn't about good taste. Knowing what you are not is very important – once you've worked that out, you can be what you truly are.

8

Round Table

1964 WAS A FABULOUS TIME to graduate from the Royal College. Having grown up in the grey, dreary post-war period, my class-mates and I were determined to live differently from our parents. The scars of the Blitz remained and bomb craters served as phys-ical reminders of how battered we'd been by the war, but there was an explosion of young people who wanted to change the world, whether in politics, fashion or music. Beatlemania was in full swing, Mary Quant had made clothes fun again and society was changing at a frenzied pace. Our world felt vivid, as if the saturation dial had been turned up to the max. The energy was phenomenal.

Everyone was setting up businesses just for fun; there was opti-mism and glitter in the air. No one in my circles ever had any money, but there was a shared sense that you could somehow make it work with enough enthusiasm and hard graft and, besides, we weren't driven by profit. This period brought a huge change in the way people lived their lives. It was a wild, whizzy time of change and fashion was at the centre of it as we kicked back against the colourless world we'd inherited. There was an influx of extraordinary creativity from designers like Biba's Barbara Hulanicki, Mary Quant, Jean Muir and Ossie Clark; and street style emerged – everyone became their own designer and created their uniquely individual look. Clothes were one of the easiest ways to express who we were and offered a clear rejection of conformity. What had until then been a snobby industry based mainly in Paris underwent a huge transformation. If you were even remotely creative, you blossomed.

In fact, the biggest, trendiest new names in art and culture came from working-class backgrounds: David Bailey, Michael Caine, Twiggy, David Hockney, the Beatles, Brian Duffy, to name a few. It didn't matter where you were from: if you had something new to say then people wanted to work with you. I suppose you could say that the class structure in Britain was almost like a caste system, but the sixties shattered it. No one had to speak with a plum in their mouth any more, which was a relief to me: I still have a Kentish twang.

With the Royal College behind me and endless opportunity ahead, I moved in with my boyfriend Alex McIntyre in September 1964. We'd been together for two years and were very much still bound by our intense work ethic and a shared drive to experiment and create. While we looked like hippie free spirits, me in clothes copied from the fashion magazine *Queen* (now known as *Harper's Bazaar*), which my mother had made, and he with his long hair, Spanish heeled shoes and pin-stripe trousers, we were ferociously keen to steam ahead with our desire to design and produce prints. Neither of us had any issue with relentless graft; in fact, it was something we understood as essential to make anything interesting. We ended up moving into a small ground-floor flat in St Stephen's Gardens in Notting Hill. It's a bit twee for me now but Notting Hill was a very different place back then. Creative people flocked to West London. Hockney lived nearby, our friends Janet and Tim Street-Porter were based in Fulham. Unlike today, renting in central London was accessible even to penniless artists at the time. I think our flat was ten pounds a week, and we even had our own bathroom at a time when a lot of people shared theirs with other apartments, and many houses still had outside loos.

Having graduated without a job to speak of, I lived a very hand-to-mouth existence. Alex and I would routinely run down to Portobello Market to buy the cheap fruit and veg that hadn't sold that day. We washed our clothes at the local launderette and on one occasion we couldn't understand why one of the driers was making a loud, repetitive banging noise. It transpired that someone was trying to thaw a frozen chicken in it. When we weren't working, which we nearly always were, we would drink endless cups of tea at a place called Mike's Café where Mick Jagger and Marc Bolan also hung out.

It was all pretty makeshift and art school-like, but it didn't matter to us. In our flat, we decided to create our own world inspired by the Pop Art with which we were obsessed. We wanted our home to make a statement about who we were personally and professionally. I didn't have a separate workspace then, so it was also our design studio. Eventually, we rented a studio a short walk away, but for now our home provided an opportunity to show the world who we were as designers and people.

We wanted to live in a space that felt truly 'designed', a reflection of the art we loved. Alex was then working for Thames TV as a set designer, so would bring home bits of unused props or materials for us to work with. First off, we covered everything in plastic, including the TV, which was more of a box then. We sourced a plastic grass carpet, which wasn't all that comfortable to walk on but looked fabulous. For the furniture, we drew abstract, wiggly shapes on the floor as patterns for the laminate and foam seating we built. We created a mad curved sofa from plywood and foam, which we covered in a blue woven fabric. That sofa followed me to two or three different places before it eventually disintegrated. We built a bar in the corner of the sitting room and constructed odd-looking platforms in unexpected places and steps where there hadn't been any before. We used cheap materials in an untamed, blatant way and bright colours. Combined, these were the essence of our Pop interiors. It wasn't about Pop imagery: we wanted to create a Pop manifestation, making Pop objects and furniture. We made Hockney's place look conventional in comparison.

I suppose it was terribly trendy but we weren't doing it to be cool. Perhaps you could say it was quite avant-garde. We weren't borrowing from anyone, we were reinventing decor. We had no interest in making the most of the Victorian cornices or detailing; we wanted to do away with all of that to create something new. If anything, we wanted to obliterate the Victorian style. At the time, my dear friend Piers Gough, now a very successful architect, said our flat had the strength of environment you might find in a shop, not someone's home. I also remember Ossie coming over and saying with mild horror, 'I can't believe you live like this.' (He and Celia had a more comfortable flat nearby.) But Alex and I loved the idea of a perfect world of plastic, a place that was honestly artificial.

At the centre of it all was a huge table that Alex and I designed together. I wanted to create something that would accommodate plenty of friends, so I made sure it could sit fourteen people. I had come from a family who rarely had guests for dinner, so the idea of entertaining appealed. It enabled us to socialize in a very personal way – cooking for people you like and love is much more intimate than going out to a restaurant. What you choose to feed your guests, who you invite and how you present and decorate your table says a lot about who you are. It's another form of

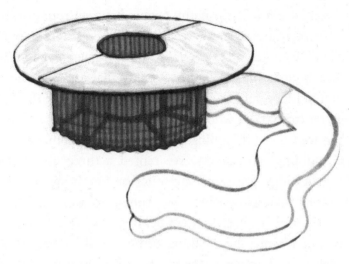

My round table and curved sofa

self-expression. It was also a way of socializing within our small budget, which in those days was very important. It was made from two semicircular pieces of plastic which could be stacked differently if we wanted it to serve as a stand or a bar. The green-trimmed silver-grey Formica top stood on top of a corrugated translucent orange acrylic base.

Alex and I would entertain most weekends and, at the time, I was famous for my beige meals: cream, pasta, potatoes and cheese. There were a few mishaps: once I dropped a whole salmon on the floor. I didn't tell anyone. We'd all listen to the Beatles and do the twist; sometimes a joint would be passed around. Friends tell me they still remember those parties, which is a great compliment. Many people passed through, and some even stayed on mattresses on the floor, such as Emmanuelle Khanh's sister-in-law, who came with Paloma Picasso when they were skint students, arriving on motorbikes.

That table is just as useful today in my penthouse as it was when we first made it. So many people have sat round it, from Larry Hagman and Diana Vreeland to John Waters and Alan Rickman. I like introducing people I think will get on and watching them bounce off each other. I enjoy that aspect of hosting very much. I love cooking in the kitchen and hearing the sound of laughter from those who have only just met.

When we weren't designing or entertaining at home, Alex and I were building our careers. We rented a three-storey studio nearby in a dingy corner of Bayswater on Porchester Road and set up a print company where we printed my work and that of other fashion labels. I can't remember how this work came about exactly, but I remember making prints for the designer John Bates, who was famous as the creator of costumes for the TV show *The Avengers*. It wasn't lucrative, but it covered our costs. Without much money, we heated the place with paraffin stoves and kept our outgoings to a minimum. I also got a part-time job, teaching one day a week at Ravensbourne College of Art in Chislehurst, and a second day at High Wycombe College of Art and Technology (now called Buckinghamshire New University). I loathed it. All I wanted was to create my own work, but teaching enabled me to do the thing I loved so I persevered. Former students, who include the designer Betty Jackson and the writer and illustrator Michael Roberts, say I was an inspiring teacher, but I'm not so sure. Students deserve your undivided attention, but my mind was always elsewhere. I simply didn't want to be there. Every hour I spent teaching was an hour not creating my own designs.

At the time, my work – like my home – was influenced by Pop Art, taking inspiration from neon signs, electric sculptures and comic-book motifs. I wanted my prints to be so radical and distinctive that a garment would be incomplete without them. They had to be more than just a pattern that would work anywhere: I wanted to establish a new concept of textile design where the print dictated the cut and shape of the garment.

Having been advised by my tutors at the Royal College to pitch my textile designs to big companies, one weekend not long before I moved in with Alex I went to Manchester – where the major fabric wholesalers were then based – to tout my wares. I spent the day presenting my paper prints to different uninterested men in suits. Every single one told me they were too bold and extreme to have any commercial appeal. In return, they showed me terrible but profit-making prints that had apparently sold by the bucket load. I don't know why, but this didn't put me off. I decided that what we find ugly today will be beautiful tomorrow, and not to compare myself to others. What I was aspiring to do hadn't been done before; I was tired of good taste and wanted to break every rule previously adhered to. I had to follow my own beliefs not those of others, something I champion as an approach in life.

I returned to London empty-handed and knew that, in practical terms, if I was to have any success, I would have to work doubly hard. I would arrive at my studio at seven thirty in the morning and finish at ten at night, often later. Grafting seemed the only way through – how can you expect to be original without constant re-examination? If I was to create prints that didn't look like anything else, I had to keep collecting ideas. I wanted to do the opposite of what had already been done. During this time, I would, of course, still host dinner parties for which I would come home earlier to prepare, but I always ended up falling asleep at the table. I would never expect guests to leave when I conked out, and thankfully no one did. Nor did they seem to mind.

As mine wasn't an approach that the mainstream textiles businesses wanted to back, I decided to reach out to Marion Foale and Sally Tuffin. Marion and Sally had been a few years above me at the Royal College and, together, they'd launched their own label, offering playful, daring clothes that were so popular they had opened a store on Carnaby Street. They were the first to introduce the women's trouser suit to a wide audience. David Bailey had already photographed their work for *Vogue* and they were exactly the sort of open-minded, boundary-breaking creatives I wanted to work with.

With a fearlessness that amazes me now, I looked up the shop number in the phone book and called out of the blue. I got through to their secretary and convinced her to arrange a meeting where I would pitch myself. I arrived at their shop in the summer of 1964 wearing my best Biba white boots, clutching my folder under one arm. If I felt nervous, I don't remember it – I approached it all rather pragmatically as I believed in my designs. If I couldn't sell myself to the people I admired, no one could.

The decor of the Foale and Tuffin shop was minimalist and contemporary – scaffolding poles hung across the width of the interior, with hangers of clothes neatly suspended at either side. The label name was lit up in red and blue light bulbs on the walls, the counter was bright white and a mannequin designed to look like Twiggy stood in the window. It was easily one of the coolest boutiques in London. I introduced myself to the girl behind the till, who sent me upstairs to meet Marion and Sally. They were both dressed in their own designs, the living, breathing embodiment of fresh-faced, fizzing London.

After a few rudimentary niceties, I opened my folder and laid it on their desk. 'I think we should work together,' I said. 'You make the sort of clothes I like, and I think you might like the sort of prints I make.' Marion and Sally took one look at my designs and saw a synergy in my energetic, lively prints and their playful design aesthetic and gave me my first job on the spot. I was thrilled, I knew it was a wonderful opportunity. All I had to do now was deliver. They chose three designs from my final college show and I created three prints specifically for them – one a star print in red, white and blue, the colours of the Union flag, which was very much an emblem of sixties British fashion. As part of our deal, I also insisted that every time I made a print for Marion and Sally a separate label with my name must be sewn into the garment, and that if any of my designs ever appeared in the press, so must my name. It was rare in fashion at that point – and even now – that a print designer be credited for their work, but I knew I had to try to get my name out somehow. It was through this credit that the *New York Herald Tribune*'s star fashion writer Eugenia Sheppard first saw my name and decided to interview me when she visited London in 1965. Press wasn't global then, as it is now, so to achieve any international press coverage was a huge coup and one I never took for granted.

In the end, that first collection turned out to be tricky to produce because Sally and Marion were keen to use wool, which is a very difficult fabric to print pigment on. I had to use acid dyes with a laborious technique of steaming and washing to finish the dyeing process. But it was worth the work. In December 1964, six months after graduating from the Royal College, I landed my first ever magazine cover on *Queen* with my Star Trellis print made into a trouser suit modelled by Jill Kennington, who was the supermodel of her day. I was over the moon. My memory of how we celebrated is dim and distant, but I'm sure it would have been at that big round table, no doubt with a bowl of delicious beige.

I would continue to work with Foale and Tuffin for four seasons. Sally and Marion were dynamic, savvy designers but I had begun creating more experimental designs that, after a while, no longer chimed with their vision. I wanted to work with crude, disquieting colours to create something new in which the print led the garment – I was hell bent on the idea that ugliness accentuates beauty. I didn't want my patterns to be cut out at random: I felt there were more possibilities in what the garment and print could do together. I had to be me, so we parted ways. Ahead lay more people to meet, and a rocky, volatile collaboration that was finally to set me on my own wiggly design path.

9

Alex's Mini

OVER CHRISTMAS 1967, ALEX AND I went on a road trip to Rome with Ossie Clark and Celia Birtwell that somehow broke our friendship. Ultimately, our work separated us, but the tension began that strange week in Italy.

By the time we decided on the trip, we were all a few years out of college and in the early stages of our careers. In many ways, we were very similar. We were all interested in art, print and quality design. Alex and I had a romantic and creative partnership, as did Ossie and Celia, who had been working together since 1965. They were a fabulous pairing – her pretty, feminine prints were the perfect juxtaposition for his hard-edged, beautifully cut designs. They balanced each other personally too. Celia was always more of a homebody while Ossie was the star of every dinner party. They were regulars at our round table in St Stephen's Gardens, and I always knew that if Ossie was there, the evening would be entertaining. He was gregarious, clever and a fantastic conversationalist. Ossie liked making friends with new people, although if you started to bore him, he'd move on to someone else. Celia was quieter, and a grounding force.

Although Ossie and I were both very ambitious, he was at a far buzzier point in his career than I was. The King's Road shop,

Quorum, where he was co-designer, was one of London's coolest hangouts and his clients included Mick and Bianca Jagger, Twiggy and Anita Pallenberg. He was already being hailed the King of the King's Road and socialized in far starrier circles than I did. Celia and Ossie were great friends of David Hockney, who would go on to draw a portrait of them in their Notting Hill apartment. I had recently stopped designing for Foale and Tuffin and was still working part time as a teacher at Ravensbourne amid accepting commissions from textile companies. My name had appeared in *Vogue*, yet I was at a strange impasse. I had big goals, to establish a new conception of textile design in which the print dictated the construction of the garment, but I didn't yet know how to move forward. I knew not to give up, but I was experiencing a creative block. Worry has often been a huge hindrance to my ability to experiment. It clogs my brain, which I need to be free for new ideas to blossom. The idea of a holiday seemed pragmatic as well as fun – a way of hitting reset, which would enable me to concentrate on my work again.

The idea of taking a road trip to Rome probably came about over dinner at the round table. I imagine Ossie engineered it, he being the most domineering and dazzling of our four-piece. It sounded like such a whizzy adventure. The plan was to drive through France and Switzerland, then to Rome over a few days. We'd stay at an apartment of one of Ossie's friends who lived there, bury ourselves in exhibitions, architecture and pasta, then drive home. As Alex was the only one who could actually drive, as well as being the only one with a car, we were to travel in his fabulous cream Mini, already *the* car to be seen in if you were a twenty-something Londoner. It was youthful and punchy, but also, as became clear over the course of the trip, cramped and uncomfortable. It was a four-seater with only two doors, which required you to assume the most experimental yoga poses to get into the back seats. Furthermore, the interiors were also cream, which Alex always insisted were kept clean. He loved that car. He'd seen it through the window of the Stewart & Ardern showroom in Berkeley Square, Mayfair, and bought it on the spot for around five hundred pounds. It was easy to run and stylish without being pretentious.

We decided to go to Rome over Christmas. We were all workaholics but I think we accepted that the week of 25 December would not be productive anyway. We got so swept up in the romantic idea of a road trip to Italy that we forgot we didn't know each other very well. That was our first misstep.

We set off the week before Christmas. It was freezing in London and our luggage sagged under the weight of our expectations and sketchbooks. The journey was expected to take two days but ended up taking five. Alex's Mini broke down twice – once in northern France where we had to spend two nights in an ugly motorway hotel waiting for it to be fixed – and then again in Switzerland where we had to stay overnight in an equally unpleasant hotel that cost even more money. None of us had any cash at that point so it was all very hand-to-mouth. For all of Ossie's fame, he was no businessman and had zero idea of how to manage his money. The sheets were damp and there was a bluebottle nest in the corner of our bedroom in France. The window overlooked a wall in Switzerland. It was so far from our idea of the Italian *dolce vita* that it was almost laughable, except we weren't laughing. None of us could speak much French, and very few French mechanics in the sixties could speak English. Every night we stayed in those squalid hovels was financially ruinous, but we had no option. It would have put a strain on the best of friends, but for us four – who knew each other only as industry friends – it was disastrous.

Eventually, we made it over the Great St Bernard Pass into

Italy. It was a beautiful part of the journey and Alex's Mini chugged past wild snowy mountains and icy lakes, but it was bitterly cold inside the car. Celia and I sat shivering in the back seat, knees bunched up over our bags, her in a big fur coat that Ossie had made for her and I secretly coveted. We must have been a real sight to behold – this flamboyantly dressed group of twenty-somethings all jammed into a tiny cream car, winding round the Alps in uncompanionable silence.

We arrived in Rome late in the afternoon to find the city covered with snow. I think we all hoped that the mood would lift, but our combined malaise stuck to us like mosquito spray. I had travelled abroad before, to Paris with my mother and sister, and to Austria as part of an exchange programme, but I'd never been to Italy. Rome was spectacular, all fountains, snow-capped sculptures, spaghetti and astonishingly beautiful churches. It smelt of exhaust fumes, cigarettes and pastries. Everyone stared at us – Celia and I were wearing miniskirts and huge dramatic coats, mine a white and orange mini style from the finale RCA show of Brian Godbold, who went on to become design director at Marks & Spencer. It didn't bother me and my thick skin a jot, but it unnerved Celia, who seemed uneasy.

I can't remember which museums and galleries we visited, but I do remember how reluctant we all were to talk about what we thought of what we saw. None of us, not even Ossie, who was usually very generous with his opinions, volunteered information about what they loved or hated. We were four creatives of the same generation, all part of the same scene. It should have been a gorgeous cross-pollination of ideas and inspirations, but it wasn't. Everyone was cagey, non-committal and guarded. No one wanted to impart the wrong opinion, which I suppose shows a shared respect between us at least. I valued the opinion of Celia and Ossie, but perhaps I wasn't comfortable enough with them to be truly open. The rest of the trip continued in a similar vein – stilted conversation, bravado and half-truths about who we were and wanted to be. We returned to London a week later and didn't speak to each other for a while. Our paths crossed at fashion events and mutual friends' dinners, but not as friends. Our trip to Rome didn't solidify our friendship: it revealed the cracks that would widen as time went on.

When I look back on it now, perhaps we all realized after spending a chunk of time together that we were more in competition with each other than we'd initially thought. Perhaps at the start of that trip, Ossie still thought of me as a textiles designer but after a week he realized I was a textiles designer who wanted to create clothes too. When you're young, which we were, you can feel threatened by someone whose work is similar to your own. I'm not saying that was how Ossie felt, but I think we all experienced a strange competitiveness that week. As you grow older, you hope that you become comfortable enough in your skin and confident enough in your own abilities to know that there is room for everyone. The fashion world, particularly, needs lots of differing viewpoints and voices. I've been around long enough to know there will be times when friends feel ahead of you professionally, and other times that you will be ahead of them. To agonize over other people's successes turns you into a sour old grape. Competition is inevitable, like it or not. The trick is to let it propel you forward and enrich your life, not destroy it.

10

Duggie Fields Painting

BEFORE THE LATE ARTIST DUGGIE Fields and I became friends, he wanted to sue me. I first met him in the mid-sixties through a mutual friend and stylist, Chelita Secunda, who famously created Marc Bolan's glam-rock look. She took me to Duggie's Earl's Court flat, where he worked. It was a large, messy and artistic space, made up of three giant rooms he shared with Pink Floyd singer Syd Barrett, whom he'd met at Regent Street Polytechnic where he briefly studied architecture. Cigarettes had been painted into the floor, mannequins stood in corners and large-scale canvases were propped up on every flat surface.

I saw the art before I saw Duggie, and it was love at first sight. Leaning up against the whitewashed wall was a huge square cartoon-like painting of a magical landscape, where a graphic blue river zigzagged through a green field. The water was peppered with fish and flanked by tall trees. To the right stood a big house; its windows were framed by bright curtains and a woman with brown hair looked out from one. The image was speckled with vivid geometric shapes, red, white, yellow and green triangles and odd-shaped slabs that were confetti-like in their distribution. It was so colourful and innovative: the lines were all straight and immaculately executed to a standard that only hours

upon hours of hard work can produce. There were top notes of
Mondrian and Dalí, but there was also such clear-sighted singu-
larity. It was a crisp, clean-edged post-Pop masterpiece, and it
represented everything I love – colour, creativity and originality.
I wanted it.

The problem was, as usual, I was broke. I was fresh out of the
Royal College, and although I was still working with Foale and
Tuffin, cash was far from abundant. Just as I was pondering how
on earth I would pay for it, Duggie entered the room from the
kitchen, an art-school dandy with an outsized quiff and a kiss
curl that sat on his forehead like a reverse question mark. His
eyes were rimmed with dark kohl, and he wore a colourful,
sharply cut suit and polished shoes. He simply didn't look like
anyone I'd ever met. He must have been twenty-one or twenty-
two then, but his look, as in his art, was already fully formed. It's
been said that he looked like a living painting and that is how I'd
describe him: a walking version of his work. Duggie never could
see the difference between art, style and life, and I suppose we
had that in common.

I asked him how much he wanted for it. He said he'd need a
ten-pound deposit, and that I could pay the remaining £110 later.
I agreed, knowing full well he'd be waiting a long time for that
money. I would repay my debt, but I couldn't say when that day
might come. Thankfully, Duggie didn't set a date so I brought the
painting home with Chelita, who helped me drag it on and off
the bus. It didn't occur to me that I might have bought a future
collector's item, I just knew I loved it. Alex and I put it up in a
room that didn't have much light and covered the small existing
window with the painting. *Big House in the Landscape*, as the
piece was officially called, was the view we wished we had. I
draped curtains either side and we placed an uplighter beneath to
make the image really stand out, which I then concealed with

hardboard panels that I'd cut out to echo the forms in the painting. Finally, I placed plastic flowers around it, which brought the picture right into the room.

A few months later Duggie knocked on the door to collect my outstanding debt. I had already received a call from his solicitor chasing me for the money and even threatening to sue me if I didn't pay it immediately, but I still didn't have it. Feeling terrible, I had stalled him, hoping I'd somehow be entrusted with a windfall. But here was a fairly cross-looking Duggie in person. I ate humble pie, apologized profusely and invited him in for a cup of tea. He reluctantly came inside and I showed him what I'd done with the painting. He loved it. I think he could see how much I appreciated and understood his work. We came to an arrangement whereby I would pay for it in instalments, a far more manageable solution. I did repay Duggie eventually, so thankfully we never got as far as the courts.

After that, Duggie and I became close friends. He was a lynchpin of my round-table dinner parties, a quiet, gentle guest with a discerning eye for art and style. After Syd Barrett left London when his drug habit worsened, Duggie remained in the Earl's Court flat where he lived until he died in 2021. He turned it into a maximalist temple covered with murals and filled with stacks of his beautiful paintings. Duggie was much more interested in the party scene than I was and regularly went to hip haunts, like Blitz and Embassy, with all the other beautiful weirdos. You'd never see him drunk on the dance-floor, though: he was a voyeur – someone who liked to watch and observe – and because of that he was very interesting. I think he always thought of himself as an outsider, so it wouldn't have felt natural to him to force himself into the mêlée.

We were both very work-led people who loved colour and Duggie's output was prolific. He would spend months trying to

My sketch of Duggie Fields' Magic Landscape Painting

create the illusion of a curve with straight lines, or how to perfectly construct an image using geometry. Watching him at work
was an extraordinary experience and it galvanized me. Without
intending to, Duggie and I and a few other friends, including
mirror and glass sculptor, artist and jewellery designer Andrew
Logan, filmmaker Derek Jarman and artist Kevin Whitney,
formed a loose gang of creatives that became known as 'Them'.
The name was coined by cultural historian Peter York in a 1976
article that appeared in *Harpers & Queen* to describe a tribe of

people who lived 'art-directed lives' and were interested in looking 'interesting rather than sexy'. I suppose you could say we were
the British version of Warhol's Factory. None of it was deliberate,
just an ebb and flow of creatives who enjoyed riffing off one
another. We all wore Andrew's jewellery, bought one another's art
and hosted parties at our respective homes.

Duggie and I spoke on the phone every day for more than sixty
years. We understood each other's visual language and had great
respect for it. I would call him whenever I was stuck on a design,
and he would help me through, suggesting exhibitions to visit,
films to watch and buildings to research. He must have spent
hours coaxing me out of creative black holes and evaluating my
work. It was Duggie who first suggested I consider doing a punk-
inspired collection, which would become one of my most
influential after its release in 1977. Our mutual friend Andrew
Logan said he could be quite critical and, although I don't remember that aspect of him, it's true that he always spoke his mind. He
was very direct: if he didn't like something I'd designed, he'd tell
me, and he was one of the few people I'd listen to. There was
complete honesty between us. Perhaps that's one of the joys of
friendship – finding people who see the best in us even when
we struggle to see it ourselves. Duggie was a brilliant and astute
sounding board and I cannot emphasize enough how much he
influenced my work. Every collection I've ever done was improved
under his exacting eye.

Inexplicably, fame never arrived for Duggie. He became a huge
star in Japan after cosmetics firm Shiseido hosted an exhibition
of his work in the early eighties and, aged thirty-seven, he became
the face of its teenage line, Perky Jean. He was a household name
there and was mobbed in the streets of Tokyo by young girls who
had seen the campaign. In 2007 he appeared as a model on the
Comme des Garçons catwalk, but his artistic genius was never

recognized fully in this country. I campaigned for him to be honoured as a Royal Academician, which would have been a way of
recognizing and celebrating his talent, but was ultimately unsuc-
cessful. He died of lung cancer on 7 March 2021 and the world is
a duller place as a result. I miss talking to him, I miss his advice,
but I try not to think about the loss of it too much – focusing on
the past rather than the present never did anyone any good. Duggie's goal was never to have his work showcased at high-culture
museums and galleries. He would have thought that terribly
bourgeois. His goal was always to be a true bohemian, which he
was in its truest sense.

I still have *Big House in the Landscape* on my wall in my Bermondsey penthouse, a perfect abstract view. It reminds me of
Duggie, and how he enriched my life.

11

Joe Cocker Album

IT'S IMPOSSIBLE TO KNOW WHERE and when you might meet the people who will shape the course of your life. Each tripwire leads to a different set of circumstances from which a new path opens. All we can do is approach life with enthusiasm because whatever route we take will deliver good and bad. If I run at life with excitement and passion I've found, by and large, I'll be met with it in return.

I met Sylvia Ayton, my first ever business partner, when I was working at Ravensbourne College of Art. I still hated teaching, it was a distraction from my own designs, but I needed the money. It enabled me to do the work I wanted to do so I stuck at it. If I hadn't, perhaps Sylvia and I would never have come across each other and I would not have learnt from the mistakes I made in our partnership.

Sylvia also taught fashion at Ravensbourne. She didn't hate teaching as much I did, but we would sit on the train from London together and discuss what we wanted to do with our careers. Sylvia was a good friend of Sally Foale and Marion Tuffin, whom I had recently finished working with. Having trained at Walthamstow School of Art and later at the Royal College, she drew beautiful fashion drawings that I loved, and aspired to become a designer.

She was an excellent pattern-cutter and her designs focused on a simplicity that felt interesting and clever. We were sitting in the dreary college canteen one day in early 1967 when I suggested we create a collection together. It's not enough just to moan about your lot: if you're unhappy with your life, do something about it, no matter how small the step – push for something you believe in. That little speck might lead somewhere, as it did for me.

I was looking for the right vehicle to keep progressing with my work, and Sylvia, with her technical understanding of garment construction, felt like the perfect partner. I believed in my textiles, but I didn't know how to make clothes. The initial deal was that I would design the prints and she would design the garments. If she had any trepidation about our venture, she didn't show it or maybe I was too bullish to notice. We began by selling our designs wholesale to high-street brands including Topshop and the now defunct luxury American department store Altman & Co. We were good at marketing our work, which was how we found stockists. Every moment that we weren't designing, we were enlisting the help of friends to create promotional images, which we'd then send to the press. Jacqui McLennan, one of my friends, also a textile designer from the Royal College, would model for us. Jacqui had infinite legs, a blonde bob and angular features, the perfect canvas for our designs. Another of our Royal College friends, Roy Giles, took the photos. No one was paid anything: we were all keen to build up our portfolios and exchange skills and talents. Alex would drive us around in his Mini early on weekend mornings when London was still asleep, trying to find suitable locations for photoshoots. Jacqui would get changed in the back seat and would hop out once we found a backdrop we liked. Our first piece of press arrived in April 1967 after the flamboyant fashion editor Molly Parkin ran a piece about us in *Nova*, then a groundbreaking, new magazine known for showcasing the brightest, most cutting-edge fashion. It was an exciting moment, and it really felt as if things were taking off.

Sylvia and I both felt we could drum up more business without relying solely on shop buyers. We wanted to go direct to the public. What we needed was our own boutique, somewhere to showcase our work in exactly the environment where we wanted it to be seen. It would be a way of communicating our vision to our customers and extending our design world. The only tiny, insignificant obstacle was funding: neither of us had the spare cash to rent a shop. Our collection was doing well, but we were hardly overburdened with money. As has happened many times in my life, a friend swooped in to help, A photographer from the Royal College, Annette Green, had recently worked with the actress Vanessa Redgrave on a shoot, and had told her about our hopes to open a boutique. Such an interaction would never happen now – you'd never dream of pitching a friend's business to a celebrity on set: it would be seen as unprofessional. It was different in the sixties: there was such an open, positive energy. It was all very DIY, and often a little ramshackle, but creatives wanted to help creatives. We all thought anything was possible.

Incredibly, Vanessa – who had just appeared in the decade's buzziest arthouse film *Blow-Up* – agreed to invest £1,000, roughly the equivalent of £30,000 today. We went to see her in person and I think she was swept away by our enthusiasm and self-belief. It's amazing what you can achieve if you come full throttle at something you care about. We didn't have much to do with her after that, but we did create a fabric design in her honour which read 'We love you Vanessa'.

The next decision was where the shop would be. Carnaby Street was a little too mass, and most shops there sold very cheap clothes. I had nothing against that, but I knew our product was high-end. The most cutting-edge, forward-thinking shops were on the King's Road in Chelsea, where Quorum, Granny Takes a Trip and Mary Quant's Bazaar were based. Fulham Road was also on the rise. It wasn't far from King's Road, but it was more affordable. Terence Conran had opened the first Habitat there three years before, which sparked its reputation as a district with real potential. Sadly, it never lived up to the hype: it didn't have the footfall of King's Road, or its star pull. Arguably, the Fulham Road Clothes Shop was destined to fail as soon as we'd settled on that location.

Nevertheless, Sylvia and I decided to proceed with the shop, continuing with the same way of working, me on prints and her on garment design. Her minimalist, clean silhouettes were an ideal bedfellow for my bold prints. It was a formula that had so far served us well in terms of sales and press attention, but I was already feeling an itch to design at least some of the clothes. I kept my feelings to myself initially, as we started working with Alex to devise the concept for the decor of the shop, which we wanted to be revolutionary and high art. This was the start of another mistake: the interior design didn't work commercially. We blocked the windows so you couldn't see in, and retrospectively I think people found that too difficult – it looked too exclusive and intimidating. The only displays we had on show were flashing neon lights: there were no clothes on mannequins. The entrance led straight downstairs to a cavernous space with white walls covered with huge photographs of our designs. The changing rooms were concealed inside mirrored pillars and the clothing racks were made using illuminated fibreglass. We made our own rubber furniture and colourful slides showcasing the collection were projected onto one wall. It was piercingly modern and looked more like a gallery than a shop. Artistic vision is all very well, but designers must consider the customer first and foremost, which we didn't in the case of the Fulham Road Clothes Shop.

That became clear much later. To begin with, it was a big success. There was still so much buzz around London at that time, and when we opened in June 1967 it was to huge fanfare. Sylvia and I wanted to host an opening party but had no idea how big it would end up. Fashion was such a small world back then, everyone knew everyone else, and if something was happening, you would find out about it if you were in any way connected to the scene. Nothing was off limits, or exclusive. Hundreds of people turned up that evening. At one point, Fulham Road had to be closed because of the throngs milling around outside. We staged a very ad-hoc fashion show, where friends of mine, Penelope Tree and Janet Street-Porter, modelled various pieces from the collection. I remember concealing Penelope's spots with blue sequins, and off she went up the stairs to twirl amid the guests. She looked fabulous. The clothes were youthful, bold and wearable, which fortunately seemed to strike a chord with the free-spirited mood of the sixties. I think it's important not to romanticize any past decade too much, though: I've always thought the most exciting thing is still to come. I have always absorbed what's happening around me and taken it forward.

I asked every friend I'd ever known to help us hand out drinks and to help dress the models, and I paid them in chiffon scarves and dresses. Annette, who had already done so much for us in persuading Vanessa Redgrave to invest in us, came up trumps again by enlisting the great Joe Cocker to perform that evening. He was riding high after the release of his single 'With A Little Help From My Friends', which we all thought was such a soulful alternative to the Beatles' original. I remember standing outside in the midsummer evening sunshine listening to Joe's gruff, raspy voice singing and feeling an undiluted, delirious happiness. I don't play a lot of music, but every time I hear Joe's records I remember that perfect June evening when it seemed as if the universe was truly opening up.

For a time, the shop ticked over. Fashion magazines including *Women's Wear Daily*, *Nova* and British and American *Vogue* gave us coverage, which generated more hype and custom. We became known for my vibrant, playful, Pop-influenced prints and Sylvia's modern shapes. I toyed with disquieting colours, faded yellows, oranges and blues, fusing them with light-bulb patterns. I came up with my now famous lipstick print after seeing a Christian Dior beauty advert, in which photographer Guy Bourdin had shot an almost surrealist image of a woman's side profile with three fingers lined up next to each other, each nail perfectly painted. I reinterpreted the fingers as lipsticks and drew them alongside lips. It worked well, especially in punchy red shades, and became a signature of mine. We also began selling paper dresses in fluorescent pink and yellow purely because they worked so well as a backdrop to the prints. A few months later, we came up with the idea of turning the patterns into body transfers, almost like temporary tattoos, which we sold exclusively at Harrods. They felt unconventional without being too subversive, and ultimately a new way of showing off the prints. Our bestsellers were our printed chiffon caftans, which turned everyone who wore them into glamorous fairy-like bohemians.

We worked hard, creating two new styles each week to ensure that we always had something fresh to present to our customers. I'd be up at 5.30 a.m., printing at my studio by 6 a.m., and would finish around 10 p.m. I'd pop into the shop a few days a week, but I wasn't there full-time like Sylvia, who designed in a tiny room at the back. I was also still working two days a week at

Ravensbourne, but I had become more at peace with that side of my life: I was creatively fulfilled, so it mattered less.

Cracks started to appear after I asked Sylvia to show me how to create a garment. I wanted to know more about pattern-cutting. I knew I was stepping on her toes, but my prints each had their own personality and we were starting to have different ideas about how the clothes should look in terms of print and shape. I wanted the freedom to allow the print to dictate the silhouette, not the other way round. I knew I was on to something original and I didn't want to compromise any more. The prints needed to be so powerful that the garment would be incomplete without them. Sylvia was keen to follow a more conventional way of design and was concerned that my vision would render the clothes undesirable and unwearable. I believed in my core that I must continue developing and pushing the concept I had in my mind. Progress means doing something different, even if it feels horribly uncomfortable.

By Christmas that year, six months after the shop had opened, relations had started to sour in earnest. I used to work late into the night, which added to Sylvia's resentment. My work has nearly always taken precedence over anything else, and I think that must be very frustrating for anyone who wants to go home on time – it must make you feel like you have to do the same. I wanted to spend more time on the prints and the construction, and I didn't mind putting in the long hours that most people object to. Sometimes I doubted my humanity as I never prioritized domesticity over my professional life. I was lucky that Alex was obsessed with his work too, so my beavering away at all hours wasn't a problem. My goal wasn't to be famous. I did things because I believed in them and I didn't want to teach any more. If I wanted to do a design with cars on it, I just did it regardless of what anyone else thought.

My increasingly extreme appearance became a real sticking point. I shaved my hairline back so I had more of a canvas for my make-up. There were no beauty brands like MAC then, so I bought make-up from Woolworths and drew red curls on my face using lipstick. My hair was dyed blue and black, which I sometimes covered with a turban, and I shaved off my eyebrows and replaced them with a line of blue glitter dots. I outlined my eyes with Pentel felt-tip pen, then glued two sets of false eyelashes to each lid. It was the sixties after all, so I wore the tiniest of pelmet skirts, which barely concealed my knickers. To me, it was experimentation, but to Sylvia it was worrying. She'd tell me to hide in the back of the shop in case I frightened the buyers and customers. People were more open-minded than they had been, but there was a still a hangover from the conservative fifties, and she was sensitive, perhaps, to that.

I truly didn't care what Sylvia thought, but it was more of a problem that Alex didn't love my theatrical look either. No one wants their boyfriend to dislike their appearance and I pretended not to notice when he'd scoff at a particularly bold eye-shadow or a pattern I'd scrawled on my face. I was usually too busy worrying about work to take in much from either of them. When I look at pictures of myself from that time, some of it looks extreme but I didn't think so. I've always been a believer that if you design clothes, you should wear the clothes you design. It's like saying, 'I'm a cook, but I don't eat my own food.' Why should anyone else wear it if you don't? You have to show you believe in it.

Sales started to wane, as did the buzz surrounding the shop. We were no longer the hot new thing, and the press had moved on. I don't know whether it had anything to do with my appearance, but I suspect it was more rooted in the location, our unapproachable-looking shop and the fact that we didn't have a strong business infrastructure. Neither of us knew the slightest thing about how a company should work. Neither of us had a salary. I was living off my teaching money and I think Sylvia was leaning on her partner. We began to build debts and Sylvia remembers having to hide in the toilet when the bailiffs arrived, which they did on multiple occasions in the spring of 1968. The location of the shop was becoming an obvious issue: Fulham Road never took off in the way King's Road had. Very few people came in. The pressure on both of us was huge, and we were hardly talking.

One morning in May 1968, Sylvia called a meeting. We sat in the back room of the store, and she told me she'd secured a new designer job at a big high-street brand called Wallis. Her leaving brought the boutique to a close, which was probably a good thing – left to my own devices I'd probably have dragged it out to the bitter end. I usually refuse to give up on anything, but Sylvia saw the writing was on the wall long before I did. We closed the Fulham Road Clothes Shop a year after it opened. I don't know why, but I didn't feel too downbeat. I should have been devastated when all I had left was that horrible teaching job. The truth was that I had learnt a lot from the past twelve months – not only how *not* to run a shop but also that I had to branch out on my own, using my prints as I wanted. I was more clear-sighted about my vision than I ever had been, and I knew then there was no room for a design partner. The store had been a financial disaster, but it had instilled clarity that I was hell bent on following. That's the thing about failure: it doesn't have to crush you. It can be a starting point for growth. All I needed to do was work out my next steps. I would return to my sketchbooks and design my way through.

12

Knitted Landscape Scarf

I SPENT THE SUMMER OF 1969 creating my first solo collection. I had decided I wasn't or couldn't be a designer who fitted into someone else's mould. My ideas were too bold, too strong for any enduring partnership, so I had to launch my own label. You could say I failed upwards into running my own brand. I am, ultimately, a textile designer who couldn't find a job, and if I'd been better at working with others and less dogged about my vision, perhaps Sylvia and I would still be in business, but I wasn't so I was left to decide what my first collection would look like.

There were days when I felt flat, when instead of leaping out of bed at 5.30 a.m. I would lie in until seven, thinking I would never have another original thought. I began filling my sketchbook with drawings of things I saw in parks and museums, but none of it set off the ions in my brain as happens when I feel inspired. Ultimately, my mother's tenacious spirit pulled me through from beyond the grave: there was no choice other than to keep going. This had to be the start of something new and exciting because, frankly, the alternative was too depressing to consider.

I quit teaching altogether, which flabbergasts me now. I had the odd commission coming in from furnishing companies, but not many. Money was very, very tight, and it wasn't a very balanced decision, but I've never been a balanced sort of person. Perhaps imbalance has kept me feeling young enough to do all the things I want to do. My focus was the collection and, after a few weeks of feeling stuck and morose, I decided a change of scenery might be the jolt I needed. Alex and I were great friends with Janet Street-Porter, who was then working as deputy fashion editor at the *Daily Mail*, and her husband Tim, a rising photographer. We'd met four years earlier at a house party in 1965, and got on straight away. We both looked extreme – Janet was going through a phase of wearing a lot of silver and streaking her hair with silver spray; she looked like a noisy piece of tin foil in platform shoes. Like me, she was also very enthusiastic and strong-minded. We were both absorbed by our work, but she was better at striking an equilibrium between work and play – Janet made time for socializing and having fun. I never had any interest in clubbing or fancy restaurants, not at that point anyway. The glittering allure of Studio 54 would grip me in a few years' time, but back in 1969, my life was my work, Alex and the odd beige dinner at our big round table. I revolved around this small orbit, but when you love what you do and the person you're with, you don't need much else.

Except I did. I needed to find inspiration, so I took Janet and Tim up on their invitation to stay at his parents' holiday cottage in Tregaron, an ancient market town in Wales. We decided to go for a week that summer in 1968 and all four of us travelled there in Alex's infamous Mini. You'd have thought our road trip to Rome would have put us off making the long journey but, thankfully, it didn't. The drive was gruelling and we arrived late in the evening; all you could see was the outline of the grey stone cottage and the star-covered sky.

As usual, I woke early the next morning and peered out of the window – it was breathtaking. Mountain ponies munched on heather-covered hills, and sheep pranced around the fields as lively as Janet on a night out. There were miles of crumpled fields covered with springy grass and tufts of wild flowers. It was a very different countryside from the one I had grown up with in semi-rural Chatham, more akin to the wild, harsh beauty of the north. Everyone else was still asleep so I got up and made bread, a skill Nanny Twigg had taught me when I was young. I felt at peace for the first time in months.

We spent the days walking for hours around the remote hills, and my renewed love of nature spilled over into my clothes – hemp bags, beaded earrings and peasant blouses worn together with macramé vests. It was a popular look at the time, home-spun pieces that sang about who you were. My hair was tinged red and black, and Janet's head was still tipped in silver, so we must have stood out to the farmers who gamely ignored the mad-looking bunch of Londoners. In the evening, it would get cool and we'd wrap up in chunky jumpers and sit on the saggy old sofas where Janet and I would knit or embroider patches and detailing onto our dungarees. It was all very wholesome food for the soul.

Over the next six months, we travelled to Tregaron at least another three times for long weekends. As the seasons edged into autumn and later winter, our evenings at the cottage became deliciously cosy. I'd make a huge pot of soup on the stove in the kitchen while listening to *The Archers*. Then we'd light the fire in the living room, eat, knit and talk until midnight. I've never been very good at knitting, but it is a cathartic craft. The repetitive, rhythmic motion of weaving the yarn between the knitting needles, or with a crochet hook, is enormously calming. It requires great focus, which helps me to switch off. We were wrapped up in layers of wool, knitted jumpers, cardigans and scarves, to keep warm in the creaky stone cottage. Alex had a green cable-stitched jumper that I became fascinated by – I wanted to come up with a way of reinterpreting the cable design flat. I decided to create a print that had the feel of a hand-worked knit but couldn't possibly be knitted.

Back in London, I went to the Victoria & Albert Museum to see the textile items on show: beautifully knitted sixteenth-century bedspreads and wall hangings made in chain stitches. I was interested in how to form patterns using stitches and differing colour combinations – the print had to feel as if someone had picked up needles and knitted it by hand rather than using a machine. I started designing knit-like prints in circles, incorporating all I had seen, but also weaving in Pop Art bright shades of red, blue and yellow. My first piece was printed on a long, fringed scarf, like those the four of us wore on the cold nights at the cottage. The key pattern was a print landscape inspired by the views I had absorbed while stomping around the fields and hills of Tregaron. I used my signature wiggle print for the first time, which brought freshness to the homespun knitted designs. I can't say with certainty where the wiggles stemmed from – perhaps they were a hangover from my childhood jigsaw puzzles. A designer or artist never really closes their eyes: everything you see and experience is potential inspiration that can inform your next work. My energetic wiggles bring vitality to any given piece and have become a recurring motif over the years.

I faced a small, but not insignificant, issue: I was still not well-versed in the making of clothes. I was designing original, statement prints, but turning them into a wearable garment was a whole new adventure. While we'd been in partnership at the Fulham Road Clothes Shop, Sylvia had taught me the basics of

My 'Knitted Landscape' design

pattern-cutting, but I knew that if I was to make a success of my label I needed to become an expert in garment construction. Fashion design couldn't be this enigmatic, unknowable craft. I asked two fellow Royal College fashion-design students, Norman Baines and Leslie Poole, to show me everything they knew. It didn't come as naturally as print design did, but I could learn it if I practised enough. Together, they taught me how to make a pattern, about the grain of a fabric and how to do a flat lay of a design. I let my prints guide me, draping them over my body as I had done when I had presented my work to Marion Foale and

Sally Tuffin five years before. I needed the right fabrics – silk chiffon, heavy felt, quilted satin and Lurex, rich, fine materials that could be printed beautifully.

My Knitted Circle print, as it was later called, was designed in circles so I cut around them to produce the silhouette of the garment – swirling, dramatic. whimsical shapes. In six months, I conceived and created fifteen dream-like pieces I was extremely proud of: dresses, caftans and a thick felt coat. The experience was utterly exhilarating. I was designing prints in the way I wanted. There was finally no compromise. The Zandra Rhodes vision had crystallized at last.

13

US Vogue

It was Richard Holley, a friend and interior designer, who told me to go to New York in 1969. Richard was a man about town, a fabulously dressed Texan with the most wonderful deep drawl. He wasn't the only one urging me to cross the Pond that summer. Two Ukrainian-American models, Oxana and Myroslava Prystay, whom I'd met at the Fulham Road Clothes Shop, also encouraged me to go. They reminded me of beautiful, chattering parrots and were most commonly found zipping along the King's Road draped in my printed silk, with floaty scarves wrapped round their heads. 'They'll love you, darling. Go to America and make your fortune.' They proved the adage that the closing of one door often leads to the opening of another.

I had been teaching myself pattern-cutting, the basis of fashion design, since the closure of the shop and had reached a point at which, although designing prints would always be my strength, I felt proficient enough to present my clothes to the world. The problem was that I was known in London solely as a print designer rather than a clothes designer. Back then, people picked a job and stuck to it; very few changed their career mid-stream and explored new avenues as we do today. Having trained in textiles rather than fashion, people assumed I shouldn't be making dresses, so I wasn't taken seriously. I had no intention of giving up, but I knew I needed a new audience who didn't know me.

New York had always been a mystical, far-flung place that had existed for me only in my mother's *Vogues* while I was growing up. For some wild reason, perhaps propelled by the momentum of swinging London, I had the vaguest feeling that I'd attract more success there. I hoped I'd have more chance of finding a backer, not just in terms of finances, but someone influential who believed in what I was doing. I didn't have anyone specific in mind, but I knew I had to find a patron who understood and recognized my work if I was to progress. I wanted to go somewhere where they wouldn't say, 'You're a textile designer, you can't make dresses.' In America, I could be taken at face value. Something made me think New York would be where it would happen.

Once I'd decided to go, I spoke to British *Vogue* fashion editor Marit Allen, who had already featured my work in her 'Young Ideas' pages, dedicated to supporting homegrown fashion talent. Marit thought it was a great idea and spoke to Beatrix Miller, who was then the editor of the magazine. Beatrix decided to write to the legendary editor of US *Vogue*, Diana Vreeland, introducing me and suggesting she meet me during my trip. Incredibly, Mrs Vreeland agreed. With that, Alex and I booked cheap flights to set off in September, using money my mother had left me when she'd died five years previously. On the way there, I wore seven key looks from my collection – all layered on top of one another – so that I could get through Customs without any trouble. I must have looked absolutely deranged, a five-foot-two bundle of bright silk chiffon, heavy felt and quilted satin, but it worked. I got through the airport without a hiccup.

I very much believe you can fall in love with places. London is my home, I love Australia and India, but New York was the city I truly fell for. For me it holds the memory of a twenty-something on the cusp of a fairy tale, a siren call of excitement, success and adventure. We arrived the week after Woodstock and everyone looked as if they hadn't changed clothes since the festival. It was a mess of flares, embroidered tunics and electric colour. Looking back, I suppose most of the looks and the music had actually come from London, but it felt new to me because at home Alex and I spent the majority of our time working. We didn't parade around the streets on Saturdays, absorbing the atmosphere.

We were in New York for work, but thankfully we had a few free days to wander without a plan, simply for the pleasure of exploring this new world. It felt as if this bouncing, smoking, sweaty, kinetic city was there just for us. I loved the skyscrapers. I realize some people find them too imposing, but they seemed to me like man-made mountains that were utterly liberating when you reached the top. Below, the streets clanked and cracked. The song of the moment was the Rolling Stones' 'Honky Tonk Women', and the film was *Midnight Cowboy* with Dustin Hoffman.

Although everyone was dressed to express themselves, I suppose I must have stood out. I had dyed my hair green and glued feathers to the tips, which was a big deal as no one was yet dyeing their hair, let alone adding extensions. I had already begun to realize that I was the best canvas for my work. No one would ever believe in my designs unless I wore them. Possessed with the determination to succeed and for my work to be seen, I floated about the city in my chiffons, often with my hair wrapped up in a dramatic turban to keep it off my neck and stay cool in the still sweltering late summer air.

Richard Holley had kindly offered us a room in the spacious flat he shared with his friend Stephen Naab on West 81st in Manhattan, not far from Central Park. From there, they introduced us to their bohemian social circle. We met Karen and Ron Bowen, an artistic married couple who had recently returned to New York from London after doing a flat swap with the Irish artist Michael Farrell. Ron was a painter and Karen was a graphic designer, with pixie-like features, who was pleased to be free of English fry-ups. Michael and Donna Malce were antiques dealers with a store in the Village. The central player was Jo Lombardo, a tall, thin artist who had a thousand opinions and hosted fantastic dinner parties. Jo renamed himself Jo Jewel, for the amount of jewellery he wore – layer after layer of necklaces and bracelets that went up to his elbows. He was, quite simply, electric.

After a few days spent exploring New York City, walking around Central Park, the Metropolitan Museum of Art and the Village, the day of my meeting with Mrs Vreeland – the grand empress of the fashion world – arrived. I zipped up my white canvas Biba boots, threw on one of my printed chiffon caftan dresses and wound my hair into one of my scarves, like a turban. I shaded my eyes with a bold blue and drew two curls down the side of my face with lipstick, so that they looked as if they emerged from my hairline. And with that we were off. Richard and I trundled to the *Vogue* Lexington Avenue offices on the bus, dragging my collection in what looked like a body bag.

Mrs Vreeland's reputation was legendary: she had an amazing eye for talent and had already launched the careers of future icons such as Lauren Bacall, whom she made a magazine cover star before she became a famous actress, and the designers Oscar de la Renta and Halston. She famously never dressed until noon, working from her bed in the mornings before arriving in the office at midday. Mrs Vreeland had exacting taste and if you were granted an appointment with her, you'd better have something special to offer. I was terrified and couldn't stop talking to Richard on the way there – a lot rested on our meeting. I knew that my work was different; I made no concessions to the commercial, the acceptable or the ordinary, but I also knew I needed a patron. In fashion, it was as obvious to me then as it is now that you are only as good as those who support your work.

Waiting in the *Vogue* reception area, I hoped that this most terrifying of editors would see the value of my designs. Suddenly her secretary appeared. 'You can go in and see Mrs Vreeland now.'

Approaching her office, I stood bewildered in the doorway. The room was painted lipstick red, the floor covered by a leopard-print carpet and the walls decorated with beautiful artworks, sketches and photographs. Most extraordinary, though, was the strength of Mrs Vreeland's character, which was so imposing it took my breath away. She looked like a magical witch with a wonderful hawk nose and dyed black hair. Her face was outlined with dramatic rouge and punctuated with a bright red circle on each cheek. Even her earlobes were coloured with rouge. Swathed from head to toe in fine black cashmere, she held an elegant ivory cigarette holder between red-polished fingernails. With each considered puff, the smoke wafted upwards.

'Zandra Rhodes?' she asked, looking up from her desk. She had the most incredible voice, deep and divinely commanding. Even the way she said my name had a clipped, theatrical quality: she emphasized the Z and the final A with a flourish: 'Zzzzandraaa'. Nodding, I gabbled how nice it was to meet her and pulled my designs out of the dress bags one by one. I watched as her eyes glided over me and on to my chiffon dresses. She paused and then, with all the drama of a RADA-trained actor, exclaimed, 'My dear, these are spectacular! You are an idea-ist who knows how to execute things. You have a great sense of colour. These are wearable dreams.'

I tried to remain confident and not to let my voice waver, particularly as it seemed she had just coined the word 'idea-ist' to define the creativity of my designs.

'Thank you, Mrs Vreeland,' I stammered, and steadied myself by explaining the origin story for the collection. 'The prints are based on knitting,' I said. 'I was fascinated by the stitches, but also by the patterns formed by knitting and, of course, the combinations of colours.'

As I continued to show her my pieces, she continued to rave about my clothes: 'We simply must shoot these for the next issue.' She summoned a member of staff and instructed her to start organizing the pieces to be photographed on Natalie Wood, the brightest young movie star at the time, thanks to her roles in *Rebel Without a Cause* and *West Side Story*. She then picked up the phone and called two of New York's best-dressed, most-photographed socialites, Mica Ertegun and Chessy Raynor, and told them they simply must buy my clothes. Mica was the wife of Ahmet Ertegun, the co-founder and president of Atlantic Records, while Chessy was a former *Vogue* editor whose style was widely copied. They placed orders on the spot. Next, Mrs Vreeland called Geraldine Stutz, the president of luxury women's department store Henri Bendel. 'Geraldine, you've got to see these clothes!' she implored. A few days later, I would meet with Stutz and our conversation would result in the store becoming a stockist of my work, a major milestone for my tiny business.

That day, in just one hour, Mrs Vreeland transformed my entire life. She was so over the top. Everything about her was glorious and I was simply dazzled by her. She was like a magician, summoning all these wonderful people to invest in me and my work. I've never met anyone like her before or since. At the end of our meeting, she asked, 'My dear, how do you plan on travelling around the city during your stay?' I told her I'd be using the bus. She looked horrified. 'You will NOT be dragging your work around on New York's filthy public transport. You'll catch a disease. I'll organize a car for you.' With one more call, she arranged for a chauffeur to drive me around the city for the remainder of our three-week visit.

That evening, as I sat in Richard's flat revelling in the wonder of the day, I looked out of the window to see that the driver was still waiting outside. I was mortified; I hadn't realized he'd be stationed there until I gave him further instruction. I had no idea how to manage a chauffeur – it was all so new.

On reflection, I don't know whether I fell in love with New York before it fell in love with me, or whether I fell hard for it because the city treated me like a rare gift. It invested in me almost immediately and it's hard to resist anything that scoops you up and woos you so completely, which was what happened that first time. By some amazing quirk of fate, my work looked different from anything Mrs Vreeland had ever seen. People talk about David Bowie and how different he was from anything that had come before, and maybe it was a bit like that with my clothes. I had been working in this cloud of my own, burrowed in London, unaware of how revolutionary or original my ideas might be.

Two weeks later, I returned to the *Vogue* offices with the dresses Mrs Vreeland had selected for the shoot with Natalie Wood. Mrs Vreeland said I wouldn't be needed that day other than to drop off the pieces, so I arrived at the studio and shot off as instructed. I still couldn't believe any of this was happening. The photographs were taken by the esteemed Gianni Penati, a favourite of US *Vogue*, who had worked with Lauren Hutton, Anjelica Huston and Marisa Berenson, and were to be published in the January 1970 issue. At the time, it wasn't easy to obtain international editions of magazines, so I was sent a copy by Mrs Vreeland's secretary. All monthly issues go on sale four weeks early, so every time the postman came during that December, I would rush to the door to see if that precious package had arrived. Eventually, it did – an A4 brown envelope containing what I knew could only be a magazine. I ripped it open and leafed through its pages until I finally found my shoot. Natalie Wood swirled around in flutterings of colourful chiffon, looking wonderful. She also wore my printed felt yellow circle coat, holding up each side to show off the full silhouette and the print, albeit including a slight crease that bothered me. But, crease or no crease, it was the best Christmas gift ever. 'Yards and yards of purest fantasy – the cloud of pink and blue is like an enchanting figure floating across a Chagall sky,' read the accompanying description. It felt like a fairy tale.

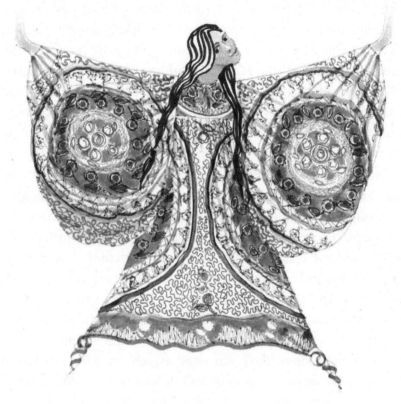

Natalie Wood in my knitted circle dress in US Vogue, 1970

Mrs Vreeland and I were great friends until her death in 1989. I hosted dinner parties for her at my apartment in London where we sat at the round table, and we went to the Met Gala together after her appointment as the Costume Institute's special consultant in 1972. She remains my dream dinner-party guest: she had such enthusiasm for talent and a way of conducting herself that, despite her grandeur, meant she wasn't remote or snobby. She wasn't afraid to show how much pleasure she derived from spotting and nurturing talent. She loved beauty and originality. Towards the end of her life, André Leon Talley and I used to visit her apartment to read to her because she couldn't see.

If I tried to get hold of anyone at US *Vogue* today, I probably wouldn't succeed. Now, magazines are led by advertising: if you're an American juggernaut with a big budget, you're likely to feature in the fashion pages, whereas independent British brands like mine are ignored. I was lucky to be in New York at the right time and to have reacted in the right way, with lashings of enthusiasm and energy. Mrs Vreeland's endorsement reaffirmed the work I'd been doing and supported my approach of doing things my way even when people told me to tone it down or follow more commercial routes. The US fashion editors and buyers knew what to do with my style and work; they knew how to market it with the right models and photographers. They made what some might have deemed eccentric make-up and hair look first class. They took me from being different to being desirable. America put me on track.

14

Biba Boots

WHENEVER I WAS UNSURE WHAT to wear in the late sixties and seventies, I would turn to my trusty Biba knee-length boots. I bought them from the label's Kensington store at some point in 1969 and was drawn to their futuristic boldness. They were white canvas with a zip up the side and a mid-block heel that meant I could wear them all day. I used to wear a lot of heels, but as one grows older, comfort is increasingly important. Now I've traded platforms for pink-sequined trainers, but back then, if I wanted to feel pulled-together, I would reach for those Biba boots. They required a certain amount of upkeep (I would regularly apply a liquid whitener to them to ensure they were always bright white), but they were very versatile and more interesting than an average black boot. They were also a perfect match for my heavily printed, way-out ensembles.

Those Biba boots went to some fabulous places with me – they were the shoes I wore when I took many of my post-show catwalk bows in the seventies, and the footwear I chose to spin around the legendary nightclub Studio 54. They were also the style that accompanied me to meet the great Oscar de la Renta in the early seventies when I rejected his job offer. It was a crossroads moment and I'm still glad I made the decision I did.

My introduction to Oscar came via Mrs Vreeland, who continued to be an enthusiastic supporter of my work. She had known Oscar since the early sixties when she had sagely advised him to turn down an opportunity to design ready-to-wear for Christian Dior. Instead, she'd told him to go with a different position, creating custom clothes at Elizabeth Arden, where he was more likely to be promoted. 'Arden is not a designer, so she will promote you,' she said. 'At the other place, you will always be eclipsed by the name of Dior.' She was, as usual, right, and Oscar went on to launch his own ready-to-wear label in the late sixties, earning him multiple awards. His designs had already been worn by Jackie Kennedy, and he was interesting enough to host parties with the author Truman Capote. He had worked with Cristóbal Balenciaga and at Balmain. In short, Oscar de la Renta was a big deal. I liked his vibrant use of colour and how joyful his clothes were. Anyone who wore his pieces looked not only glamorous, but also really, truly happy. He wasn't the sort of designer where the clothes were really about him: he simply wanted women to look and feel amazing.

The fact that I liked Oscar's designs was a minor detail. Even if I wasn't interested in his work, I would have arranged to meet him anyway – one ignored the instruction of Mrs Vreeland at one's peril. His Manhattan office was a grand building with high ceilings and expansive windows. The decor was elegant without being dull: books spanning art, architecture and fashion were neatly stacked on shelves, plants grew out of bamboo baskets and pictures of women he had dressed hung on the wall behind an elegant mid-century desk. It was a very different space from my ramshackle studio in Porchester Road. Oscar was a suave, twinkly-eyed figure, dressed in a navy three-piece suit and tie. His hair was slicked back like a fifties movie star's and he had the broadest smile. Over the years, I never saw him in anything but a perfectly tailored suit. He was the sort of person you can't imagine ever being dishevelled, which might have been intimidating for someone as chaotic as me, but Oscar put me at ease right away. 'Take a seat, Miss Rhodes,' he said, beckoning me to a chair in front of his desk. 'Mrs Vreeland tells me your prints would be a perfect match for my clothes.'

Together, we went through my sketchbooks, and I showed him my Knitted Circle designs that had recently been photographed on Natalie Wood for *Vogue*. He was terribly kind about my work and told me I had a strong understanding of colour and fashion as fantasy. At the end of our meeting, he wondered whether I would consider working for him. 'We'd have you on print design,' he said. I asked, as I had with Marion Foale and Sally Tuffin a few years earlier, whether my name would appear alongside his on the label. If he thought it was an imposition for an emerging designer to raise such a question, he was far too gallant to show it. 'No, Zandra, you would be working in-house for me,' he said politely. 'That means my name only on the label.'

I immediately declined. It was an incredible offer and I was fully aware of how successful he was, but I knew I had to focus on my own collection. Textile designers were mostly nameless (they still are even now), so I had to ensure I was credited if I wanted to pursue a career in fashion. Oscar was utterly gracious. We shook hands, and he told me he was sure he'd see more of my designs in the press in the future.

Not long afterwards, I received a similar request from Yves Saint Laurent's office in Paris. One of his staff members called my London studio and wanted to know if I'd be interested in selling prints to him. Saint Laurent was one of the most famous designers in the world, following the launch of his iconic Le Smoking tuxedo suit in 1966. He had been credited for rejuvenating crusty French fashion with his daring modern looks. Once again, I said my name would have to feature on the labels, which he refused, so my answer was clear. Over my dead body, Yves. Later, he asked the model Loulou de la Falaise not to appear in any more of my fashion shows.

I don't regret turning down either Oscar or Yves. If you live with regrets, you're not living. You have to live in the present, whatever you do. A should-have-could-have mentality gets you nowhere, and I never would have made a name for myself if I'd dedicated myself to making prints for other people. Working with Sylvia Ayton and Foale and Tuffin had taught me that I didn't want to spend my life watching other designers make a success of my prints. That was the right route for me, but there's nothing wrong with saying yes if you want to make beautiful textiles but not to go through the exhausting rigmarole of launching a brand. Running a fashion label is hard work, and in my experience involves putting it above everything. Not everyone wants their life to be dominated by what they do. I don't think I knew who I really was in the early seventies. Neither did I know where I was heading. None of us do really, but you just have to put on your best Biba boots and pretend. It's always worked for me.

My Biba boots

15

Show Feather

IT WAS FEBRUARY 1971, THE day of my first fashion show, and I was standing in a room inside a New York townhouse rammed with models, clothes and dyed feathers. I was presenting my latest collection, Elizabethan Slashed Silk, inspired by my British roots. Model Pat Cleveland whizzed by in an airy printed silk dress, with a trailing zigzag hemline that I had carefully cut with a knife. Her hair, like mine, was tipped with feathers that had been glued on by Leonard, the leading hairdresser of the day who had famously created Twiggy's pixie look back in 1966 and had now flown in from London to realize my vision with feathers.

I had been obsessed with feathers since they inspired my previous year's collection. Some of the clothes from that collection would also feature in this show. They were too beautiful not to make an appearance – I had cut out each printed feather and hand-rolled them to create feathered edges that formed the hemline, if you can even categorize it as that.

Another model, Loulou de la Falaise, drifted past in a kaleidoscopically bright but entirely sheer caftan, the bottom of which I slashed into pinked-edge ribbon streamers. Her wrists and neck were festooned with gold jewellery designed by Mick Milligan.

My friend, the stylist Chelita Secunda, played Janis Joplin, which we had chosen as the soundtrack to the show. The room smelled of hairspray and adrenaline. It was noisy, crowded and chaotic. I was wearing blue striped stockings with cut-silk mini shorts and green-heeled platform boots. My feather-tipped hair was also decorated with tufts of rainbow-bright extensions. I was set to make an impression, but in that moment I was absolutely terrified.

My debut catwalk show had been a few years in the making. Since my first visit to New York in 1969, I had visited the city three times. It was unusual to travel somewhere so far so often back then, but increasingly it was where my business was. I never felt too extreme or idiosyncratic to New Yorkers as I occasionally did to Londoners. I was not only accepted but loved by my new friends, and by American fashionable society. Mrs Vreeland had continued to support my work in *Vogue* and I was racking up wealthy US customers for whom I created bespoke pieces. I still sold my pieces in Henri Bendel, where sales were going well. I was in demand. Back in London, my business was blossoming too – I was now stocked at influential department store Fortnum & Mason – but New York was where it was really happening.

During one of my visits to New York, my friend Richard, who had suggested that first trip in 1969, introduced me to a high-end interior designer friend of his called Angelo Donghia. At the time, Angelo was working with Halston, and had created the decor for his decadent, pattern-heavy showroom. Donghia was always dressed in a well-cut suit, and strongly believed in making one's surroundings attractive. If you were a member of the New York style elite in the seventies and eighties, you went to Angelo, or Dongo as he was known to friends. I can't remember exactly where we met, but I do remember what he said. Angelo took one look at me, with my flowing headscarf, experimental make-up, Biba boots and printed caftan, and said, 'Well, if you look like that, your work must be wonderful, and I have to see it.'

The following day, I brought my designs to his studio and, on the spot, he commissioned a line of hand-printed wallpapers and furnishing fabrics, spanning my signature wiggles and cut-out circles. From that point onwards, Angelo and I became firm friends. Although fashion was always my focus, my textiles still lent themselves to the world of interiors so we had a lot to talk about. One evening over dinner, he mooted the idea of a catwalk show. At that time, fashion shows were still mostly held in the respective designer's showroom or their flagship store. Although orders were coming in thick and fast, I still didn't have enough capital for either. I was telling Angelo this, when he asked quite simply, 'Darling, why don't you do it at my place?'

My heart nearly skipped a beat. Angelo lived in a sprawling townhouse on the Upper West Side. No one except his closest friends had ever been inside, so to host a catwalk show there would be a huge coup. People would want to attend for that reason alone. I said yes immediately, and Mrs Vreeland put me in touch with the great American fashion publicist Eleanor Lambert, who helped me to organize it. I decided that this show had to be about more than just a collection of dresses: I wanted my guests to feel as if they were enveloped in my fantasy world. It had to be entertaining and theatrical, not stuffy and staid, as most catwalk shows were. It had to feel alive and fresh. It was important to me that everyone there understood that my ideas extended to a full look beyond clothes to jewellery, hair and make-up.

Angelo's home was the perfect venue, not least because he'd just returned from Morocco where he had practically emptied the souks of fabric. Famed for his heavily upholstered furnishings, he had been hugely influenced by the embroidered silks and rugs that now covered his sofas, beds and cushions. In one room a Bedouin tent was draped with intricate, vibrant Moroccan rugs. It looked very bohemian and avant-garde, a completely unconventional approach to presenting a collection. I didn't want guests to sit on chairs next to a dull, straight catwalk. I was all about the wiggle, so I planned for the models to come up the stairs and dance round the furniture through different rooms, culminating in Angelo's bedroom. This, I hoped, would create energy, and if it flopped, at least I'd have tried something new. I chose models known for their personalities like Loulou, Pat and Elsa Peretti. All of them were supernaturally beautiful, but they also brimmed with individuality. I wanted to show that anyone could wear a Zandra Rhodes. I wasn't overly prescriptive about how they should move through the house. I knew it was best to encourage them to be themselves. I wanted them to project themselves with intensity. That's all of any of us can do in life. What's the point in being a half-measure of yourself?

All I can say is that, on the day, it worked. The hard thing about being a designer at your own show is that you don't get to see much of it because you're so busy backstage, but I was told afterwards that it felt like a private party. What I do know is that the turnout was better than I could have imagined: Mrs Vreeland and Halston sat on Angelo's giant four-poster bed, while all my other guests – society ladies, buyers and, of course, my friends – sat on Moroccan cushions strewn around the two rooms. There was a free-spirited, hippie jet-set glamour amped up by the interiors and confirmed by my clothes. Those slashed hems and decorative prints – a deconstructed take on Tudor England – felt like a blend of art and punk, not that the latter had even been invented yet. It was a ragged, kinetic kind of beauty. The models resembled dreamy dancing sculptures, weaving among the furniture with such grace. I'm not sure how I feel about the word 'elegance' because it's so bound with restriction and rules, but 'grace' – there's something in that. Moving with grace is about possessing a positive attitude, which is a much more realistic and inclusive way to be.

Janis Joplin's music turned out to be the perfect choice, her soulful, raw voice, which blasted out of a stereo, infusing the room with emotion. It was a noisy show: amid Janis's rasping vocals, I could hear clapping from the audience after each model stepped out.

At the end, after the last of my chiffon-clad visions had spun round the room, Mrs Vreeland jumped up off of the bed. 'She's a genius!' she cried, and everyone gave me a standing ovation. I remember taking a deep breath, walking up the stairs in my platforms and doing a quick bow in the doorway. It was the most amazing feeling, and I do hope I never took any of it for granted. Whenever you're whisked off your feet, as I was during that period, it's so hard to remain grounded. I was told later that it was an early example of fashion as theatre, but I just did what felt instinctive, which is all any of us can do. I hope with all my being that, over the course of my career, I have helped others on their way up, just as I was helped up each step of that staircase.

16

Australian Opal

IN THE CENTRE OF MY big round table sits a collection of at least three hundred rocks that I've picked up from around the world. The ring-shaped formation includes geodes, stones from Petra, pebbles from Sardinia and even a piece of the Berlin Wall. I ought to label them, but of course I haven't, so they just kick around on the table and gather dust. They're a reminder of all the places I've been and that beauty is in small things. When I'm stuck, this eclectic array of odd stones nudges me to look deeper and to keep going.

Among the most precious is a polished slice of opal presented to me at the end of my first trip to Australia in 1971. No two opals are the same, and each has a unique pattern and irregular colour bands – it's me in rock form. Mine was given to me by Sekers Silks, a Sydney-based company with whom I had done a very successful collaboration. A miniature spectacle, it's around four inches wide and two and half inches deep and was the start of my entire rock collection. It has an ocean-like quality, coated in the most wonderful iridescent pale blues and greens. On one side it opens up to turquoise crystals, and the other is covered with curvy lines that look like waves. There is so much to see in such a small surface area. Australia has played a huge role in my work,

Australian opal

and it's a place I've returned to many times since the early seventies, with big shows held in Adelaide, Melbourne and, of course, Sydney. On each visit I'm reminded of its upbeat, enthusiastic outlook, its warmth and honesty.

My love affair with Australia began in 1971 after I received a call from Sekers, a silk and rayon fabric print company that had previously been used by Christian Dior, Givenchy and Pierre Cardin. The company's fashion director, Vera Kaldor, had heard about me through the press attention I was receiving in New York and wanted us to collaborate. Would I design twelve exclusive prints that would be sold by the yard for Australian women to make their own clothes? I said yes immediately. It would be a big departure from my own luxury line, where the high price tags meant the clothes could only be worn by the wealthy. This collaboration would enable me to reach a broader market and would be another way to showcase my work.

I spent the next few months working on a collection, drawing on my signature wiggles, chain-link stitching and stitched flower prints, which were to be made into bright shades of blue, pink and purple. Australia hadn't been a country I'd planned to visit, but I was excited to travel somewhere so far-flung.

Its distance was one of the most appealing prospects of the project – things between Alex and me were starting to sour. He was increasingly irritated by my extreme hair and make-up. On a brief trip to rural France, we'd been spat at because of how I looked. He'd been really bothered by it and didn't understand why I was so insistent on looking so dramatic. Alex had a more understated approach to style. I'd tried to convince him to wear a few bold printed shirts I'd made for him but he refused, saying they were ridiculous. During one trip I made to New York, he took two bags of my clothes to a charity shop. When I returned, furious to find my precious pieces gone, he said they were in the way, and walked out. I immediately went to the shop to try to retrieve them, but they'd already been sold – I think I managed to buy back a fur coat.

It sounds like a superficial disagreement, but it ran deeper than that: we were going in different directions. Our differences, which we used to find charming, were becoming unworkable: his fastidiousness was increasingly at odds with my creative chaos. I was running into the fashion industry full throttle but Alex wasn't interested – his world was furnishings – although we were still working together. The other issue was that we were spending more and more time apart as I was so often in New York. While I was abroad, Alex had more time for other 'distractions'. We would have huge arguments in front of my small but growing design team, and I'm sure the atmosphere at that time was less than serene. I knew Alex and I were in a bad place. Rather than deal with our situation head-on, I buried myself in work, and my visits to the States became longer. A trip to the other side of the world couldn't have come at a better time. Just before I left, I received a call from Vera at Sekers.

'Zandra, we hear you have green hair. Would you change it?' she asked. 'We'd like you to make a few television appearances, and we worry you might come across as too bold for some of our customers.' I don't know why, but I agreed over the phone, but as soon as the call ended, I thought, *No way!* My hair stayed forest green with reddish tones in the front and I made sure to attach feathers to the ends. In life, but especially in fashion, you have to stay true to yourself. Find your uniqueness and stand by it. Do not, whatever you do, let others crush you.

In the end, my wild appearance was what the Australians loved about me. I framed my eyes with rainbow colours and sequins, shaded my cheeks rosy red like a clown's, and used a deep purple on my lips. During my initial three-week visit to Australia, I was treated as if I was one of the Beatles. The press described me as a 'bird of paradise', which was rather lovely and a delicious ego boost. There weren't nearly as many flights to and from Australia back then, so very few high-profile figures visited. I was a rarity, which added to the traction surrounding me. I met the beautiful Margot Fonteyn, who was also visiting. A chauffeur drove me from place to place around the country: I made special appearances in various shops, was interviewed in television and radio studios, and went to glamorous parties in the evenings. My collection took over the expansive windows of Myer, the largest department store in Australia. I featured in multiple magazines, including *Australian Women's Weekly*, which dedicated several huge spreads to my work in which I was praised as 'revolutionary'. The collection sold like hot cakes, and I was made to feel like a star.

I met a whole new crowd of people who lit up my world: the late Australian artist Martin Sharp and his then girlfriend Nell Campbell, who later became famous playing Columbia in *The Rocky Horror Picture Show*, and a talented but quiet photographer called Grant Mudford, whom I ended up dating after Alex and I split up twelve months later. Grant was kind, handsome and had deep dark eyes that were calming to look into. We travelled a lot together, from Australia to Mexico. Ours wasn't an everlasting love, but he was a motivating and supportive presence in my life for a few years.

Those unforgettable three weeks in 1971 had turned me into a household name in Australia. I returned as soon as I was given the next opportunity, which came in 1973, when I was asked to design a collection for a Sydney-based label called Daily Planet. Amid the parties and television appearances, I was determined to visit Ayers Rock, now reverted to its Aboriginal name Uluru, a mystical-looking, sandstone formation I'd seen on the front of multiple postcards during my first visit. I'd asked my hosts at Sekers about it, but they were dismissive and told me to go to Fiji instead. I have never been interested in sitting on a beach unless I'm drawing. I haven't got time to waste. Now, of course, the Aussies are very proud of their magical desert landmark, but at the time no one cared about the big lumpy rock that sat in the middle of nowhere.

This time, I wasn't taking no for an answer. With a friend, I drove two hundred miles in a four-wheel-drive Toyota from Alice Springs across unmade roads through what felt like no-man's land. We kept the windows open to stay cool and became coated in red dust – it got everywhere, my hair, my clothes, the pages of my sketchbook, my camera. The desert was unlike anything I'd ever experienced, scorched red earth that went on for ever, broken by tufts of spinifex grass that looked like Mother

Nature's version of cushions. Then there was the sound, or indeed the absence of it. It is a very strange sensation to be anywhere completely bereft of noise – even in the most remote countryside, we hear sounds of birds or the wind, but in the desert there is nothing. It is both unsettling and soothing. We stayed in very basic cabins that offered school-dinners type meals. Tourism simply didn't exist in that area back then.

Uluru blew me away. The light bounced off it to almost super-natural effect, and changed as the day wore on: in the morning it was a rich pink, at noon it glowed orange, and at sunset it switched to deep ochre. It had so much force, that dazzling sand-stone monolith. Its untamed surfaces rolled and bulged under an expanse of electric blue sky. The mornings were freezing, but I'd get up at dawn, wrap myself in my rainbow fur coat and draw for hours until dusk. I wanted to give myself to the Rock and to capture its ever-moving light. It had an awe-inducing presence and I felt entirely submerged in the sublime, a sense of being almost winded by the might of nature. It was an intensely inspiring experience and resulted in one of my most famous prints, 'Ayers Rock', which I have since renamed 'Uluru'. The work that I did, sitting at the humbling base of Uluru, is perhaps among the pieces of which I'm proudest. Sometimes my sketches make their leap into fashion print in a more indirect way, but my drawings of what I saw out in the desert are a literal interpretation of my Australian experience. They would go on to make their acclaimed public debut a year later at my 1974 show spectacular in New York.

Australia is one of the first countries after America that made a lasting impact on me. Travel is a crucial source of inspiration; all of my trips and experiences have been useful in terms of drawing. I love finding out how people live and looking for artefacts or keepsakes to influence and inspire new fashion collections. I collect things consciously, always thinking about how something might be of use, and my shining opal is one such example.

My long flight back from Australia in 1971 was broken by another destination that inspired and enriched me. My next stop was Tokyo.

17

Lily Tattoo

ON MY LOWER HIP, I have a tattoo in the shape of my famed lily print. I had it done in LA, perhaps five years after my initial trip to Japan in 1971, which was where I first developed the design. Nowadays, tattoos are so popular that I probably wouldn't have bothered, but back then it was a daring, nonconformist form of creative expression. Over the decades, the black outline has faded a little, but I don't regret it. I've always been a walking, talking canvas for my ideas, and I suppose being inked was inevitable. It's my body and I'll decorate it however I like. My tattoo is an indelible reminder of my time spent in Japan, where I came up with some of my best work.

My first introduction to Japan came in London, where I initially met the fashion designers Kansai Yamamoto and Issey Miyake. They were both friends of famed restaurateur Michael Chow, who was an early patron of my work and eventually helped me to stage an unforgettable catwalk show at the Roundhouse, London, in 1972. All that was still ahead of me when I made my entry into Japan. I admired the work of both Kansai and Issey, but it was the latter who suggested that I make a pitstop in Tokyo on the way back from my trip to Australia.

Issey and I designed very different clothes, but I think we were bound by a similar ethos: practical originality. His signature was his fabulous use of pleating, and mine was my innovative approach to prints, but we designed garments that were experimental, yet wearable. There was a mutual respect between us. Through his bulging address book, he instigated and arranged a show at Seibu, Japan's equivalent of Harrods. The store's owner was so confident I'd be a hit among its clientele that he hosted the event for free and invited their highest-spending clients and fashion editors. It was held in a big hall and was on a much larger scale than anything I'd staged before. Among the guests was my friend Michael Chow, to whom I introduced a then rising model called Tina, whom I'd cast as part of the catwalk line-up. The two had an almost instant chemistry – she was a match that lit things and helped them glow brighter, and Michael adored her. They got married the following year, in 1972, with gorgeous Manolo Blahnik enlisted as the unofficial wedding photographer. We had lunch afterwards at Mr Chow, in London's Knightsbridge, because where else?

Overseas travel was still uncommon in 1971, which added to the buzz surrounding me. In Tokyo, I was whisked into television appearances, press interviews and a whirlwind of parties. It was a great compliment to find myself a success in such an unfamiliar place, but it was also a deeply confusing, overwhelming city. Alex had flown out from London to join me and tried to explore the city, but the streets didn't have names, and if they did, they certainly weren't in English. He would come back to the hotel frustrated and stressed at having spent hours being lost. He lasted a few days before returning to the UK. I understood: life's too short for staying in places that make you feel unhappy. I had to be there for professional reasons, but he didn't.

Tokyo felt incomprehensible, claustrophobic and overwhelming. It was hard work, and without Alex it was even harder. I hated not being able to do anything on my own without getting lost. The smallest things were big challenges. I couldn't speak Japanese and few Japanese could speak English. I didn't know how to use chopsticks, and the restaurants didn't have knives and forks, so I drank a lot of miso soup. Most of the streets existed under a canopy of tangled electricity wires, which made me feel even more discombobulated. Even the smells were strange – the tempura, teriyaki and gyozas sold at wooden *yatai* food carts gave the streets a deep-fried, unfamiliar scent. I wandered around the narrow alleys of Shinjuku Golden Gai on my own, only to find each of the tiny bars full. Nothing was recognizable to me.

For all my feelings of isolation, I was blown away by the precise beauty I saw there. The Japanese are almost obsessed with perfection – the perfect way to fold something, the perfect blossom, the perfect bonsai tree, the perfect way of arranging food so that it looks like a work of art. Everything felt designed. I was fascinated but intimidated in equal measure. My Seibu show went ahead successfully, but flights to London were still irregular and I'd given myself an extra week in Tokyo to explore. After multiple failed attempts to seek out the city's famed gardens, I decided to hide in my room, feeling overwhelmed and lonely. I'm sure I won't be the last person to take refuge in a hotel after finding the intensity of a new city too much, but I felt angry with myself for not making the most of what should have been an incredible adventure.

Just as I was feeling very low, someone new and brilliant entered my life. Before my trip, Issey had arranged for me to meet a friend of his, Noboru Kurisaki, a master of flower arranging. Kurichan, as he was known among his close friends, had a tiny dark club where we drank tea and men sat in drag, all of us shrouded in cigarette smoke. It was a magical, otherworldly place. He worked under the ancient practice of *ikebana*, which operates from a very rigid and precise set of rules, but key to it all is being selective about the flowers – less is often more. Kurisaki couldn't speak any English and I had no Japanese, but we understood each other on a deeper level. He became a great friend to me, and made Tokyo feel less alien.

The day after we met in his club, he sent the most beautiful bouquet of lilies to my hotel room. They smelt exquisite. I grabbed my sketchbook and began to draw them. Holed up inside, I went into myself and created something new – fields of lilies, lily petals, lily collars, my hand glided over the page at speed. I remembered a black-and-white photo of my parents on their wedding day, my mother wearing lilies in her hair. These flowers were a perfect mix of known and unknown. I interspersed my drawings with calligraphy, inspired by the flashing neon lights outside, the impenetrable posters and placards, and handwritten signs. Writing on fabric wasn't done back then, but I loved the way it looked, the words dancing among the drawings. I was beginning to see Japan's beauty: it was a land of neon, newness and mystery.

When I returned to London, full of beans and lily-shaped visions, I developed the method of reversing the silkscreen to produce a mirror image of the print to create a larger repeat. This in turn influenced many of my future significant prints, such as 'Lace Mountain', 'Cactus Volcano' and 'Scribble Turnaround'. I covered my Lily dresses with beading, which also became a signature. My 'Lovely Lily' looks were worn by Twiggy, Lauren Bacall and Anjelica Huston, and the original paper design was chosen by the V&A for its textiles collection. It became my most popular print of all time. It's hard to pinpoint why. Sometimes you're just lucky enough to introduce something at the right time, but I suppose you'd never find that sweet spot if you didn't do the

My lily tattoo

research and legwork first. Lilies have an inherent femininity and the lace and chiffon they were printed on have a certain romance. They're princessy but without the froth, which I suppose is quite modern.

I returned to Japan on multiple occasions over the years. On one notable trip in 1981, I travelled with Karl Lagerfeld, Perry Ellis, Giorgio Armani and Hanae Mori to stage a catwalk show that was designed to cement Tokyo as a leading fashion city. It was a spectacular event called the 'Best Five', celebrating the world's five leading designers of the year, but what I remember is taking Karl, who was by then a dear friend, to meet Kurisaki and the three of us travelled to the magical city of Kyoto to see the

Shinto shrines. Karl wasn't keen on the idea of my lily tattoo (you can't please everyone), but he adored the sublime architecture and Japan's regimented, ordered approach to beauty.

Britain is a small island, like Japan, physically detached from anywhere else. Both places have developed their own creative identity and sense of originality. Both have a clear sense of design and a deep appreciation of it. I owe much to Japan, and have loved being in Tokyo since that first meeting with Kurisaki. There are few places in the world that care so much about design. It permeates the most ordinary parts of Japanese culture, from food to flower arrangement. In discovering the beauty of Japan, I discovered the key to one of my most treasured prints. It's a uniquely intense country that isn't for everyone, but it's very much for me.

18

Andrew Logan Bust

I'VE NEVER UNDERSTOOD THE PHRASE 'blood runs thicker than water'. My best friends are my family, the people who have listened to me, inspired me and put me back together when I've fallen apart. They have celebrated my achievements, accompanied me on my travels and told me when I've been in the wrong. When you're younger, you have friends for different things, but if you're lucky, by the time you're of age, you might have a few people around who tick every box. The sculptor and jewellery designer Andrew Logan is one of those friends for me – we know and love the very bones of each other.

It's difficult to talk about a friendship like ours because it's instinctive, part of who we are. Andrew is and always has been a route back to myself. Society talks a lot about romantic relationships, but the older I get, the more I understand the importance of friendship. It's terribly important to be open to new friends of different ages, but it's equally important to appreciate those who have been there long-term. Find friends who lift you up, help you see beauty and leave you smiling. Ideally, find an Andrew.

Ours was a slow-burn friendship. We were introduced by our mutual friend Duggie Fields in the early seventies when creative, arty types naturally bumped into one another at parties; he was known as an artist, but also for throwing London's best parties. In 1973, he asked me to judge his subversive beauty pageant called Alternative Miss World, which I instantly agreed to do. Inspired by the original Miss World contest and Crufts dog show, Andrew had launched his inclusive spectacular the year before, when people of any sexuality, shape and age were invited to compete. Andrew dressed as half man, half woman – his costume was split straight down the middle. Later, I designed the woman's half of all of his Alternative Miss World costumes. The winner was chosen based on their poise, personality and originality rather than their beauty, and the judging panel included an array of arty figureheads.

The first event was held at Andrew's Downham Road studio, a former jigsaw factory, on the borders of Islington and Hackney, an area we all thought of as a distant wasteland. That any of us bothered going so far east was a testament to how much fun Alternative Miss World was. My fellow judges that year were mostly people I already knew: David Hockney, Ossie Clark, Celia Birtwell, Barbara Hulanicki, Thea Porter, Bill Gibb, Amanda Lear, Molly Parkin and Angie Bowie, who was married to a certain David Bowie. There was such a buzz around Alternative Miss World that when the Starman pulled up in his Rolls-Royce, to support his wife, it was so overcrowded inside that he wasn't granted access. Apparently, people tried to climb in through the windows to watch.

The winning contestant was an actor called Eric Roberts (not Julia's brother), known that evening as Miss Holland Park Walk, who dressed up as Scarlett O'Hara from *Gone With the Wind*, decked in a mix of black lace and red velvet. In the years to come, the filmmaker Derek Jarman won as Miss Crêpe Suzette, a vision in a white A-line gown and pearls. Alternative Miss World became bigger and bigger, and more recent judges have included Grayson Perry and Jarvis Cocker. Today you'd describe it as a counter-culture celebration of queer identity; then, it was very ahead of its time. I don't think Andrew ever thought about it in those terms. He just saw it as an entertaining expression of joy and fun, but it became those things by default.

It was obvious to me from very early on that he was a true original, and being in his orbit made life more exciting. Over the course of that decade, we got to know each other well. As with so many of my close friends, work was a uniting force. I loved his art, beautiful mirrored decorative sculptures and jewellery that brighten rooms. I featured his jewellery in my catwalk shows. Like me, he'd still be making things even if they didn't turn a profit, and he is always happiest in his studio – we'll both be working until we drop. I wear his jewellery every day. Colour inspires us both and boosts our mood. When you look at the world, it's filled with saturated shades. There's a myth that black and navy hide flaws while colour exposes them, but I disagree. Colour makes you glow and I think Andrew understands that too.

In 1981, we took the first of many working design trips together to India, a country I fell head over heels in love with from my first visit there. I'd been invited by Indian scenographer and cultural and design curator Rajeev Sethi, who has since become a very dear friend, to celebrate the first Festival of India. The country deserves a chapter of its own just to begin to describe its influence on me. Andrew and I have since been all over the world together, from Morocco to China to Sri Lanka to New Zealand to Norway, and had a great many adventures along the way, sometimes sleeping on bare floors or in freezing tents, yet we've never had a cross word.

Travel is a test of friendship, as I'd found out with Celia and Ossie back in 1967, but I love being abroad with Andrew purely because we like doing the same things. We're early risers and will always get up to see the sunrise before drawing for a few hours; he does watercolours and I sketch with Japanese paper and Pentel pens. Maybe we'll explore a museum before doing some shopping, then dress up outrageously for dinner in the evening. Draw, museum, shop, repeat. We both find excitement in doing things and going to places that might not appeal to everyone.

In the early nineties, during a trip to Morocco's Atlas Mountains, we drove a tiny hire car along a narrow road into the king of Moroccan deserts, Erg Chebbi. I can't remember how long we travelled for, with the wavy sandy dunes whistling past us, but suddenly the road stopped and two young men in their late teens stood in front of the car. Talking in a mix of French and English, they offered to show us an oasis further ahead, but we'd need to let them hop in. We could have turned back, but we threw caution to the wind and let them get into the car. We drove across the desert for perhaps thirty minutes to an hour, speeding across the minimalist expanse of dunes. It was as clear to our guides where we were going as it would be to me if I directed someone from London Bridge to the Tate Modern.

We eventually began to see a smudge on the horizon – the clay guest house where we would stay overnight. We arrived at sunset when we felt as if we were surrounded by gold. Our accommodation was simple, a bedroom and toilet we shared, but there was a chef who made us a delicious lamb tagine. Not dissimilar to my experience in Australia of Uluru, the clay guest house was surrounded by complete nothingness, scorched earth and sand dunes as far as the eye could see. All sense of commerce, work and stress ebbed away. The sun slipped down behind the dunes and finally gave way to night. The stars were different from anything I'd ever seen in my life, as if someone had punched dazzling holes in the sky. I hadn't known there could be so many. When we woke the next morning, it was freezing cold and we layered up in as many of our clothes as we could, looking like crosses between Lawrence of Arabia and art-school students. In lieu of a shower, we washed with water from a neighbouring well, and watched as a local young boy tobogganed down the dunes on a cut-out plastic canister.

The same teenage guides from the day before offered to show us back to the road where we'd first met them and, en route, took us to a local Berber cave where the floor was scattered with black ammonite fossils. It was an overwhelming experience and, as with so many of my trips, I arrived home with a set of ideas that I could interpret into new designs.

The more you get to know someone, the more they get to know you. They understand better how you might respond to something, and what makes you tick. Andrew understands that my big love is my work and that I'll never go out to lunch. He knows that if we meet up I'll always need to get back to designing at some point. That's the beautiful thing about friendship – you either accept your friends as they are, or you give up. We all have our idiosyncrasies, especially as we get older. In the early nineties when minimalism was in fashion and my maximalist aesthetic was decidedly out, Andrew suggested I buy an abandoned building on Bermondsey Street, with a view to turning it into a museum. We'd been friends for so long that he knew I needed a change in direction and a new focus. I bought the old building, which I converted and turned into the Fashion and Textile Museum, London's first and only museum to be solely dedicated to fashion and textiles. Andrew knew what I needed before I did.

Andrew has created several grand mirrored portraits of me, one of which stands in his museum in Wales. Of all the jewellery and work I have of his, the glass mosaic bust he made of me is my favourite. In 1979, there was a terrible fire at Andrew's house at Butler's Wharf on the South Bank of the River Thames. I had some spare rooms and invited him to work at my place in Notting Hill so he could continue with his sculptures. It was during that time that I sat for him and he made the sculpture of my head. I would climb the ladder into the yet-to-be-converted attic room where he was working, and totter along the unfinished floor where I'd sit for him. I always fell asleep so he'd shout at me to keep my eyes open. Slowly it evolved into the colourful bust I've drawn here. It was bought by the National Portrait Gallery, and he gave me a copy of

My sketch of the bust Andrew Logan made for my birthday

it for my fiftieth birthday, which I have displayed in my rainbow penthouse. Most of Andrew's sculptures aren't happy or sad. He says there's a moment in people's faces that he calls the inward pose, where you're between everything, and that's when you see someone's soul. He says the bust captures my fragility and my strength. It is one of the most precious objects I own.

Friendships that inspire lead to more creativity. If you're creative, don't hide yourself away – cross-fertilize and collaborate. Bounce ideas off someone you respect and love. There is a misconception that artists need to work in solitude, but I can't think of anything worse. I don't know where I'd be personally or professionally without fabulous Andrew.

19

Andy Warhol's Wig

IF MY 1960S BELONGED TO London, my 1970s belonged to New York. Over the course of the decade, I spent a great deal of time travelling back and forth across the Atlantic, New York being where I promoted my work but also indulged in partying. In London, I would hunker down and work 24/7, often heading straight to my studio in Bayswater upon my return without pausing for breath. Even when I spent great swathes of the year promoting and selling my work in America, London has always been where I can truly focus and feel grounded, the place I go to design and assimilate my ideas. New York, however, was quite different: meeting brilliant new people and going to fabulous happenings was so intoxicating and exciting. I quickly became addicted to the city's frenzied energy and cultural scene. Every time I left, I craved it again.

At the time, rents in New York were low, which meant creatives could afford to live in the thick of it. The downside to this was that crime rates were high: tourists arriving in the city were issued with pamphlets bearing a drawing of a hooded death's head and the bold headline 'Welcome to Fear City', advising them on how to stay safe. But while New York was dangerous, it also hissed with possibility and hedonism. The city was full of monolithic skyscrapers and glamorous fashion parties. Everyone knew everyone – artists knew musicians knew designers knew writers – and we all mingled with each other. No one was inaccessible. We were all flawed, and we made up for it by expressing ourselves in ways that made us feel beautiful.

I continued to experiment with my hair and make-up, seeing myself as an extension of my work. I shaded my eyes with bright blue, drew squiggles across my face and dyed my hair with streaks of colour. I was willing to go to great lengths to be me. In a city where artists came together to celebrate their difference, I revelled in the freedom such nonconformity celebrated.

My social life was a messy blur. In New York, I broke my no-lunch rule to dine with the likes of socialite Babe Paley and novelist Truman Capote, whom I remember as a quiet, wry man with a fantastic drawl and an even more fantastic Perspex cane that he carried everywhere. I spent weekends in Fire Island off Long Island, home to a fabulous pre-AIDS gay party scene, with Angelo Donghia, his boyfriend the designer Clovis Ruffin and the then king of fashion Halston, where we would smoke marijuana and dance until dawn. Halston was a shameless self-promoter, always trying to convince me to use whatever new thing he'd just launched. 'Darling, you must try my fragrance,' he'd purr at me.

The lunches, dinners, parties and events were wild, but I always refused to stay out too late. I would often end up feeling over-stimulated, as if my brain was doing a war-dance. An abundance of ideas would flow through my mind and I had to make sure I was able to translate everything into my work. My job was to look, look, look for the next inspiration, the next big idea. That I had a habit of falling asleep at the table also tended to put a stop to the late nights, although there was one social occasion for which I managed to stay awake throughout – an extraordinary dinner with Salvador Dalí.

I have always loved surrealist work, with its reliance on the subconscious to subvert reality, so I was very much looking forward to meeting the god of the movement. I still don't know why I was invited to that intimate dinner at the Plaza Hotel, but I didn't question it. So much of what happened to me during that time feels like a dream. Dalí had taken over one of the hotel's grand rooms with impossibly high ceilings, down the middle of which ran a long, exquisitely appointed table. Karl Lagerfeld, whom I came to know very well in the years that followed, was part of the mêlée, as was Andy Warhol.

When I first laid eyes on Salvador, it struck me that he looked exactly as he did in the pictures with that spindly, waxed moustache and wild dark eyes. He would have been in his mid-sixties, speckled with sunspots and walking with a bronze-tipped cane. A fabulously flamboyant character, he was decked out in a ruffled shirt and a double-breasted striped suit. His wife Gala had drawn a replica moustache across her face as a tribute, which she claimed was a tattoo – she'd have said anything to shock. They looked like cartoons. I was thankful that Dalí didn't bring the ocelot he was known to cart around with him as that would have put me right off my food. Time slipped by, like one of his melting watches, and I was delighted to be part of that magical moment surrounded by the key players in New York's art and design world.

In direct contrast to the Plaza, the epicentre of the downtown arts scene, Max's Kansas City, was a hangout for the young, beautiful and artistically inclined. A few years before the arrival of Studio 54, it wasn't grand, but it was where everyone wanted to be, myself included. The entrance opened into a long room with low light and red walls. Two piranha-filled fish tanks lined one side, but the main attraction was always the art, which was everywhere: an Andy Warhol soup can, a Dan Flavin light sculpture and a plate-glass window sandblasted by Michael Heizer, to name just a few pieces. A hallway at the back and a waitresses' galley (which, rumour has it, stored a bowl of prescription amphetamine pills to help them get through their long shifts) gave way to a back room with red booths on either side and round tables in the middle. This was where Andy Warhol and his entourage held court.

In the late sixties and throughout the seventies, Andy was undoubtedly the city's most famous artist. At Max's, he would sit at the biggest table, which subsequently became known as 'the Captain's Table'. There was no velvet rope forbidding entry, but anyone with any social nous knew you couldn't go in unless you were invited. Patti Smith once compared the social hierarchy of Max's to high school, which was spot on. Of course, the prom king wasn't some muscular sportsman but a slight, weird-looking man with a wig plonked on his head. People like Janis Joplin, Nico, Loulou de la Falaise, Paul Morrissey, Halston and Lou Reed would perch next to him, his chosen disciples for the evening. My crowd and I were happy to stay at the front smoking dope and watching the action unfold around us.

Over the years, I would see Andy at various fashion parties, dinners and as a guest at my shows, instantly recognizable by his silhouette. I had been a fan of his work since the early sixties when I was at college and found his Campbell's soup cans inspiring. I first met him in 1972 at his legendary studio known as the Factory, through a great friend, journalist and art collector, Joan Quinn. Joan was one of his many muses and a whizzy shaker on the LA arts scene. She collected antique Cartier watches, which she wore all together on her arm, sometimes

five or six at once. After we were acquainted, I would occasionally be invited to lunch at the Factory, a regular Friday event to
host people featured in Andy's *Interview* magazine, as well as
high-spending advertisers. Andy was very commercially savvy.
He loved to sell advertising, and he always wanted me to buy
ads. For all the press I was getting at that time, the payments
were still slow to arrive and I certainly didn't have money to
spend on advertising.

The truth is, Andy was terribly distant. I didn't become close to
him, although he always acknowledged me. He was a quiet, aloof
person who never talked much, just stood back and watched
others. I suppose you could say he was a sponge: he would pick
up anything and everything. He absorbed it all, then spat it out in
his own fantastic way. He filmed one of my New York runway
shows, which is now part of the permanent film collection at the
Andy Warhol Museum in Pittsburgh. I always thought he looked
like a human mushroom, a skinny man dressed in black with a
fuzzy white wig perched on top. His wigs were amazingly
designed objects, dark at the back and blond at the front. He used
to treat them as if they were part of his body, giving them the odd
trim every now and again. They concealed who he was and projected an image of how he wanted to be seen, creating a mystique.
That raggedy, strange wig turned him into an artwork through
the sheer brilliance of self-promotion.

Looking back, Andy's wig has come to represent a period of
my life when I almost lost myself to New York's wild social scene.
The Factory was at the epicentre – I'd go and immerse myself in
all that went on there. It was buzzy and happening, but in hindsight, also very superficial and ramshackle. Like Max's, it had so
much mystique surrounding it but really it was just a big, grimy
space with a lot of half-finished paintings and exhibitionists
trying to prove themselves. Eventually Andy filled it with

Andy Warhol in his wig

beautiful furniture he bought from Karl Lagerfeld, who he was
also friends with. The wood was dirty, the walls had exposed
pipes running up them and not in an aesthetic way as you see
now, but you could go in there and make a mess, which was the
point. I did several amazing photo sessions there for Andy's *Interview* magazine – my favourite featured Pat Cleveland in my
Schiffli-lace bridal look, standing regally next to a caped Latino

model called Juan Fernández, who sits dutifully by her side. The photo – shot by Francesco Scavullo, who did a lot of celebrity portraits back then – appeared in a 1973 edition of *Interview*. The caption read: '*Interview* says: This June get married. It's the only thrill left.'

The Factory was a buzzy place to be, but I wouldn't have wanted to call it home. It was a lot of smoke and mirrors. To make it all seem more professional, a beautiful boy would sit at the front desk and ask if you had an appointment, but even if you didn't you were still allowed in. All this to give the impression of a serious business, when really it was just artists playing. While I loved my time there, I had to return to London to focus and work once playtime was over.

20

Karl Lagerfeld's Fan

A PICTURE EXISTS OF MY late friend Karl Lagerfeld and me at the famed fashion-spectacular Met Gala. I must have been in my early forties, and I'm wearing one of my own designs, a strapless printed dress with a fuchsia chiffon scarf draped over one shoulder and an iridescent statement necklace. On my head sits a hot-pink exaggerated bouffant hairpiece, a picture of eighties maximalism; my lips are painted bright red and I've drawn on my eyebrows. Karl, who would have been fifty-three, is dressed in a beautifully tailored black tuxedo. His dark hair, not yet silver, is tied into his signature ponytail and he is smirking at the camera. We are both holding fans: mine features an illustration of a woman's face and Karl's is an elegant black and white. He is holding his dramatically in the way an opera singer might, with his arm outstretched.

I love that image because it says a lot about us – I'm laughing my head off and dressed to the nines, and Karl is the epitome of self-aware grandeur. His half-smile shows he's not taking any of it seriously. I like that he's carrying his trademark fan – fans were a part of his style uniform long before his black sunglasses and gloves. He told me once that he used them for practical reasons: he never enjoyed cigarettes, but his friends did and he'd use them

Karl Lagerfeld's fan

to bat away the smoke. I don't think it hurt that they looked fabulous too, helping to create an almost regal aura. I still have the fan I wore that evening and it will always remind me of Karl, our friendship and how he tried to help me on my way up the fashion ladder.

Karl and I first met in Paris in 1971 through work. My friend David Bailey had introduced me to the pioneering duo behind MAFIA, an influential design agency that offered graphic design and publicity services. Founders Maïmé Arnodin and Denise Fayolle wanted to promote talent from outside France and invited me to Paris where they commissioned me to create multiple textile prints. London was still very much where everything was happening in the early seventies, but what Paris lacked in buzz it made up for in sophistication and classical beauty. The Parisians were a show in themselves: everyone dressed up in a very traditional sense whether they were going for dinner or just for coffee. I stood out like a sore thumb: I had forest-green hair and was decked out in my boldly printed designs as usual. People used to stare at me as I charged about town with my sketchbooks.

The fashion scene was slowly changing there too, the carefree, liberated spirit of London and America slowly making its way to Paris, challenging its more prim dress codes. The designer Yves Saint Laurent was the most famous driver of this change – everyone was talking about his modern, boundary-pushing clothes, which were transforming the way many women dressed. I'd worn trousers before he launched his iconic 1966 'Le Smoking' collection, but never had they felt like a viable evening option and many women still refused to wear them. The year I arrived in Paris for work, Saint Laurent shocked everyone by appearing naked in his fragrance advert. There was a real oscillation between the new and the old French fashion guard, and I firmly backed the former.

I was travelling fairly regularly to and from the City of Light, which I loved. Paris has always occupied a special place for me. Not only is it the ultimate fashion city and home to heavyweights such as Chanel, Dior and Balenciaga, but it is also where my mother worked at the House of Worth in the mid-thirties. It meant a lot to be treading the same cobbled roads as she might have done pre-war, pre-marriage and pre-me.

During one of these trips, Denise and Maïmé of MAFIA hosted a dinner and it was there that I first met Karl. I'd already heard of him; by then he was working at Fendi and Chloé as a designer. My name was also on the rise after my successful New York catwalk show a few months prior, and while Karl was more established than I was, we were definitely coming up together. There was nearly a decade's age gap between us, but we got on almost immediately. He wanted to know and see everything and was obsessed with learning. I love people like that because it exposes me to new influences too. He had an amazing presence and was dressed impeccably in a black suit and tie. He was impossibly grand, which could have been intimidating, but he never was. He had created a very specific look for himself, always in sharp tailoring and carrying a fan and a cane like a nineteenth-century dandy. We talked about everything from the history of costume to Pop Art and found we had more in common than it might have seemed based on our respective appearances. We had been born to and shaped by strong, sometimes formidable mothers with an acute sense of style. For both of us, they were motivating forces in terms of our careers and where we found ourselves. Like me, he had an inexhaustible approach to work, and was similarly precise and introverted. Both of us are true Virgos: neither he nor I could bear to be anything other than perfect.

We used how we looked to court attention in a way that meant we didn't need to put the essence of who we were on the line. Not that we ever discussed it, but clothes were perhaps protective armour for both of us. Karl never hid behind his image with me – he was always just my incomparably clever and kind friend. There was never a drop of pretence. Although the Parisian fashion set at that time gravitated towards glamorous spots like Club Sept and Café de Flore, we both loved entertaining at home and I spent many evenings in his beautiful apartment sitting at the dinner table surrounded by his incredible collection of art-deco furniture and shelves upon shelves of books. He drank buckets of Coca-Cola, and moved on to Diet Coke when he went on a diet and could no longer have sugar.

The company at his parties was always wonderful. Karl's friendship group was colourful and stylish, but never superficial, from the revered Puerto Rican illustrator Antonio Lopez, whose work featured in *Vogue* and *Harper's Bazaar*, to the flamboyant Italian fashion editor Anna Piaggi, whose wildly colourful outfits and theatrical make-up were, for a time, inspired by me – that was the rumour anyway. I saw our increasingly similar aesthetics as flattery. In the late seventies when I was in my punk period, the three of us went for a rare lunch at the Palace of Versailles – that's the sort of thing one did in Karl's company: he brought grandeur to the most ordinary of social occasions. I wore a white slashed punk top with beaded safety-pin detailing. I had a pointed green fringe and dramatic asymmetrical punk eyebrows, and I expect Anna was decked in something equally eye-catching. Karl never flinched. He loved people who devoted themselves to style and beauty.

We used to spend a lot of time scouring Paris flea markets for inspiration, and on occasion would travel in a spectacular glass car belonging to our stylish friends Emmanuelle and Quasar Khanh. She was a fashion designer, sometimes described as the French Mary Quant because of her fresh, youthful clothes. He was a cerebral inventor who masterminded inflatable furniture and the aforementioned glass car named the 'Quasar Unipower'. Wider than it was long, the vehicle's seats were wooden and not overly comfortable. On one trip to the flea market with Karl and the Khanhs, I bought some old magazines on lace and crochet-making, which I would use as inspiration for my later 'Lovely Lilies' collection.

The thing everyone simply must know about Karl is that he was endlessly generous with his time and himself. Everyone needs a friend who cheerleads them, and Karl was that person for me. In the early seventies when I had little business in Paris aside from my work for MAFIA, he took me from shop to shop, demanded to see the owner and suggested they buy my pieces and sell them.

Of course, my collections were still too way out for elegant, conservative Paris, and I was well past the point of compromising on my vision, but I have never forgotten the gesture. I admired Karl hugely and, looking back, I think the admiration was mutual. A later Chloé collection of his was inspired by my 'Hands and Flowers' prints, and looked nothing short of fantastic.

Karl was simply wonderful to me, and we remained friends for decades. I saw him less in his latter years because he had so many different professional commitments between his eponymous line, Fendi and Chanel. He did it all with so much style and wit. Karl was a forward thinker, who never, even in old age, lost his sense of how interesting and mysterious the world is. He continued designing and learning until he died in February 2019, and that's a philosophy to live by.

21

Anjelica Huston Roundhouse Show Poster

IN THE SPRING OF 1972, I staged my first catwalk show in London at the Roundhouse, the circular cutting-edge music venue. This marked the start of a period when the British fashion industry saw me as an artist, rather than as an eccentric-looking outlier. My designs had appeared in publications including British *Vogue* and *Queen*, and I had one stockist in the luxury Fulham Road boutique Piero de Monzi. The bulk of my business, though, was still coming from America. I wanted to boost my name in London and hopefully generate more sales as a result. A show, I hoped, might be a way of doing so. Also, my fruitful trip to Japan had provided me with enough inspiration to create a collection I felt truly proud of, 'Lovely Lilies'.

I wanted to demonstrate to my audience in London that a catwalk event could be an art form in its own right, as I had done with my debut New York show at Angelo Donghia's townhouse in 1971. I had no interest in reproducing the popular staid format in which models walked in a straight line on a raised platform towards the elite in a designer shop or showroom. I wanted to have a fantastical and immersive performance somewhere exciting and unexpected, which was why I chose the Roundhouse. Bands of the moment Pink Floyd, the Doors, the Rolling Stones and the Who had all played there, but no one had used it for fashion purposes. Guests sat round the circular centre stage, which meant that everyone had a good view. The only problem was the venue was booked up with gigs for the foreseeable. If I wanted to stage my show there, I'd have to start the event at midnight. As a morning bird, the idea of such a late start felt like death but I could appreciate that it might create a rock 'n' roll allure.

I floated the idea to my friend and mentor, restaurateur Michael Chow, who had been a guest at and key orchestrator of my catwalk show in Tokyo. He'd become an even bigger fan of mine since I'd introduced him to Tina, and was very keen to help me promote the event. Michael advised me to create a limited run of signed and numbered posters advertising the event to generate hype. You could describe it as high-end fly posting, although the posters were like mini artworks in themselves – an image that represented harmony between the clothes and the women I wanted to dress. Very few designers were marketing themselves in this way, bar the mighty Halston, who promoted his events with images illustrated by his influential creative director Joe Eula. I used photography instead as there was more room for my own creative input.

The image starred a twenty-year-old Anjelica Huston, then in the early stages of her modelling career and a favourite of Halston. *Vogue* photographer Barry Lategan, responsible for the 1966 picture of Twiggy that launched her career, took the picture. He was friends with superstar make-up artist Barbara Daly, known for her bright, bold looks – she'd often use crayons to create the look she was after. She was fresh from working with director Stanley Kubrick on the make-up for the 1971 cult film *A Clockwork Orange*, and later went on to design the wedding-beauty look for Lady Diana Spencer in 1981. I loved her work: it was dramatic, artistic and pushed boundaries.

Amazingly, she agreed not only to do the poster, but the show too. We toyed with what Anjelica's make-up would look like, but in the end decided on a mask. There was something almost rebellious and irreverent about hiding the face of one of the most sought-after rising models. I decided the masks, which we covered with pearls, would be worn by all of the models in the show. They were a powerful, subversive juxtaposition to my romantic, lily-printed chiffon dresses. On the poster, you can see only Anjelica's dark kohl-rimmed eyes, and orange tinted lips. My dear friend Leonard masterminded the hair, attaching a neon tangerine wig of frizzy curls that matched the saturated tone of the printed dress in the picture. I hand-wrote the date (Thursday 27 April 1972), the location, my stockist details and the names of my collaborators at the bottom. It perfectly communicated what I wanted to say about who I was and the unusual format of the show: fantasy fashion theatre. I spent a day driving around London, hand-delivering the posters to magazine editors and to any potential stockists. It was an effective marketing tool, and one I continued with throughout my career when it came to creating pre-show interest.

By the time the day of the show finally arrived, I'd been working eighteen-hour days for weeks before. I was exhausted but running on adrenaline. I wanted the show to be a multi-sensory experience. It had to feel like a real happening, something you'd remember. My jet-set audience included the ever-beautiful Bianca Jagger, the footwear designer Manolo Blahnik and the photographer David Bailey, along with every eminent British fashion editor imaginable. The pressure was huge, and I remember fussing backstage and getting in the way. I had enlisted the most legendary models of the day, Anjelica Huston, of course, but also Warhol muses Donna Jordan and Pat Cleveland, who both flew over from New York. I chose *Vogue* favourite Cathee

Dahmen to wear the all-important finale look – a heavy guipure lace ensemble with a trumpet skirt cut to resemble an inverted lily, inspired by my Parisian flea-market finds and my whirlwind trip to Japan the year before. I kept pulling and picking at details of the outfits such as the huge gold-foil lily-shaped necklaces and headpieces by Mick Milligan and tying and accidentally knotting the bow-ties of the garments, much to the frustration of the dressers, who were attempting to apply the finishing touches to the outfits as they helped the models into the clothes. There was almost nothing left for me to do, but I couldn't just sit there alone with my nerves so I straightened hangers and busied myself with the minutiae. I felt positively frenzied, not that I told anyone – when I'm truly nervous I resort to silence. I still become apprehensive before a show: sticking your neck out and presenting the fruits of your labour is like giving birth every six months. You've just got to hope that you bring out a healthy baby everyone likes and not a sickly thing they all ignore.

The show began as promised at midnight. I stood in the wings as the lights were dimmed and spotlights illuminated the central stage. The noisy, crowded room went quiet – the atmosphere was electric. I felt slightly sick with anxiety. The music began – joyful, rhythmic Brazilian carnival sounds reverberated around the space. Directed by choreographer Jacques Ross, my star models emerged one by one in the mysterious beaded masks and began to dance to the music, spinning around the circular platform, splaying the chiffon out over their heads to show off the lightness of the fabrics. They twirled in romantic caftans and smocked jerseys with exposed reversed seams. The Mick Milligan gold-foil lily accessories trembled round their necks and heads. The sliced handkerchief hems whirled as the models pirouetted to the percussion and bossa-nova beats. It was extraordinary – a fusion of fashion, dance and music, a major performance, as I'd intended.

After Jacques had led Cathee out as my finale bride, he motioned for me to come on stage. I moved out of the wings and took a quick bow, looking down the whole time. To my amazement, the audience stood up and gave me a standing ovation. Amid the clapping, people started dancing to the music; it felt like a dream. David Bailey and his then girlfriend, the model Penelope Tree, threw an after-party in my honour at his home round the corner from the Roundhouse in Primrose Hill. I'd love to tell you that it was debauched and wild, but the sad truth is I felt asleep on his staircase. The weeks of work and build-up had finally caught up with me.

Although I was aware that the show had been a success, it didn't dawn on me until later how new and game-changing it was. The revered fashion journalist Suzy Menkes, who was there that night, said it was her first big catwalk show – she had never seen anything of that size, scale or drama. No one else had done anything on that level before. Finally, I was a fashion sensation in my own country. It's worth saying at this point that a designer is only as good as her team, and I have been lucky to be supported by the best in the business. From Ben Scholten, who worked with me on the clothes and music concepts, to Gill Griffiths, who assisted on my prints, and Frances Diplock, whose detailed hand-finishings made my garments sing, my team has brought alive my collections and runway events. One's creative vision is worth very little if you don't have the crew to bring it to life.

Throughout my career, I have treated my catwalk shows as theatre, particularly during the seventies and eighties when I was riding high on success. Involving choreography, sets, dancers, special effects and dramatic hair, make-up and accessories, they have become a vital part of my legacy. My 'Fables of the Sea' show in 1984 featured a Poseidon character rising from below the stage, while 'India Revisited' in 1985 was soundtracked by the famous

Bengali musician Ananda Shankar. My 'Circle in the Square' show of 1974 deserves a chapter in its own right, so I'll get to that in due course.

When London Fashion Week launched in 1984, I presented my collections as part of the official calendar, but I never felt wedded to it. I have always liked to do things in my own spirit and time, and where it suits me, whether that's London, New York or LA. There will never be anything that represents the glamour and beauty of fashion quite like a catwalk show.

22

Adel Rootstein Mannequin

I HAVE BEEN VERY LUCKY that so many people have had a hand in my success. As I've already described, my closest friends have inspired and guided me through good and bad, both emotionally and professionally, but a mentor has a different role. They're usually someone who has more experience or expertise in a particular area, and offers encouragement and wisdom when it comes to work. Running a fashion label is a brilliant job, soaked in creativity and stimulation, but it's also hard work. Sometimes the ideas don't come as quickly as you'd like, and sometimes your specific aesthetic doesn't always chime with what's in at any given moment. Sometimes money is tight. Sometimes you can feel very much alone and lost. That's why mentors are so important – they can help problem-solve and bolster self-belief.

After my mother died in 1964 when I was twenty-four, I found myself without my chief cheerleader. She was never one for platitudes, but her high expectations for me came because she knew what I was capable of. Her unwavering confidence in my talent was so strong that it lay within me like a rod of iron. In the absence of my mother, as my career began to take off, I found myself at creative and business impasses without anyone to guide me in a practical sense. An unsung fashion pioneer, the great mannequin-maker Adel Rootstein arrived in my life in late 1969 as an equally dynamic, nurturing force of nature. Without her, my business wouldn't have flourished in the way it did. Her straight-talking, sensible advice and business acumen enabled me to develop. I very much relied on her and, if I allow myself to think about it, miss her still.

It was winter 1969, following my successful first trip to New York, when Adel first knocked on my rundown studio door and demanded to see my clothes. She was a small, well-dressed woman with a distinctive bob and a no-nonsense expression. She was wearing an elegant Jean Muir navy dress, the sixties label of choice for serious, cerebral women who preferred restrained, unadorned clothes. I didn't know who she was – her mannequin business hadn't been going for long at that point. I told her she was welcome to see the collection at Fortnum & Mason, where it was currently on sale. She point-blank refused and said she wanted to see the garments there and then, so I showed her in. Somehow I understood that you couldn't say no to Adel. She was fierce.

As we started going through the rails, I asked her what she did for a living. She told me a brief outline of her story: she was a Russian Jew, who was born in South Africa in a small village in the middle of nowhere called Warmbaths. At a young age, she came to London and went to work for the now defunct British label Aquascutum, creating window displays. Adel couldn't understand why mannequins all looked like lifeless, spindly droids when sixties fashion was so vibrant and exciting, so she decided to make her own using the latest fibreglass technology and a talented sculptor called John Taylor.

Her mannequins were beautiful and innovative. They were like nothing that had ever been seen before – dramatic and exciting, flying and leaping in the air, striking poses. They looked like real

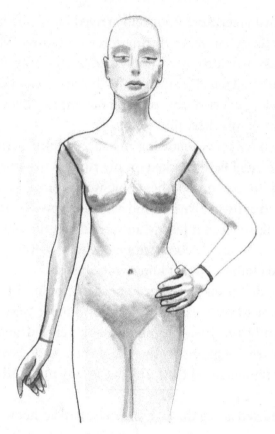

Adel Rootstein mannequin

people. She always said that whatever was selling the clothes in a magazine should be selling them in a window display. She had a great idea of creating mannequins to look like the biggest stars of the day, usually immortalizing them before they became huge – style icons like Pattie Boyd, models including Donyale Luna, Twiggy, Tina Chow and Marie Helvin, then actresses such as Joan Collins and Joanna Lumley. Adel's eye for a future trend or style maverick was so esteemed that it became a huge honour if she used your likeness as the focus of one of her visions.

She believed in giving customers what they didn't know they wanted, which is a dictum to live by in fashion. The make-up was hand-painted, going as far as to recreate even facial pores; her attention to detail was acute. Far from the stiff, dull window displays of the fifties, Adel's mannequins were embodiments of contemporaneous trends, manifesting as three-dimensional models. She was also an early pioneer of diversity, launching plus-size and petite lines not long before she died in 1992. Her business went international very quickly, and she did a roaring trade in the US where she created eye-catching window displays at Saks Fifth Avenue. I loved her work, and when I opened my Grafton Street shop in 1975, I used her mannequins – my clothes need bodies. I know all garments do, but my prints are best seen on something that looks alive. Adel's exuberant mannequins were the perfect vehicle. It's hard to imagine now, but people would come up to London to visit the window displays, and Adel's were always the star attraction.

In the decades that followed, I learnt so much from Adel. In the early days, when money was tight and I couldn't afford to pay my staff, she loaned me what I needed, always trusting that I'd repay her, which I did. She set me up with her accountant, who helped to manage the financial side of the business. When I hosted my first show in New York in 1971 at Angelo Donghia's townhouse, she allowed my friends and me to stay in her studio there. At one point, our respective offices were just minutes apart in Kensington, so we saw each other often. We were very close. She forced me to believe in myself, even when things went wrong. After my Grafton Street shop closed in 1990, her encouragement made me carry on. She always believed that my brand was worth saving. She had faith not only in me but also in my work. Adel never accepted things as they were: she was critical and forced you to really look at a situation. She always pushed boundaries and wanted to be innovative, qualities I hugely admired. She was softly spoken, but very wise and direct. I didn't always appreciate her honesty, but she was always right. If she hosted a dinner party, she'd decide when everyone was leaving by simply telling them that a black cab was waiting for them outside. She was elegant, but you didn't want to get on her bad side. What a wonderful way to be.

Like me, Adel was a perfectionist. When she found out she was dying of cancer, she organized her own funeral and obituary; that's the type of woman she was. In her will, she donated a number of her mannequins to me; I have them at home in my penthouse, much treasured objects. I was glad to see Miuccia Prada use a selection of Adel's statuesque works in Miu Miu's 2017 pre-fall collection. They looked just as contemporary and fresh as they did when they were first launched more than fifty years before.

23

Freddie Mercury's Cape

ONE MORNING IN EARLY 1974, I received a phone call from a musician who introduced himself as Brian May, the guitarist in a new band called Queen that I'd never heard of. Although I wasn't known as a menswear designer, I had been featured in both British and US *Vogue* so had begun to build a name for myself with my distinctive clothing. Furthermore, I had designed some bespoke looks for Marc Bolan of T. Rex via my stylist friend Chelita Secunda. Chelita, who was married to Marc's manager Tony Secunda, felt that my clothes would be a good match for Marc, so she regularly came to the studio to select pieces she knew he'd like. I wasn't particularly aware of T. Rex's music either, although I think my boyfriend Alex played me some when he knew I was designing pieces for him. I was a Radio 4 listener even then and was more interested in *The Archers* than pop music. Brian told me that his group had recently had a top-ten hit with 'Seven Seas Of Rhye' and asked if he and his bandmate Freddie could come over and look at some clothes in the next few weeks. He said the group needed new outfits for a few gigs. I agreed – to me, they were just prospective customers.

As I say, if I have the radio on, it's always Radio 4. My knowledge of new records has always either come from *Desert Island*

Discs or from friends putting on something at a dinner party. For all my dressing of musicians over the years, music as a medium has never been a big part of my life. I have simply helped them look the part. When music and image blend perfectly, you hit the sweet spot. Perhaps being detached from the music helped me dress them more objectively – I was never influenced or bogged down by the weight of fandom. Glam rock was in full swing at the time and although Bowie had revealed his flamboyant alter-ego Ziggy Stardust a couple of years before, it was Marc Bolan who really introduced conspicuous androgyny to that decade. When Marc cried glitter tears on *Top of the Pops* in 1971, the pretty pixie man and his guitar changed everything. Rock stars didn't have to look typically masculine or wear Brut aftershave: it was better to look exquisitely otherworldly. Suddenly we saw an explosion of sequins, lamé, colour and mascara. From all the glamour, flamboyance and camp theatrics emerged this new band called Queen.

I told Brian they'd have to visit in the evening once my staff had gone home if they wanted privacy. My rickety studio above the travel agent in Bayswater was three floors of chaos, a real tangle of sewing machines and print screens, and we certainly didn't have changing rooms. Before they left, the girls in the studio played me Queen's hit record so I had a sense of their music.

When the doorbell rang, I went to meet Brian and Freddie. Escorting them through the nondescript, dusty old door, I noticed immediately that Brian was the chattier out of the two. Freddie seemed shy; he didn't come barrelling in like a big rock god. He had black nail varnish and a fabulous head of hair. I don't think you can always tell if someone's going to be a star, especially if you're meeting the man rather than the performer. No doubt if I had met him fresh from the stage, he wouldn't have appeared so unassuming and quiet.

Freddie and Brian didn't flinch at the state of my studio. Instead, they clattered up the narrow stairs quite happily in their platform boots, dodging the rolls of fabric and cannabis plants along the way. I knew not to converse with them about their music because I had little idea who they were. I focused on the reason they were there and my area of expertise – clothes. I asked them about how they wanted to wear the pieces. How physical was their planned concert going to be? How much did they want to move on stage? What did they like wearing? What made them feel good? What colours did they like wearing? Brian was clear that they needed to be able to play their instruments and move without restriction. Freddie told me, 'I need to look bold – I need something that helps me become a showman.' He seemed to have an innate understanding that what he wore on stage was as important as what he sounded like.

When we got to the top floor housing the machining and cutting room, I pulled a few pieces off the rails for them to try on. I had made no special edit for them: these were just pieces I'd recently finished working on, including a wonderful pleated bridal top. I told them they must move around the room and see how they felt. Clothes need to do different things if you're a musician: they have a purpose, and part of that is to enable the wearer to move well. Another part is to project an image of who the individual wants to be perceived as – though that's much the same with everyone, musician or otherwise.

Freddie picked out a few things to try on based on my suggestions, including the white pleated bridal top made in heavy ivory silk with a lace bodice and giant pleated butterfly sleeves. 'They look like angel wings,' he said, holding it up against himself. 'It's amazing.' Inspired by one of my favourite models, Tina Chow, and some drawings of lilies I'd made while visiting Japan, I had designed the top as part of a wedding two-piece, complete with a matching skirt. His choice didn't surprise me – it had a theatrical quality that I think we could both see working well on stage. As soon as Freddie put it on and started to move around, I knew it was the one. He looked like a flamboyant bird. Spreading his arms like wings, the fabric swirled around him and the pleats worked perfectly.

So much of how we look in clothes depends on how we feel in them. That top helped Freddie blossom into the showman he

Freddie Mercury in my cape design

wanted to be. To create any sort of magic, there has to be chemistry between the wearer and the garment, and it can't be forced. Rod Stewart, for example, didn't feel right in my pieces when I fitted him a few years later. He flew me out to Paris for the occasion, but the chemistry wasn't there. When that happens, it doesn't worry me – I want the wearer to feel spectacular in my designs and if they don't, well, I never expect them to buy anything. But Freddie transformed in that top because it helped him become what he wanted to be – a flamboyant, boundary-breaking peacock. In that moment, when someone tries on my clothes and starts to radiate a different energy – whether it is joy, confidence or glamour – there's nothing like it.

That said, it was a subversive choice. Despite the popularity of glam rock and how its artists challenged conventional masculinity, homophobia was rife in the seventies. Although the Sexual Offences Act had been introduced seven years before, it only partially decriminalized homosexuality. The age of consent was set at twenty-one for sex between men, as opposed to sixteen for heterosexual sex, and any sexual acts had to be performed in the privacy of someone's home. Underage homosexual men and women were arrested for as little as kissing or holding hands in public. The atmosphere towards gay sexuality was still largely intolerant. Outside my arty enclave in West London, men simply weren't talking about their sexuality. Even Freddie had to hide that side of himself at the time, but that design did something for him. Like Marc, he found that my designs allowed a certain type of man to feel able to express something of himself without outwardly saying, 'I'm sleeping with men.' They could come to me for clothes that revealed much more of themselves than their clothes had done previously.

Freddie was clearly taken with the top and I agreed to make one for him. After a few more sketches, we made a version in a heavy cream satin with quilting at the chest rather than guipure lace, which he felt was a touch too bridal. I've never had a problem altering pieces for clients – the customer is always right. It's crucial that they feel wonderful in the garment: they're wearing it. I hate the idea of dictating what someone should wear. I'd only ever disagree with changing a piece if I felt it was being redesigned in a way that went against my aesthetic handwriting, but that's never happened, perhaps because my signatures are so pronounced. If you're coming to me for a piece, you know what you're getting. We agreed on a price – no one was given anything for free back then, regardless of how famous they were. He and Brian didn't stay much longer, Brian having chosen a printed pleated jacket, which I would have to continue remaking for him over the years as it kept getting stolen. I'd hate to romanticize crime, but I will take those instances of theft as a compliment – it's clearly a hot property.

Not long after our first meeting, Freddie and Brian invited me to watch Queen play at Earls Court Olympia. Freddie called in advance to tell me he was pleased with the piece and would be wearing it that evening. I went along with dear Duggie Fields and we felt like the oldest people there by at least ten years. That night, a few photographers got the rub of what Freddie wanted to be, capturing him flying about the stage in my pleated design. He looked like an ethereal hallucination. He was a god on stage. It felt wonderful to know my work had been part of his transformation, but, to be honest, it's nice when I see anyone – famous or otherwise – wearing my clothes and clearly feeling fabulous. It's an affirmation that I've done my job well.

I designed a few more outfits for Freddie and Brian but we didn't stay in touch other than professionally. People often think that because I have pink hair I must have constantly partied with the musicians I dressed, but that was never my scene. When

Freddie died in 1991, I was invited to the memorials because I had created that iconic look – people even asked me to sign pictures of him. It just so happened that Queen became one of the biggest bands in the country and I was there early, fantastic luck. Success is a mix of good fortune and hard work, and I've certainly harnessed both over my 83 years. Of course, I had no idea that the unassuming man who knocked at my studio door in 1974 would become a global icon, or that the piece he chose from that rail of clothes would go down in fashion history. It's only later that these things become apparent, but he certainly wouldn't have known who I was or come to me had I not been so dogged about creating a style that was bold and original. That billowing white top became part of Freddie's story, so he became an integral part of mine. Our names were linked in a way I could never have foreseen.

24

Princess Anne's Engagement Portrait

To be a success in fashion, support from the right people at the right time is crucial. As you've read so far, I was lucky enough to have that, although to quote Samuel Goldwyn, the harder I worked, the luckier I got. I don't think you can always engineer your good fortune, but in my experience, knocking on doors and dogged persistence help because they put you in prime position for others to see and appreciate your work. I'm also a firm believer in originality – it's the hallmark of good design, and forces people to form an opinion, good or bad. Ultimately, it all boils down to a very subtle alchemy – making the right clothes at the right time, which are then worn and seen by the right people.

This was what happened when Princess Anne chose to wear one of my gowns for her official engagement portrait in 1973. It solidified me as a heavyweight on the British fashion scene. I was not only someone who dressed wealthy socialites, models and musicians, but someone whose appeal stretched to royalty.

By 1973, I was still living in Notting Hill and working in my chaotic Porchester Road studio. My clothes, which regularly appeared in *Harper's Bazaar* and *Vogue*, were being worn by as diverse a group of people as Marc Bolan, the ever-stylish Bianca

Jagger and the beautiful Ali MacGraw, then at the height of her fame after her starring role in *Love Story*. Orders were coming in from America as my customer base grew over there.

My personal life was in less great shape – Alex and I had finally split up. I still can't pinpoint an exact reason why it all fell apart. When you've been together so long, there's rarely just one reason. My tendency to put work above almost everything has made it hard for me to sustain romantic relationships and my partners have probably all felt sidelined at times. There is also a certain level of fame that comes with dating me, which many men I've known have found off-putting. Alex 'distracted himself' with the affections of others. We continued working with each other for years afterwards regardless. The results of our creative partnership were fantastic, the atmosphere less so. In fact, a former colleague described it as an intense war zone. I can't remember the situation ever being so acrimonious, but as I tend to block out pain or hardship it's possible that it was.

When I received a call from one of the fashion editors at British *Vogue* asking me if I would submit a few designs for a VIP who would feature in the magazine, I jumped at the chance. The identity of the VIP was to be kept anonymous, and the only criterion was that I send ballgowns. I had no idea that the dress was for the newly engaged Princess Anne to wear to announce her engagement. In fact I thought the celebrity in question was Elizabeth Taylor, and I was dying to dress her. (My wish came true in the eighties when she wore a few of my designs.) I sent a selection of gowns to the British *Vogue* offices, including a romantic white net gown with a full skirt and a finely stitched bodice. It had featured as my finale bridal look in my most recent collection and was covered with intricate Schiffli embroidered lace shells. It was also very flattering, cinched at the waist and splaying out at the hem to create an hour-glass silhouette.

After the designs had been couriered to Vogue House, I didn't think much of it. Fashion editors often ask to borrow pieces to be worn by models or high-profile figures on photo shoots, and you never know if they'll be used or not. I didn't find out that my dress had been chosen for the engagement portrait until the day I saw it in British *Vogue* that November, the month she married. I was abroad at the time, probably in New York where I was doing a lot of business. I couldn't believe it: to dress the royals at any time was a huge coup, but to do so for such a historic occasion – well, my feet barely touched the ground all day.

The princess looked like a dream – the images had been photographed by my dear friend, the late Norman Parkinson, who had become an official royal photographer in 1969. Not only was Norman wildly talented, he was also very discreet, making him a perfect candidate for the job. The final pictures were taken in the Long Gallery at Windsor Castle, showing Anne holding hands with her fiancé Captain Mark Phillips. The background is a haze of regal furniture and the couple stand isolated in the centre – it's a soft, very romantic picture. The dress itself looked wonderful, as feminine and beautiful as the photographs and the occasion required. It was a huge honour to have been part of those images, and I owe Parks a great deal for any role he played in ensuring my dress was chosen. I still don't know what happened at the photo shoot because I wasn't there, but from what I understand, Parkinson presented Princess Anne with a rail of clothes and singled out mine as a favourite. Apparently, she fell in love with it as soon as she tried it on.

Princess Anne has excellent taste in clothes and wears them well, but there's a sense that she's more driven by easy practicality than anything else. I love that for her engagement portrait she went for something completely different – a gown weighted in fantasy and glamour. I was told by a member of the *Vogue* team

My design worn by Princess Anne for her engagement portrait

that Anne wore a simple Gina Fratini piece underneath my shells gown because Prince Philip, who was present on the day, thought it too sheer and daring to wear solo.

When I arrived back in the UK, in the days following the release of the engagement portrait, photographers crowded round the plane waiting for me. I wasn't used to attention like that, but everyone assumed that because I'd made the engagement gown I'd designed the wedding dress too. In the end, they were wrong: that job went to Maureen Baker, the head designer at a fashion label called Susan Small.

It would have been a great honour to design that wedding dress, but if you look at the designers who have created gowns for British royalty, it's clear what enormous pressure it puts on the designer and their label. David and Elizabeth Emanuel's joint business collapsed less than a decade after they had designed Lady Diana Spencer's dramatic wedding gown in 1981. And when the then Kate Middleton wore a beautiful blue Issa jersey dress for her official engagement photos in 2010, the brand didn't have enough money to finance production on the mass scale required to meet the new-found demand for their clothes and went bust two years later.

Before a dress for a royal is revealed, a designer needs to have the infrastructure to deal with the ensuing demand and be able to manage the pressure that comes with all that publicity. I'm not sure my business had those components in place back in 1973. That said, the outcome of making Anne's engagement look was hugely positive. I don't think I can definitively say that it made other royals look in my direction, but it did build greater public awareness of my work, at home and abroad. As a result, we received orders from around the world and, even if I didn't make the wedding dress, my name was still closely associated with the event. In December that year, the shell gown was enshrined in the windows at Fortnum & Mason, the London store that stocked my designs, and crowds queued round the building to see it, which was very gratifying.

In my opinion, Anne is one of the most underestimated royals.

She works tirelessly, really does her homework and doesn't have any pretence about her. We've met several times since that engagement picture, although we've never spoken in depth about the dress. Most memorably, in February 2015 on the day of my investiture as a Dame of the British Empire alongside a few hundred others, I saw that Anne had memorized every single person's name, who they were and the achievement that had led to their honour – quite a feat. Having my gown chosen for her engagement photograph was a huge milestone for me professionally, and one of which I'm immensely proud. I cut out the picture in *Vogue* and had it framed and hung in my studio. It was the start of an enduring relationship with the Royal Family that went on to include designing for Princess Margaret and Princess Diana, two women I would grow to respect for very different reasons.

25

Princess Margaret's Gongfu Teacups

I'VE ALWAYS LOVED THE ROYALS and it's been a great honour to dress a number of them throughout my career. One of the most memorable encounters I've had with the Royal Family occurred when I was called to Princess Margaret's apartment at Kensington Palace in the spring of 1979.

I'd first met her at a party in the seventies hosted by Bubbles Rothermere, a client of mine who earned her nickname on account of her love of champagne. On that occasion and at subsequent events where our paths crossed, I found the princess very formal and aloof. While other royals I've known and worked with can be a bit awkward when it comes to all the pomp, Margaret was very much at ease with it. You could only ever ask her a question if she spoke to you first (not what I would call a conversation) and she expected you to curtsy and follow the correct procedures. In fact, Margaret would sometimes appear to exploit royal protocol for her own benefit – for example, no one was ever allowed to leave a party until she had decided to retire for the evening. As someone who gets very tired and falls asleep very easily, I found that difficult. I recall an evening event at the Italian Embassy on Grosvenor Square when it was well past midnight and all the guests were willing her to hurry up and go so we could head home. She continued chatting away, completely oblivious, or perhaps she just didn't care.

If you're British (Americans don't see this in the same way), I think you understand that if you are in the company of the royals, they are always quite unknowable because of the power imbalance that exists between civilians and royalty. Right or wrong, that is how it is. They might be very nice to you (and Princess Margaret was always very nice to me), but they are always guarded and you are always aware that they are many rungs up on the social ladder (in my case, about a hundred). Princess Margaret knew who she was, and that person was very, very royal. She had no interest in putting anyone at ease. Like me, she had decided she didn't want to be a mousy person and lived by the standards she had set for herself. As lofty as she was, I had a lot of respect for her.

Having met Princess Margaret on a few occasions, I thought I knew what to expect when I was called to her apartment at Kensington Palace that spring day in 1979. I had been commissioned by the high-society philanthropist Drue Heinz to make the princess a ballgown as a gift. I walked into Margaret's apartment past several pairs of muddied wellies and a battered old suitcase, which I assumed she took on trips to the country. A member of staff swiftly led me upstairs to the sitting room where the fitting would take place, one of at least twenty rooms in the four-storey building. The focal point in the room was a grand piano, with pictures of all the family on top, including Margaret with her mother and sister. Behind it, the large window looked out over the private gardens. Altogether, the palace was much like a country house. Don't get me wrong: it was very lovely, but not grand.

As I ambled around the room subtly admiring its many antiques, a maid with a square piece of freshly pressed linen appeared and placed it on the floor; apparently the carpet underneath wouldn't be protection enough for Margaret's feet. When she arrived, we swiftly got on with the fitting, which went well enough. I remembered my ma'ams and curtsies. One thing you must know about Margaret is that she was tiny, even smaller than me and I am five foot two (I've since shrunk to four foot eleven). She didn't tower over me, but she made up for it by being lofty at all times.

After we'd finished the fitting, Margaret asked me if I'd care for a cup of tea. I obliged and followed her to what she called the library, a sumptuous room that was covered with oil paintings hung over ornate wallpaper. As I went to sit down on the couch, I noticed a petit-point cushion with a message embroidered on it that read 'It's not easy being a princess.' To this day, I still wonder who might have given it to her.

Margaret summoned a maid and asked politely for tea for two. We exchanged pleasantries about the weather before the maid bustled back in with a silver tray, on which the first thing I spotted were three of the tiniest biscuits I'd ever seen. I was ravenous but knew I couldn't touch them before Margaret did. Next to those tiny treats stood a beautiful teapot and delicate, but expansive,

Princess Margaret's Gongfu teacup

Gongfu china teacups and saucers. Mine was empty, I presumed because the tea was still brewing. However, upon glancing at Margaret's cup, I noticed that it was already full. Why would her tea be already poured when mine was still brewing? I wondered whether, in fact, it contained something a little stronger, perhaps her favourite tipple.

I never saw her wear the dress from that fitting, but I heard that she wore it to one of the Heinzes' lavish balls. Whenever I see that dreamy Norman Parkinson portrait of Princess Margaret wearing one of my pleated jackets, I always remember that extraordinary day, and her elegant way of surreptitiously slipping in an afternoon gin and tonic.

26

Diana Ross's Turban

I MUST HAVE BEEN IN my mid-thirties when Diana Ross threatened to crush me under her garage door. It was a simple misunderstanding, but it's not the sort of thing you forget in a hurry. You simply don't expect to be told by a world-famous diva that she might kill you if come any closer.

Diana's and my story started in 1976 when she bought a few of my pieces to wear as part of her European tour. She was due to perform at the Victoria Palace Theatre in London, a sell-out concert that everyone was talking about. She was at the height of her fame, and although, as I've already said, I was no music buff, even I'd heard her hit singles 'Ain't No Mountain High Enough' and 'Touch Me In The Morning'. Disco as a musical genre was building serious momentum, with Donna Summer's 'Love To Love You Baby' the soundtrack of 1976. Diana Ross was, of course, a key part of the scene. Andy Warhol loved her and had featured her in his *Interview* magazine. We all loved listening to her, but we also loved looking at what she wore – she was pure style dynamite.

Diana booked an appointment with me at my Grafton Street boutique where I fitted her, a service I only offered VIPs. In the end, she chose an elegant red pleated chiffon skirt, matching top and a red pleated satin jacket, complete with a red turban by Graham Smith, a talented milliner with whom I'd collaborated on a few collections. She looked gorgeous – the colour and cut worked very well on her. I was also wearing one of Graham's turbans that day – a plain white jersey style that hid my then green hair. She had a reputation as a diva, but there was nothing haughty about her. She was warm and friendly and had a clear sense of what suited her. We got along well enough for her to invite me to the show and after-party in a few days' time. I didn't need to be asked twice. The concert was sensational – watching her transform into Diana Ross the superstar on stage is something I'll never forget. There was so much sparkle, swooshing and sashaying – she was champagne in human form.

We caught up at the party afterwards where I congratulated her on an incredible show and complimented her outfit, the design she'd picked out at the fitting. It was a great moment.

A year later, I was in Los Angeles for a show I was doing with the department store Neiman Marcus. I had developed a client base there following my successes in New York, and was staying with my friends Joan, who had introduced me to Warhol a few years before, and her husband Jack Quinn. He was a hotshot lawyer and the youngest ever president of the Los Angeles Bar Association. They had a huge circle of artistic friends, including David Hockney, Jean-Michel Basquiat and Ed Ruscha, and often threw dinner parties at their 1930s Beverly Hills home. Joan loves introducing people, and she was instrumental in spreading the word about me to the rich and beautiful of LA.

One afternoon, Joan and I were driving through Beverly Hills in her Cadillac after a client lunch, when Joan saw Diana Ross driving into her garage outside her home on leafy Elevado Avenue. She stopped the car and told me to go and say hello. The idea of accosting one of the world's biggest stars outside their house didn't fill me with immediate joy, but it's very hard to say no to Joan – she's a terribly enthusiastic sort of person, and her enthusiasm is very persuasive. I reluctantly got out of the car, took a few paces up the path and waved at Diana. She looked at me with seething contempt and said in an icy voice, 'If you take one step closer, I'll shut this garage door down on your head.' I made a sharp U-turn, bolted back along the path and jumped into the car, shaking. I had no idea what I could have done to upset Diana so much, but tried to block it out as best I could.

The next morning, I came downstairs to find Joan and Jack at the breakfast table with dark rings round their eyes. They'd received a call from an apologetic Diana Ross at 3 a.m., she having worked out that the mad-looking woman she'd seen on her property was not a hippie stalker, as she'd suspected, but the designer Zandra Rhodes. Without the white turban and chiffon dress I'd been wearing when we met in London, she hadn't clocked who the green-haired, flamboyantly dressed figure in her garden was. Diana had been talking to a friend that evening about her unwanted mystery visitor with feathers glued in her hair when she'd realized who I was. She then did some calling around to find out where I was staying – the LA arts scene wasn't extensive then, and it would have been easy enough to track me down. Eventually she called Joan and Jack in the early hours, explained what had happened and asked if she could come over and look at some clothes. Thankfully, they were very understanding and found the situation amusing. Diana arrived later that morning in a tracksuit without a trace of make-up and we went through a rail of the punk-inspired clothes I had brought over from London. I didn't raise the events of the preceding day, and neither did she – I had no desire to provoke any further death threats.

I have a Polaroid that Joan took of me that morning fitting Diana, she in the pink version of my punk bride ensemble and me with my neon green fringe and printed caftan. You'd never know that the same woman had made me tremble with terror less than twenty-four hours before. Diana and I met again a few times at various events and I dressed her for other occasions, including a beautiful shoot she did with the legendary photographer Richard Avedon for US *Vogue* in 1981.

Of course Diana Ross isn't the only great diva I've designed for. Barbra Streisand and Shirley Bassey are also loyal customers. Shirley has become a good friend, and we've had a few dinners at my round table over the years. During the mid-eighties, she performed a sell-out show at the New York Coliseum, for which I designed her beaded finale outfit. I was there as a guest when, mid-concert, she stopped everything and announced that her dress designer was in the audience. She asked me to stand up in the spotlight, while the audience cheered and clapped. It was overwhelming and amazing in equal measures.

Women like Shirley, Diana and Barbra are dream customers, not just because of their fame but also because they're unafraid to stand out. I can't and won't design for people who hide in a corner. Fashion should always be about becoming a peacock.

27

Lauren Bacall's Dress Pin

It was Halston who told Lauren Bacall that she needed to meet me. She was one of many famous, stylish women to have worn his clothes, and Halston – who had been a friend since I'd first started travelling to New York – recommended that she invest in my designs. If Halston believed in you, he was generous with his industry connections and network. For all his grandeur and self-promotion, he could also be very kind. He passed on my number to Lauren, and at some point in 1975, she called my Porchester Road studio and arranged to come for a fitting.

I'd had no idea who Freddie Mercury was when he'd visited the year before, but I was fully aware of Lauren Bacall's stardom. My friend Duggie and I loved going to the cinema together, and I'd watched her in *The Big Sleep* and *How to Marry a Millionaire*. She had innate style and looked wonderful in everything she wore. I was extremely flattered that she wanted to see my work. To me, good style is to have personality. What you wear doesn't have to link to the latest thing in fashion, it's about how you put yourself together, your panache and adding a personal touch to something. Style doesn't have to relate to fashion. It can, but it doesn't have to. Anyone can blindly follow a fashion trend if they have eyes and money, but it takes creativity and imagination to decide what looks good on you and inject it with something new. Lauren Bacall had that skill – she brought such poise and attitude to her clothes. She mastered tailoring – has anyone ever worn high-waisted trousers quite as beautifully? She also liked fluid, silky dresses, which was where I came in.

When the day of the fitting arrived, I wasn't nervous. A number of high-profile stylish American women had found their way to me and my attic studio, including socialite Marietta Tree and the beautiful wife of the US ambassador, Evangeline Bruce. Lauren appeared at the door wearing not even a smudge of make-up, looking incredible nevertheless. She was beautiful because I expected her to be, which is often the way with famous men and women. Some people just have that rare, almost indescribable quality called presence. Mrs Vreeland and Karl Lagerfeld had it in spades, and so did Lauren Bacall. I invited her up the same staircase that Freddie Mercury and Brian May had clattered up the year before and made small-talk to which she responded politely. If she was in any way fazed by the state of my chaotic, shabby studio, she didn't show it. There is nothing more vulgar than bad manners, and I can tell you that Lauren Bacall's were impeccable. It feels almost pointless to talk about her voice as so much has been said about it, but I remember it so vividly – it was as raspy and deep as everyone says, but more than that, she had a way of talking that could almost flatten you in a sentence. It was confident, strong and intelligent; the delivery made you listen. She was as poised in her speech as in her dress. We got down to business. Lauren didn't want to be dressed for a specific event so I had pulled together a rack of recent pieces I thought she might like – fluid, elegant looks that I felt chimed well with her personal style.

Lauren pulled out a one-shouldered evening gown from my 1974 'Uluru' collection and held it against herself. The dress was made using jersey, so it clung to the body, but the asymmetric neckline was trimmed with a gold satin band, from which two layers of slashed silk chiffon cascaded to the floor. This created a graceful fluidity, and a beauty of movement.

Lauren was changing into the dress behind a screen when I heard her let out a horrible scream. It's not every day you hear a world-famous actress screech in your company, so I rushed round. She was howling, 'Oh! Oh! Oh!' The poor woman had stepped on a dress pin that had unfortunately been lying around on the floor. She'd slipped off her shoes to try on the piece and was barefoot. The pin had gone straight into her flesh and she was hopping around holding her sole. Her cool, controlled voice disintegrated into a high-pitch squeal. I had broken Lauren Bacall. I felt utterly mortified. I got down to the floor and asked if I could try to extricate the offending article. She nodded, closed her eyes and held out her foot. It was all very unpleasant – not Lauren's feet, they were as elegant as the rest of her, but the incident. I managed with my fingers to prise out the pin, a surreal experience if ever there was one, and discarded it in a nearby bin. Lauren regained her composure, and pragmatically continued trying on the gown.

When she finally stepped out from behind the screen, she looked sensational. She gazed at herself in the full-length mirror I had in the room and swooshed the chiffon from side to side. I could tell she felt good in it. The pain of the pesky pin was mercifully forgotten. Lauren Bacall would have looked fantastic in anything she wore, but she made my dress sing. She asked if I could make it in black, rather than the dusty pink I'd designed it in. I happily agreed and offered to bring it to New York where she lived during my next planned trip in a few months' time. I was frankly delighted she hadn't held the pin accident against me.

As promised, I hand-delivered the gown to Lauren's apartment. I arrived with my then boyfriend, Grant Mudford, the photographer I'd met in Australia, and she told me off for not coming alone. I was firmly put in my place, and felt terribly embarrassed for not realizing that a Hollywood star probably wouldn't want everybody and anybody knowing her address. Regardless, she wasn't put off and continued to buy my pieces, including a V-neck gown with butterfly sleeves. It's difficult to know what impact it had on my business because I wasn't strongly involved with the numbers at that point, but it's always a thrill to see anyone you admire wearing your pieces.

I never found out where Lauren wore that first Uluru dress, but a year later Jackie Onassis bought the same asymmetric gown. I opened a copy of *Life* magazine and there she was in a red version. I was elated: Jackie O was one of the most famous and stylish women in the world. Who knows whether the two things are related, or if Lauren influenced her by wearing it at an event she also attended? Whatever, that gown became a classic of mine and I've reinterpreted it using other prints throughout my career.

Thirty years later at the opening of the Fashion and Textile Museum, I chose that specific piece as my favourite for the inaugural exhibition 'My Favourite Dress', which included a number of personal favourites chosen by famous designers. It's very much proof that clothes carry power purely because they so often remind us of a moment or an emotion – my one-shoulder Uluru dress will always send me back to my mini adventure with Lauren Bacall and a runaway dress pin.

28

Paper Fan

FOR SOME DESIGNERS, FASHION SHOWS live in our memories as a favourite book, album or film might; the best of them take on additional weight with the passage of time. Although I have staged hundreds of catwalk events over the years, my milestone 1974 show at the Circle in the Square theatre in New York is among the most memorable. It is part of my mythology and, to my amazement, fundamentally changed the direction of fashion shows for evermore.

Compared with how we know them today, catwalk shows were very different in the early seventies. This was long before the days of John Galliano and Alexander McQueen, and the idea of fashion as theatre was yet to exist. Only the upper echelons of the industry were invited to events, fashion editors or high-spending customers who would take a cushioned seat in a department store or designer showroom to watch models lurch stiffly down a carpeted catwalk. But despite the prevalence of this stuffy approach, a few small labels, like mine and Ossie Clark's, were trying to do things differently.

My clothes were and are about fantasy, so it was important to me that my shows created a sense of wonder in the audience. We have enough reality to deal with so, for a moment, I wanted people to feel something else – shock, freedom, vibrancy, joy. In the same way a band must be seen performing live for their audience to appreciate the merit of their songs, I feel my designs needed to be seen 'live'. Clothes aren't just something to appreciate visually: they have an emotional appeal that you can only truly feel by wearing the garment, or seeing someone else wear it well. I struggle to put my emotions into words so clothing has always been a vital vehicle for me to express myself. Sometimes I worry that these important aspects of design are diminished in today's collections. Other considerations seem to get in the way and while commerce is vital – crucial, even – so is the idea and the way the execution of that idea makes someone feel when they're wearing the clothes.

Determined that fashion could be entertainment in the same way as music, film or television, in 1972, as you know, I held my debut London catwalk show at midnight at the Roundhouse. It was such a groundbreaking success that a friend of mine, the interior designer and painter Maxine Smith, suggested doing a similar style of show in New York. When her husband, the Emmy-winning television producer Gary Smith, proposed a Broadway theatre called Circle in the Square as a location, I was immediately taken with the idea.

The fact that no one had ever hosted a catwalk show in a theatre spoke to my need to do things differently. I've always wanted to push boundaries, drive things forward and contribute to the evolution of fashion, so in this event I saw the perfect opportunity to do something game-changing, a spectacular on a scale the city hadn't experienced before. It would be colossal and terrifying, a watershed moment for me, but also for British fashion. Very few luxury designers had yet crossed the Pond to host a solo runway show. It wasn't the norm to go global, but that was the scale of my ambition.

The weeks leading up to the show were manic. Every day, I worked until midnight, waking at five in the morning to begin again. I was always the last to leave the studio and the first to arrive, and I expected the same level of commitment from the dream team I'd enlisted. Although I can be single-minded about how I want things done, I've always understood that you're nothing without your collaborators and so many amazing people worked alongside me on this event: Jerry Pennick on choreography, Barbara Daly on make-up, following her brilliant work with me at the Roundhouse show; similarly Leonard, who had not only done the models' hair at the Roundhouse show but also at my first private show in New York at Angelo Donghia's townhouse. Clive Arrowsmith photographed actress and model Marisa Berenson for the poster in faded sepia shades, hot on the heels of her various best-supporting-actress nominations for playing Natalia in *Cabaret*. The artist and ceramicist Carol McNicoll designed the porcelain hair ornaments; her work transformed the British ceramics scene. Every single one of those people was at the top of their game in their respective fields.

The collection was based on my recent travels to Australia, where I had fallen in love with Uluru and the surrounding red-earth desert. I had drawn and redrawn those images in all their colours, translating them as *Toile de Jouy* style scenes on felts and chiffons. It had been a painstaking process, involving fine line drawings that were then turned into two colour finely-drawn images. The drawings had been cut up and I'd moved the pieces around in different combinations until I found an authentic-looking depiction of Uluru with spinifex grass. I had also designed another form of lace, which formed collars and trims.

As well as perfecting the garments, I spent a great deal of time making printed paper fans to give to every guest, each folded by me. I liked the idea of offering something tangible that could act as a record of that moment: a programme of the event. It featured my Uluru print outlined in green, the rock silhouetted against rays of light that splayed out to form the pleats of the fan. On the reverse was listed the show credits and, importantly, my US

My 'Circle in the Square' show programme

stockist, the department store Henri Bendel. Each was hand-tied with a pistachio-coloured satin ribbon printed with my name in pink.

In later shows, I would start using fans as the basis of the invitations. I liked to think of them as mini artworks, reflecting who I was at the time and what I wanted to say professionally. Over the years, some things have stayed the same – they use vivid colour and my handwritten scrawl – but the combinations of shades, the chosen prints and collaborator names have changed as my inspirations and ideas have. They are a reminder that hand-drawn art and print are my for-ever focus, and the thing that sets me apart.

As the weeks passed and we approached the day of the show, I became utterly convinced that something would go wrong. I was probably unbearable to be around. I am always nervous as to whether people will appreciate the work but the event had become so big. Knowing the venue had a capacity of around six hundred and fifty people – a huge number by any stretch – I had decided to sell tickets to the show so that the public could attend. I've never thought of myself as an elitist designer: fashion will never move forward if it reaches only a select few, so accessibility was important to me. With lots of seats to fill, I called Priscilla Tucker – a fashion editor at *New York Magazine* – in the hope she might cover the show in her 'Best Bets' column. Sure enough, an article soon appeared with the headline 'Getting the Rhodes on the Show', reporting that a number of famous models, including Bianca Jagger, would be appearing. There weren't a million publications back then, so if you were interested in fashion, you were likely to read that column, and anyone could attend if they went to the theatre box office and bought a ticket.

On the night, I was so busy backstage that I wasn't aware of quite how much buzz there was front of house. Mobs of people with tickets turned up, descending the theatre escalator to a crammed lobby. The leading lights in the fashion world, including Mrs Vreeland, Halston, D. D. Ryan, Bill Blass, Diane von Fürstenberg and Elsa Peretti, were all there, mingling alongside students and shop girls. New York's most stylish women, Mica Ertegun, Nan Kempner and Chessy Raynor, bumped alongside those who idolized them. The show was a pivotal moment: audiences evolved from being watchers to participants, dressed in every form of fashion of the day, from rock 'n' roll to establishment, and looked not only at the clothes on stage but at each other. As this eclectic group began to take their seats, I remember hearing the roar of the crowd from backstage and thinking that this was how Mick Jagger must feel before a gig. It truly had the atmosphere of a rock concert.

As the show got under way, a hush descended, and the magic began. I wanted the models to appear as if they were floating, so choreographer Jerry and I had them emerge from dry ice and dance around the stage. Led by Pat Cleveland, one tableau featured three models who appeared like strange hobby horses, wearing square felt cloaks in black, faded yellow and green. Perhaps it was sleep deprivation, perhaps it was relief, but seeing that scene on stage – the magic of the choreography combined with the movement of the clothes – brought tears to my eyes. Donna Jordan, Orson Welles's daughter Beatrice and the actresses Apollonia Kotero and Little Nell also featured in the model line-up, their brightly dyed hair glowing under a stark spotlight as they arrived on stage. The squiggles, the sequins, the hand-painted prints all whirled past. The models looked if they were levitating. It was spectacular. I'm told there was a standing ovation at the end, but I don't have a clear memory of it. I suppose I must have walked out and taken a bow but, honestly, I think I was too overwhelmed at the time to take in what we had just achieved.

In the weeks that followed, it became clear that the Circle in the Square show had given me new credibility in America – it was all anyone in the industry was talking or writing about. If I was seen as a rising star before, the show had turned me into a serious fashion heavyweight. Notably, it led to another major stockist in Martha Phillips, more commonly known as Miss Martha, deciding to buy a number of my pieces for her chic New York and Florida stores. She was known to have an eye for blossoming talent in fashion, having already helped to launch the careers of Halston, Valentino and Yves Saint Laurent in the US, and she was very well connected. Martha's clientele included wealthy, well-dressed women such as Brooke Astor and Gloria Vanderbilt, the type of women you wanted wearing your clothes. One picture of the right person in one of your designs is worth its weight in gold in terms of influence, so to have her backing was a huge coup and doubtless raised my profile in New York.

Many years later, when the revered fashion designer Anna Sui became a much-loved friend and collaborator, she told me that the Circle in the Square set the tone for every show she attended thereafter. She always expects to be dazzled, but few shows made her jaw drop quite as mine did on 23 April 1974. Anna even kept the paper fan, which she treasures at home in New York. It reminds her of her first ever fashion event, and of how far she's come. It serves the same purpose for me.

29

Grafton Street Shop

I'D KNOWN EVER SINCE THE Fulham Road Clothes Shop closed that at some point I would open another boutique. I would take the mistakes I'd made the first time round and turn them into something positive. There's no point in dwelling on the things you've done wrong: it's a waste of energy and holds you back. You just have to try to be better the next time round, and that was what I did when I was given a second chance at retail.

By the time 1975 rolled around, I was riding high and it seemed like the time was right to open my first solo store. I was regularly featured in the pages of both US and British *Vogue*, and *Harper's Bazaar*. I was travelling the world with work and was freshly in London after a trip to Tokyo where I had featured in the 'Best Five' show. The runway event had been organized by revered fashion trade magazine *Women's Wear Daily*, who had selected me among five other design talents, including Karl Lagerfeld, Perry Ellis, Hanae Mori and Giorgio Armani, to present my work. In my industry, striking while the iron's hot is crucial. Fashion changes incredibly quickly, which is why one must always jump at an opportunity as soon as it presents itself.

There are certain elements that must be in place before a designer considers launching a boutique. The first is clarity of vision and originality – there has to be a reason customers come to you over anyone else. The second is a clearly defined customer base. I had acquired a high-profile clientele, which spanned musicians, including Freddie Mercury, Cher, Donna Summer and Diana Ross, actresses Natalie Wood and Lauren Bacall and, by that time, the Royal Family in Princess Anne and Princess Margaret. I had more and more orders coming in from the States and in the UK, many from people who would have to trek to my little studio for fittings. A shop would create a more beautiful environment to showcase my collections. It was perhaps time for a space where my clients wouldn't end up standing on a dress pin or have to change behind a screen while listening to my machinists at work in the background.

The other prerequisite of opening a store is money, or an investor. Even with orders flying in from around the world, luxury materials weren't cheap and the workmanship that went into each garment meant we didn't have the infrastructure to produce masses. Stockists were often late on payments and I was far from feeling flush. As I've said before, there were occasions when my mentor Adel Rootstein kindly loaned me the cash to pay my staff. Another solution came from an unlikely source, a former cab driver called Ronnie Stirling, who, with fellow cabbie Jeff Cooper, launched one of the sixties' most successful fashion brands, Stirling Cooper, a favourite of Mick Jagger.

A clever and forward-thinking entrepreneur, Ronnie was a friend of my accountant, and saw expansion potential in my business. Perhaps because of the media buzz around my name, he put together a proposal and offered to finance it. I'm eternally grateful that he believed in my work – I certainly didn't have the money to fund a shop myself. Ronnie's business package meant a great deal: it enabled me to develop my label without having to come up with the funds. I was in.

The next step was finding the right person to manage the shop.

I knew from my experience at the Fulham Road Clothes Shop that perhaps this was a role best delegated to an expert, rather than something I attempted again myself. At the time, my clothes were sold at the elegant Chelsea-based shop Piero di Monzi and at Fortnum & Mason, which was where I first came across Anne Knight. Anne was an intimidating character in charge of the shop's buying department. She chose which brands were sold at Fortnum's and how much space they were given. She had a huge contact book, knew how shops should be run and the environment that needed to be created for customers to spend. Anne also had an acute eye for talent and had been instrumental in bringing my collections to the public. I approached her about leading the day-to-day running of the shop and, to my delight, she agreed. Having a shop meant I wasn't limited to wholesale, or to clients travelling to my studio, and it allowed me to show the public what my brand was really about. Anne, Ronnie and I were aligned in our vision: we wanted to create a unique shopping experience in which being in the shop was as beautiful and intoxicating an experience as wearing the dresses.

The three of us scouted London for the right location, eventually landing on an empty space on Grafton Street, a road just off the luxury shopping stronghold of Bond Street. It was exactly the right spot – cheaper than Bond Street, yet with a guaranteed footfall of the same moneyed clientele. It was also less than a ten-minute walk from high-end hotels, such as Brown's and the Ritz, which were popular with the type of wealthy Americans who bought my clothes. We signed a lease, and I enlisted the help of my interior-designer friend Richard Holley, who had first suggested I travel to New York to tout my wares back in 1969. I left him to mastermind the decor and, in the end, he managed to create one of the most beautiful and sumptuous shops in London. It became a real talking point and gave me huge visibility.

As with everything I do, from my shows to my collections, there was a sense of theatre. I wanted to display the textiles as well as the clothes, so the ceilings and walls were draped in a pink satin feather print. In the centre there was an oversized cushioned seating area where shoppers could rest under a giant artificial tree. Each of the four changing rooms was accessible through heavy, extravagant curtains that gave way to a beautiful mirror tilted at a certain angle to make the customer look their best – not that they didn't look fabulous in those dresses anyway. The space was scattered with pleated satin cacti-shaped sculptures, inspired by a recent trip to Mexico (which had also resulted in two new prints), and useful Z-shaped seats, which I've since painted in fluoro shades and now use as side tables in my penthouse. It was totally different from other shops of that time,

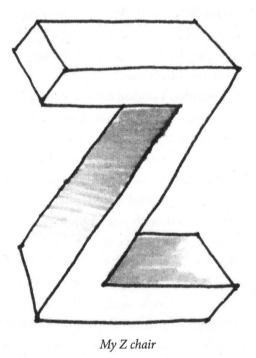

My Z chair

which were quite hard-edged. It was soft and tactile, a place where everything felt as good as it looked. It was a maximalist dream.

The dresses were so expensive that the shop staff were constantly counting them to make sure none had been stolen. We alternated the hangers in different directions to foil thieves (a little tip for any retailers trying to avoid shoplifting). Not everyone could afford the clothes, but people came in just to see the shop – it was an experience. The designer Christian Lacroix told me once that as a student he used to press himself up against the window just to look inside.

The Grafton Street store generated a huge amount of publicity, and it served as the perfect luxurious setting for my well-heeled customers to shop and be part of my world. I had always wanted to bring fantasy to any shop I opened, and I think we achieved it. I didn't spend a great deal of time there but would always attend fittings with VIPs, such as when Diana Ross came in 1976. She wasn't the only huge star to cross the threshold of the boutique – Princess Diana and Sarah Ferguson, Duchess of York, would also shop there, but that's a story I'll come to later.

The only pitfall to having such an opulent shop and all the press attention was that it became a target for thieves. In 1985, it was robbed but the criminals didn't smash the windows: they somewhat ingeniously managed to hook the chiffon dresses that were hanging in the shop window, using God knows what, and pull them through the door's letterbox as the dresses were so featherlight. After that, I made sure the letterbox was jammed shut.

The store was a huge success for more than a decade and became the blueprint for a series of ZR in-store boutiques in major department stores, from Bloomingdale's in New York and Marshall Field's in Chicago to Seibu in Tokyo. It was only fifteen years later that my relationship with Anne and Ronnie soured. I felt I was putting in more and more work and Ronnie was getting too big a percentage for what he was contributing. As we moved towards the nineties, fashion's mood changed and minimalism rose to the fore. Anne wanted to change the decor to make it more relevant, but it didn't feel authentic to me to adjust my vision just because a new trend had emerged. In the end, we all parted ways acrimoniously. The shop was doing well, but I wasn't capable of running it and so I closed the doors for good. After that, I sold my collections to retailers in America, like Neiman Marcus, and also to private customers from London. Looking back, it was a mistake to sever ties with Ronnie and Anne, but my life took a different turn. I started designing for various operas in America and set up the Fashion and Textile Museum.

All that said, I am still proud of my Grafton Street shop, a colourful oasis in the heart of the city that attracted people from the world over. Through magic and optimism, London was an international fashion destination that excited everyone – Mary Quant had created the mini with Twiggy, the phenomenon of Biba happened, there were romantic dresses from me and my fellow designer Bill Gibb, then later punk with Vivienne Westwood. That creativity flowered with Alexander McQueen and John Galliano and has now moved to Paris. Suddenly so much is gone. Thanks to Brexit, there's no affordable way for designers to trade from the UK to overseas customers: shipping alone is hugely expensive. There is so much incredible design talent here, from Simone Rocha to Erdem, but it is much harder to become a success now than it was when I was starting out. The UK has always been very good at creating forward-thinking, dynamic and pioneering fashion designers; brilliant, boundary-pushing ideas pour out of London more than anywhere else in the world, but Brexit has put such a strain on new designers at the beginning of their design careers. The current crop of amazing designers based in London are operating against all odds.

I don't think the same footfall exists because of the increase in online shopping. I don't disagree with e-commerce: if you don't adapt to what the customer wants and needs, you will lose. Yet I can't help but think we have lost some of the emotional, sensory and joyful experience that once came with shopping. I was lucky enough to be part of London's initial fashion bloom, and I hope that today's young designers are soon given the same opportunities to flower. They will rise again because one thing we can always depend on is the creativity and originality of the young. We can't let the world crush us. There will always be hurdles. All we can do is try our hardest and in the end something will happen because creativity is leading the way.

30

Thank-you Letter

IN 1974, A YEAR AFTER Princess Anne had been photographed wearing one of my gowns for her engagement portrait, my assistant received an extraordinary request from Kensington Palace. Lord Snowdon wanted to visit my Porchester Road studio with his children to see how a fashion designer worked. Of course, the children in question were David and Sarah Armstrong-Jones, who were then thirteen and ten respectively. It turned out our mutual friend *Vogue* art director Barney Wan had suggested they call in as a way of introducing the children to different artistic mediums. Lord Snowdon wanted to show them how working designers lived and worked outside royal palaces.

Lord Snowdon – or Snowdon as he was known professionally, Tony to his friends – was a member of the Royal Family, but also had a penchant for bohemia. His photography was very much a part of Swinging London; his images were uncluttered, distinctive and modern. His early pictures depicted a city rising from the dust and grey of war to become a charismatic, throbbing place where everyone wanted to be. I had sat for Snowdon perhaps six months before in a group portrait of leading fashion designers for British *Vogue*. The shoot took place in his Pimlico studio and I was joined by Ossie Clark, Mary Quant, Bill Gibb, Jean Muir,

Thea Porter and Gina Fratini. For reasons I've never found out, the portrait wasn't used and now belongs to the National Portrait Gallery in London. Regardless, it was a fascinating experience.

Snowdon loved photographing artists, perhaps because he considered himself to be one, and I think we are probably all at our happiest doing the things we are good at. Unlike other photographers, he didn't try to put you at ease. I've been lucky enough to be photographed by a number of great image-makers, and they all have different approaches. David Bailey, who has always been utterly wonderful to me, is very good at creating a rapport between himself and his sitters. He's very good at making people laugh and making them the centre of the universe for a few hours. Snowdon was very different: he didn't chat, but seemed completely consumed by the task at hand – the quest to find the perfect image. He wasn't rude, but he was cool. His detachment from his subjects worked so well because he never became more prominent than his sitter. Snowdon also art directed the *Sunday Times* magazine front cover of Bianca Jagger in one of my chiffon designs in December 1972. She looks divine.

Snowdon was certainly familiar with my work, so it must have made sense for him to visit me when the idea was put to him. It was arranged that he and the children would take a tour led by me, and I spent the morning attempting to make the studio look more presentable. I hid the cannabis plants in a cupboard, moved fabric rolls to the edges of the rooms and swept the staircase and floors. Even with the team's and my efforts, it was still by definition a design studio and therefore somewhat of a chaotic mess. I shouldn't have worried. When the Armstrong-Joneses arrived, they paid no attention to the disarray. In hindsight, Snowdon, as a friend of so many artists, was probably more than familiar with the disorderly nature of studios, and his children would have spent time in their father's inevitably messy workspace. The children didn't seem shocked by my appearance, which – given that my hair was jet black and fluoro green and I was wearing a bold pink caftan – was testament to their good manners.

Snowdon was as stylish as I'd remembered from when we'd met previously on set, in a camel roll-neck, slacks and lace-up suede shoes. He was elegant, neat and accessorized with the ultimate posh-man essential: a chunky signet ring. I hoped there was no residual paint on the floor. He was more congenial than he had been at our meeting six months before. 'How good you are to make time for us.' He smiled, full of charm.

'We brought you a gift,' chirped Sarah, and presented me with a hamper full of fruit, chocolate, biscuits and jams. They were incredibly sweet children.

I took the three of them round the studio, room by room, explaining how the process of designing a garment worked, from inspiration to printing to construction. We looked at my sketchbooks, and I explained that once I draw a print that I'm happy with, it is painted to scale, then often cut apart and reassembled. We talked about the transference to silk screens, how colour testing works, to achieve the desired combinations, and how the garment develops from there. I explained how toiles – early versions of the garment – are fitted on models to see how they move, and how the prints look. We toured the sewing room, and I introduced them to my seamstresses. It doesn't matter how often one works with the Royal Family, being in their company never feels entirely normal, but my visitors seemed intrigued by what we were doing, with such an appreciation for art and creativity. The visit can't have been longer than an hour or so, and they left with words of gratitude.

A few weeks later, a letter arrived – a handwritten note on headed paper from the young Armstrong-Joneses, thanking me for 'a very interesting and enjoyable afternoon in your colourful studio'. It was short and to the point, but still a sincere effort to show their appreciation. My mother had instilled in me the importance of thank-you letters, and I still try to send them whenever I can. They might seem like a relic in the era of mobile phones and email, but it's an act of thoughtfulness that makes the world a little nicer. Over the years, that note has survived various moves and clear-outs. You can keep a letter, but you can't keep a text. A classy move, it enables me to relive that special afternoon whenever I stumble across it.

31

Emmy Award

NOT MANY PEOPLE KNOW THIS, but I am an Emmy Award winner. In 1983, I won a Daytime Emmy Award for Outstanding Individual Achievement for designing costumes for *Romeo and Juliet on Ice*. I keep the little gold statuette next to my front door at home where it doubles as a rather fabulous key holder. The wings of the award are perfect for hanging my keys on, a wonderful mix of beauty and practicality.

I have always been reluctant to say no to new projects. I am led to exciting new opportunities by friends or industry figureheads and agree to new things even when it leaves me feeling, at times, overwhelmed. I usually wake up happy but sometimes my mood dips when I struggle to cope with the rest of the day. My girls – the team I work with in London – are constantly telling me to say no to things, but I can't help myself. I must have failed the 'Say no' exam at school. Part of it is just plain curiosity – I will never stop being interested in exploring creativity and textiles through different means. I'm lucky enough to love my work, and I want to keep doing it through various media. Sometimes I take on too much and it becomes stressful, but that's what you sign up to if you want to maintain a small independent business like mine. It's

My Emmy award

not about the money per se (although that plays a part), but about finding new routes to do the job I love.

Designing costumes for *Romeo and Juliet on Ice* was the first time I'd had the chance to create for a production, which I continued to do in the early 2000s when my ready-to-wear business went quiet. Back in the early eighties, I was at the height of my fame and simply liked the idea of adding another string to my bow.

The costume-design project came about through two friends, Gary and Maxine Smith, who had instigated my triumphant Circle in the Square spectacle in 1974. She was a top interior designer, rated among the best in the world by *Architectural Digest*, and a loyal client of mine. Her husband Gary was a lovely man and a successful television producer, who had by 1983 already won two Emmys for his 'specials' – hugely entertaining standalone shows that often interrupted episodic programming. They featured stars including Bette Midler and Barbra Streisand. When Gary approached me about designing the costumes for the American TV special of *Romeo and Juliet on Ice*, I jumped at it. I trusted their judgement when it came to new opportunities, and I knew I could do a good job. Turning fashion shows into extravaganzas was already my area of expertise.

The production was to be filmed about six months ahead of the scheduled air date in a famous studio in Toronto, Canada. The cast was already agreed: American Olympic gold medallist Dorothy Hamill and Canadian world bronze medallist Brian Pockar would star as Romeo and Juliet, and Olympic bronze medallist Toller Cranston, who was already a big star in Toronto, was cast as Tybalt, Juliet's cousin. The music, Prokofiev's *Romeo and Juliet*, would be performed by the London Symphony Orchestra under the direction of star conductor André Previn. There was no diva behaviour simply because there wasn't time – the skaters were on the ice for twelve hours at a time, gruelling physical work.

To my delight, the brief was not at all didactic and I was given a relatively free rein. Gary said he wanted the costumes to have a unique, special look. 'They need to be Zandrified,' he told me before I got cracking. 'We need your originality.' We all know what ice skating looks like – Spandex outfits with little flippy miniskirts for the girls and Spandex full-length leotards for the boys – so I decided on a look that had never been seen before. I not only wanted to challenge figure-skating norms, but also to push back against what we typically expect Romeo and Juliet to wear. I liked the idea of the costumes having a medieval look, but there should also be colour and romance too. In the same way that clothes should never wear the person, but rather enhance who they are, the costumes couldn't overwhelm the perform- ance: they had to contribute to the mood and the story. The costumes existed to say something about the characters.

It didn't take me long to come up with the designs, maybe a few months. I started with the practical elements: the costumes needed to be made in materials that the cast could skate in, so the Spandex leggings had to stay, but I conceived them in vivid colours – sky blue, rich purple and bubblegum pink. Even the skates were created in vibrant tones: I wanted the viewers to feel as if they'd been hit between the eyes with colour, movement and sound. Once I had created the initial sketches and decided on the fabrics, I was flown to Canada with the materials, including my printed chiffons. There, Gary's team created the costumes and I helped with the fittings. It wouldn't have felt me without a dose of chiffon so Romeo's tops were created with full, billowing sleeves in that fabric, and Juliet's outfit featured trailing chiffon veils that floated beautifully across the ice. It was an ice show made to look like fairyland. By the time I was done, the costumes were more like something you might see on stage rather than an ice rink – billowing, theatrical, featherlight fantasies.

The only difficulty came via a minor disagreement with the felt

I'd used to create some of the costumes. Felt is a relatively sensitive fabric and unfortunately shrinks when wet and under hot theatrical lights. Ice skating is an intense physical activity that raises body temperatures, and often involves falling on the ice, so we spent our lives ironing the costumes and trying to stretch them back out. It was my first introduction to the restrictions on the materials you can use as a costume designer, but we learn by our mistakes, and later, when I designed ensembles for various operas, I was more vigilant. My designs lend themselves well to productions because, in plain terms, you can really see them. They're bold and big, and instantly catch the eye. It's less about detail than when I'm designing ready-to-wear. I learnt to build on that thread, creating bigger, more dramatic silhouettes and broader visual statements – for *Romeo and Juliet* it was ethereal, but with a giant Zandra Rhodes stamp of colour. I loved working on the show. I felt I was flexing a creative muscle I hadn't used before but found surprisingly comfortable.

After it aired on US television in November 1983, *Romeo and Juliet on Ice* was well received, as were my costumes. The *New York Times* wrote of how the 'elaborate Elizabethan costumes designed by Zandra Rhodes floated across a sheet of ice as if it were the most natural activity in the world'. At this point, I must be honest and say my Emmy win was an anticlimax. I had no idea I'd even been nominated – this was still long before the internet. Now, award nominations are announced live and we know who is up for what within seconds, regardless of where we are in the world. It was very different in 1983. I didn't know I'd won the Emmy until it arrived in the post in a large padded box, cushioned with tissue and bubble wrap. It was a fabulous surprise, but a somewhat underwhelming way to be told I'd just won a major award. I'd have loved to attend the ceremony and accept my winged gold statuette on stage, like you see the stars do, but it was wonderful to be recognized – and I suppose it wasn't bad going to win an Emmy for my first attempt at costume design.

As proud as I am of that achievement, success isn't about the number of awards I've won. I run from one thing to another and hope I survive. The problem with awards is that they can make you big-headed, and in my business, if you rest on your laurels, you'll fall flat on your face. The trick is focusing on your work, putting your whole spirit into it and hoping the right people take notice.

32

Indian Screens

NOWHERE HAS INFLUENCED MY LIFE and work quite as much as India. It is the most confronting, contradictory place, a country that hits you with its unique cultural identity as soon as you arrive. Vibrant colours and pungent smells. Breathtaking crafts- manship and inspiring humility. Blinding opulence and thrifty innovation. Extreme wealth and shocking poverty. Hardship and generosity. On one trip in 1987, in a rural village in the desert of Rajasthan, I came across a family digging a well. They were obvi- ously very poor yet they offered us some of their lunch – a dry roti, a horseradish and some salt. I was deeply moved by that gesture.

I have never been anywhere that challenges every sense and thought quite as brazenly as India. One minute you can be smell- ing the most fragrant jasmine, and the next there's a foul waft of sewage. The noise, the scents, the colours, everything in India is mind-boggling. It is consistently surprising and ceaselessly inspiring. India isn't an easy place, and it isn't for everyone – David Hockney hated it – but I will remain enthralled by it until I die.

Everyone talks about India's poverty and – as someone who has travelled there many, many times over the past few

decades – I have been asked how I cope with seeing such destitu-
tion. There will always be the wealthy and the destitute, but I
would rather be poor in India than in LA where the homeless are
openly despised or routinely ignored. Back then, India's rich culture was not widely appreciated in the West; it was more known
for its deprivation, but the country is so much more than that.

It was this desire to change limited Western perceptions of
what the country was that partly prompted the first Festival of
India in 1981, a celebration of arts and crafts organized by the
Indian government. I was invited by my dear friend scenographer Rajeev Sethi. Rajeev's story was impressive – he started
his career in Paris in the sixties training with the printmaker
S. W. Hayter, then was mentored by the hugely influential designers Ray and Charles Eames. From there, he'd started working
with fashion designer Pierre Cardin before going back to India
where he set about celebrating and promoting Indian arts. His
idea was that I would be taken around the country so that I could
research traditional Indian crafts for an Anglo-Indian exhibition
at the Barbican in London the following year. Rajeev wanted to
bring Indian craftsmanship to the world, and has been incredibly
successful in doing so. I had never even considered visiting India
before. My travels had largely been led by my work, so the idea had
never arisen, but the task sounded hugely appealing – preserving
the legacy of skilled craftspeople. I ran at India with open arms
and have never looked back.

Rajeev invited me to bring a guest with me for the duration of
the three-week trip, so I invited my ultimate travel companion,
Andrew Logan. Thanks to Rajeev's deep understanding of the
country in all its multi-faceted, complicated form, we saw India
in plain view. We watched traditional Indian dancing, we saw
people sleeping in railway stations at night, and everywhere I
went people gazed appreciatively at my bright pink hair. Local

women would ask to touch it to see if it was real, which never bothered me. You can't dye your hair hot pink and not expect people to talk about it.

One of the many highlights of that first trip was sitting in a boat in Varanasi in the early hours, sketchpad in hand, as swarms of devotees in colourful saris or *dhoti*s arrived to immerse themselves in the holy waters of the Ganges. It was an amazing spectacle that lasted all day and what was most remarkable was the elegance of the women, who somehow managed to remove about five and a half yards of sari – and put it back on – without revealing an inch of their bodies. We were lucky in that Rajeev showed Andrew and me an India beyond luxury hotels: to experience it only in that way is to miss out.

The juxtaposition of wealth versus poverty was stark. We visited millionaires' homes – clients and friends of Rajeev's – and I revelled in the beautifully embellished saris. Then we'd go and eat somewhere very local and shack-like. I loved the spicy smells of the market: cardamom, coriander and cumin, India's culinary stars. Sights that would be so completely incongruous and wild in the UK became commonplace to me: cows in the street chewing bits of orange peel, or people brushing their teeth outside. It was of course the colour that won me over heart and soul. There was so much yellow. Far from insipid pastel tones, India's yellow is turmeric bright and hugely mood-boosting. I loved the deep orange marigold flowers that were used to decorate almost every celebration, the vivid blues associated with the Hindu god Krishna and the chilli-red saris worn by brides. Jolts of pink covered turbans, buildings and flowers. As Mrs Vreeland once said, 'Pink is the navy blue of India.'

It is the backdrop to everything. During a subsequent visit to India in the mid-eighties, Rajeev and I celebrated the Hindu festival of colours, Holi, in the city of Mathura where Krishna was born. Everyone was sprayed with pink the same shade as my hair. Decked in my typically bright clothes, I was quite at home there. I had never been to a country where colour was a way of life in the same way it was for me. Perhaps that's why some people connect to certain places in a big way: they feel understood by them. India was radiant in its colour, frantically, dazzlingly bright.

During those three weeks, we were driven, taken by train and flown to villages, towns and cities across India to meet and watch the craftspeople and artisans at work. I saw people practising an array of different crafts such as weaving, block printing or the artful technique of zardozi, which is integral to Indian textile design. Fine metal wire and thread in either gold or silver are used to create patterns of embellishment on silky fabrics such as velvet, satin and raw silk.

We visited the city of Chennai to see the embroidery, and Agra for the monumental Taj Mahal and the ornate inlay work. I was amazed by what I saw and it had a huge impact on me. These men and women did their work in shacks or outside, often surrounded by goats, yet they were every inch as skilled as the artisans working for the big fashion houses in Paris. My sketchbooks bulged with drawings and ideas.

To top it all off, I was invited back later to judge Miss World in Hyderabad for a televised audience of one hundred and thirty million people! Again, I brought Andrew along for the ride. My appearance meant that people recognized me wherever we went, a deeply surreal experience. That same trip, we flew to Kashmir to look at the Kashmiri painters. I remember the three of us floating on the vast Dal Lake in a sandalwood houseboat – it felt as if time had stood still. We were staying in the same houseboat on Easter Sunday when Andrew picked up a newspaper to discover that England was at war against Argentina, over its invasion of the Falkland Islands. That seemed so strange to us both. It was all so distant.

After returning from that initial trip in 1981, London felt like a very grey place, but I was mostly too absorbed by my work to feel blue. When it came to putting together the Barbican exhibition, I had more than enough material to choose from. My job was to reinterpret Indian crafts and skills using my own design signatures. The showcase was called Aditi, which means 'boundless' in India's classical language of Sanskrit, a reference to the limitless Indian craftsmanship. It wasn't so common to travel to India then, and I wanted to celebrate everything I had seen during my visit. In the early eighties, garments made in India were associated with cheapness and low quality, and I wanted to change that mindset, spotlighting the incredible design and heritage techniques. I designed handmade, block-printed banners, carved in specially treated wood in the Indian city of Farrukhabad and combined with my own signature squiggle print. My Z-shaped tables, which were originally conceived in my Grafton Street shop, were upholstered in fabrics with zari and zardozi embellishment. Cushions and bedcovers were decorated with Indian appliqué and embroideries.

Aditi launched to the public on 6 July 1982 as one of the first exhibitions to be staged at the Barbican Centre after its own opening five months before. The showcase was a huge success, visited by an estimated eighty thousand people. The late veteran art critic Shanta Serbjeet Singh described it as 'a glittering, glowing event which . . . will change the face of Indian culture in the Western hemisphere'. I was thrilled to have done some justice to the skilled Indian men and women who were working against all odds to preserve Indian craftsmanship. It was a privilege to have been part of it and was the start of my long fascination with India.

As the years went by, I found varying reasons to return to that country of vibrancy and colour. I have spent Christmases with Rajeev in Udaipur, a magical city based around the serene Lake Pichola; we went on to explore the cities of Ajmer and Pushkar. In 1987, I hosted sari-based fashion shows in Mumbai, then known as Bombay, and also Delhi, where I gave audiences the full Zandra Rhodes theatre. Needless to say, my relationship with India had a huge influence on my work. My 1982, 1985 and 1987 collections were all inspired by its sights, style and colours. In each, I aimed to combine traditional Indian practices with a contemporary design sensibility. I took saris, such fluid and versatile garments, and played with them in different ways – some I covered with sequined squiggle embroidery, the multi-hued beading of which I sourced in Jaipur. I cut holes into the loose ends of the garment for the arms to go through (I called it my 'holey sari'), which I again decorated with beads. To others I added shoulder pads (it was the eighties, after all), and Victorian crinolines under the draped fabric to create an alternative silhouette. Each model walked with a cane and wore an ostrich-feather headdress. It's hard to imagine now, but my interpretation was seen as outrageous at the time.

I set up a beading studio in Chennai, which employed local men to embellish many of my beaded tunics and jackets. I teamed silk chiffon trousers with matching tunics that had mandarin collars. I wanted to celebrate and credit Indian creativity as much as I could. Since then, I have designed carpets and furniture for a fair called 'Hanover 2000' inspired by the 'speaking tree' design seen in Mughal textiles, created a wiggly luggage installation for Mumbai airport and met with organic cotton farmers in rural Gujarat ahead of a collaboration with environmentally friendly brand People Tree. I've even designed a toilet seat for charity WaterAid after becoming aware of the bad sanitation in India. I remember once looking over the parapet in the holy city of Vrindavan at 6 a.m. and seeing scores of people squatting everywhere down by the river. Everyone should have access to a working toilet.

In June 2019, I returned to film BBC TV show *The Real Marigold Hotel*, which was set in Puducherry in southern India. It was a wonderful experience that ended with great sadness. It was there that I received a call to tell me that my beloved partner Salah Hassanein, had been admitted to hospital in the States. I rushed back but he died shortly afterwards. He had been bedridden before I left and I asked him first if I could go on that trip. Of course he said I must: he would never have wanted me to miss out on a visit to India. He knew how much it meant to me. Funnily enough, we never went there together. He wouldn't have liked it. He'd have wanted to stay in the ritzy, high-end hotels. There's nothing wrong with that, but it's the grit, rawness and reality of India that I love most.

My first trip to India set off a magical chain of events that I could never have foreseen. I'd spend more time there if I could, but I'm lucky enough to be needed in different parts of the world. Instead, I have filled my penthouse with slices of India so I'm surrounded by its colour and brilliance even on London's most dreary and grumpy days. It was hard to choose an object for this chapter because I have so many beautiful pieces that remind me of my favourite place, including a set of four rainbow chairs that were hand-carved in southern India. I drew on them and then the artisans carved the patterns.

The wooden screens I have in my living room, which hide a rail of clothes, are my favourite, perhaps because they make me think not only of India, but also of Salah and a very happy period in my personal life. It was the early nineties and we'd recently moved together into a beautiful beachfront house in San Diego, California. I had been given free rein to decorate the bedroom,

Filigree carved Indian screen

which I wanted to do in blue. I saw a version of these screens in Jodhpur, and thought the mellow blue was rather soothing. The carvings are so intricate – they truly honour the incredible workmanship of the artisan. I think I would have been with Andrew at the time, and he is always good at encouraging me to shop. His mantra is, 'Don't think about it. Buy it, or you'll regret it for the rest of your life.' He was quite right. I have zero buyer's remorse.

33

Straw Goat

EVERY CHRISTMAS, I DIG OUT my decorations from underneath a long wide table in my living room. It's covered with screen-printed cloths to mask the fact that I use the hollow space underneath as storage. Next to boxes of paperwork and rolls of fabric is a straw goat ornament bound by red ribbons. It's perhaps half a metre tall and a similar length wide with curved horns that curl backwards. Goat has no name but is wheeled out each festive season as a reminder of the warm, huge-hearted friend who gave it to me: the unforgettable performance artist and actor Divine. Every festive season, it occupies the spotlight under the tree.

I want to write about Divvy not only because he was one of the most lovable friends I have ever had, but also because not enough people, especially younger generations, know about his legacy and how he changed the face of drag. Those who have heard of him do so through his collaborations with cult film director John Waters, who is also a treasured friend. Divine starred in some of John's biggest films, *Pink Flamingos*, and *Hairspray* in 1988, which made him a star. Without Divine there would be no RuPaul.

Divine upended the drag world by giving performers permission to look however they wanted. Before him, most drag queens

Divine's Swedish straw goat Christmas gift

were very conservative-looking – slim, beautiful creatures, who wanted to look like Miss America. They aspired to a very conventional form of glamour. Divine had a very different look: he was overweight, wore super-sexy, tight clothes, and his make-up was exaggerated and messy. Sometimes he'd arrive on stage holding a chainsaw with scars drawn on his face. He truly was a solid eyeful. Divine wasn't trans. If he were alive today, he'd be very supportive of that community, but he didn't want to be a woman. He always thought that women's clothes, bar mine, were too uncomfortable to wear full-time. John has said that Divine wanted to be a combination of Godzilla and Elizabeth Taylor, and I think that's a fairly accurate description.

Divvy and I first met at some point in 1976 through my friend Joan Quinn. I was staying at her home in Beverly Hills while she was away for the weekend when there was a knock at the door. I opened it to find a tall, portly man wearing a Chinese-style suit with a mandarin collar and fairly standard, ballet-esque flat shoes. He wasn't made up and still had the remnants of his bleached-blond hair. I can't remember if I knew he was coming or not, but what could have been an awkward weekend in which two strangers shared someone else's home was actually perfect. We spent two glorious days in the garden by the pool, him smoking pot and us talking. From the day I met him, he felt like home.

There was a big difference between Divvy my friend and Divine the performer. Divvy was a quiet man who'd sit around with me drinking tea. He liked food and cooking. I remember going round the supermarket with him in Baltimore, picking up bits and pieces for dinner. I never felt I had to be on show with him, and I think he felt the same about me. Far from his outrageous stage persona, he was a very relaxing person. It was one of those full-monty friendships where we were just as content having a quiet night in, watching television on the sofa, as we were going on adventures. I have a picture of us somewhere bleaching our hair together using elastic bands to divide it into strands, like a couple of teenagers doing makeovers in their bedrooms. Other nights, we went out to Studio 54 and danced with mutual friends, like Karl Lagerfeld. Divvy started wearing some of my chiffon caftans, which weren't the type of figure-hugging, constraining clothing drag queens at that time wore. The designs he loved of mine were softer, comfortable and allowed for movement while still making him feel beautiful. They let his body breathe. Some of my clients from the LGBTQ+ community have come to me because of Divine and the way he wore my clothes.

As our friendship went on, he introduced me to John Waters although I can't be sure when. Again, he was one of those people I felt as if I already knew, someone who knew exactly who he was and wasn't afraid to show it. We got along from the very start. John is exactly the sort of person you want at a dinner party – funny, clever and charming. I'm sure at the time the three of us looked like an unusual bunch: I had weird green hair, John had his signature weird moustache, and Divvy was simply Divvy. We all loved rebels, outsiders and nonconformists, but at the same time we were all workaholics. Divine loved to work, John loves to work and we all know I do. We knew what we wanted and we were ambitious but, as John told me recently, none of us sold out. We stayed true to what we wanted to do. We let society come round to us, rather than us changing and going to them.

There came a point when Divvy wanted to do something without John. They had known each other since they were teenagers growing up in Baltimore, and from there they went on to make some of cinema's most camp and shocking films, in *Pink Flamingos*, *Multiple Maniacs* and *Female Trouble*. It was, of course, John who came up with the name Divine, along with the tagline 'the most beautiful woman in the world, almost'. They had been working with one another for more than a decade by the time I met them, and, while they were as close as they had ever been, I think Divvy felt he needed to try something solo. He decided to record music in London and came to stay with me in my Notting Hill home. In the evenings, he would perform on stage as a scheming prison matron in a comedy called *Women Behind Bars* at the Whitehall Theatre near Trafalgar Square, directed by Ron Link. I would go to work during the day and leave him to his own devices.

Divvy had a taste for the high life but didn't have the funds to back it up – he racked up huge bills at Fortnum & Mason where he'd go daily for afternoon tea. Eventually he was banned because he'd put it all on a tab he couldn't afford. It was very Oscar Wilde. He loved to shop and he loved eating good food. He was a huge fan of my bread-and-butter pudding and would sneak down at night if there was any left and eat the lot. I wasn't always aware of what Divvy got up to during the day because I would leave for work at 7 a.m., but he would often hold court and enter-tain guests at my place. I returned home one day to find out that David Bowie had not only visited Divvy at my house but had left by the time I had finished work. Can you imagine Bowie popping over and you're not even there to offer him a cup of tea?

Divvy liked looking at posh houses, so in my rare downtime we'd drive around the ritzy parts of town and he'd pick out the houses he'd buy one day, but really it was the lack of pretension and unaffected spirit of London that he loved most. I introduced him to people I thought he'd like, including Andrew Logan and Duggie Fields, and hosted dinner parties for him at my round table. Those evenings were a riot, full of laughing, great conversa-tion and indulgent dishes heavy with double cream. (I'm obsessed with double cream, I can't help myself.) Later down the line, I remember John coming to London with his mother, so I threw a dinner party for her too.

We also did the odd trip out of London. In 1977, the day after the Queen's Silver Jubilee river procession, which we'd watched from Andrew's studio on the South Bank, a small group of us, including Divvy and Andrew, got into my funny little car and drove to Hastings for the day. It was a bank holiday in England, so of course the weather was dreary and the sky was the colour of wet towels, but we sat on the beach and had a picnic. Divvy loved every minute of it, and asked if we could do it every weekend. He really was such an enthusiast, even on a tired old beach on a grey day. Divvy and Andrew became friends and together they co-presented the 1978 Alternative Miss World, which was made into a documentary that premiered in London's Leicester Square and also at the Cannes Film Festival. Divvy, never one to miss a moment of glamour, naturally attended both events. He sometimes stayed at Andrew's studio during his London visits, and once filled his bath so high that water slopped over the sides, flooded the studios below and blew up the electricity. It was impossible to be annoyed with Divvy, though – he was simply too likeable.

When he died of a heart attack in 1988, aged forty-two, I almost wasn't shocked. He was so young to die, but he was a big man and his size must have been a strain on his heart. I was devastated. Divvy was such an ebullient force of nature and the thought of never being able to spend time with him was too awful to bear. I was in the middle of organizing a big catwalk show so I didn't go to his funeral. I can't even remember where the show was now, but I know that wasn't about the show: I just couldn't cope with the idea that he was gone. I lost a lot of friends in the eighties during the AIDS epidemic, a part of my life which is owed its own chapter, so I learnt to deal with loss by burying myself in work. There was so much loss at that time and I had to find a way of going on. Work has always been both a solace and a sacrifice. It has helped me through the darker periods of my life, but relationships have suffered as a result and friends stopped calling because they knew I was never at home.

Although I didn't go to Divvy's funeral, I marked his passing by throwing a dinner party in London a few months later and everyone brought one of his favourite dishes. Naturally, I made bread-and-butter pudding. I hope it would have been exactly Divvy's kind of tribute. His place of burial in Prospect Hill

Cemetery, in his hometown in Baltimore, has become a destination for fans to pay homage. John Waters and two of his regular
cast members, Mink Stole and Pat Moran, have all bought plots
there, so they can spend for ever with him. They call it Disgrace-
land, and John has invited me to join when the moment arises. I
haven't decided one way or the other yet. I hope that time doesn't
arrive too soon.

No chapter on Divvy should end with his death. Above all, the
one thing that reminds me of him is Christmas. For many years,
Divvy was estranged from his parents. It wasn't as much to do
with his drag career as his habit of charging purchases to their
credit cards. Towards the end of his life, they reconciled, and I
remember meeting them, but when I first knew him, in the
absence of his biological family, he spent Christmases with me in
London. Divvy was addicted to Christmas: he loved everything
about it, the tree, the glitz, the decorations, the food, the feasting,
the sheer, shiny joy of it all.

He also adored giving presents to the people he loved, which
was how the goat came to live beneath my living-room table. It's
a traditional Swedish yule goat, and Nordic folklore says each of
these straw animals is an invisible spirit that appears before
Christmas to ensure that the festive preparations are made correctly. I don't know how Divvy would feel about being compared
to an ornamental goat, but he had similarly specific, firmly held
views on how to do Christmas properly. The first year he stayed
with me for the festive season, I made the grave mistake of telling
him that I used a plastic tree, rather than a real one. He looked at
me as if I'd kicked him in the shins.

It was mid-December and few places were still selling real firs.
I told him that the only way of buying the tree of his dreams was
to get up at 5 a.m. and go to Covent Garden. I never thought
he'd be up for that: Divvy liked his sleep. At four thirty the next

morning, he knocked on my bedroom door holding a cup of tea for me. He was wearing his coat with a hooded pixie hat ready to head off to buy that bloody tree and the other greenery. We dragged the tree back in my car, strapping the thing to the roof. When we finally got it to my Notting Hill home, he ran up to the spare room and returned with a wand. He spent the rest of the morning enthusiastically barking instructions about the placement of the decorations, using the wand like a conductor's baton as I stood on a ladder precariously reaching to where he pointed.

Divvy wasn't interested in Christmas being tasteful. What was important was that it was big and bold. If ever there was an object to represent Divvy, it is my yule goat with its similarly high standards of Christmas.

34

Beaded Safety Pin

THERE ARE THREE CRUCIAL INGREDIENTS to creating a good fashion collection: originality, wearability and relevance. Innovation is the element that makes fashion exciting, but the design has to have function. There's no point in making clothes so avant-garde that no one can wear them. Those factors still mean nothing unless your collection reflects the times. Sometimes a designer senses a social change before it happens – take Yves Saint Laurent and his decision to put women in evening trousers for the first time, or Thierry Mugler, whose padded shoulders of the seventies were laughed at until they became mainstream in the eighties.

My 1977 punk-inspired collection was a swirling combination of all three. Conceptual Chic, the name Duggie and I came up with, was an artistic experiment that told the world punk could be beautiful. I have always felt our perception of beauty is limited. There are certain sights, objects and materials we associate with pleasing aesthetics and luxury, but it's my job to see the world in a different way: to find beauty in unexpected places and to re-position it in a high-end space. That was what I set out to do with Conceptual Chic and, regardless of how badly it sold, I succeeded in taking punk into a new realm.

As a designer, one must always be open to what's happening in the world. Ignoring the news or not paying attention to what's emerging in society is short-sighted because, frankly, fashion is a dragon that needs to be fed. Inspiration has to come from somewhere and you won't find it if you're blinkered. My greatest fear is being unable to come up with new ideas; the thought of it used to panic me to the point where I'd feel almost paralysed by pressure. In my calmer days, I understand that, through keeping my eyes open and ear to the ground, I have always eventually found something for my imagination to settle on. Inspiration can and should come from many places.

Conceptual Chic was rooted in two different ideas: the first was a Norman Parkinson photograph of a dress by the surrealist fashion designer Schiaparelli in collaboration with artist Salvador Dalí. It was a truly arresting garment: a sheath-style tube of silk printed with repeated surrealist shapes of jagged, torn fabric, which looked like tears. The 'Tears Dress', as it was called, was made using a viscose rayon instead of silk, which was then the standard material for luxury clothing. There was something haunting about it and it remained in my memory.

The second influence was the rise of punk in London. Having spent so much time in America for work, I had noticed the mood shifting over the previous two years: the stage at Max's, my go-to nightclub in New York, featured a new crowd: Patti Smith, the Ramones, Blondie and the New York Dolls all offered a new, rasping, moody energy. In London, people on the street were dressing differently. King's Road underwent a makeover: the romantic, carefree looks from the sixties disappeared and instead a new form of rebellion emerged. It was grumpy, loud, smelt of lager and despised hippies.

Everyone was shopping at a small but shouty store called Sex, which sold bondage-inspired clothes and was run by a

little-known designer called Vivienne Westwood, who partied
with my friend Andrew Logan. Chiffons were out, and vinyl was
in. The young and truly cool wore black plastic bags tied up with
safety pins, laddered stockings and more safety pins threaded
through their ears and noses. Hair was spiked and dyed green
and orange. Mine was black with a neon green fringe. It seemed
to me punk was everywhere. My right-hand designer, Gill Griffiths, routinely came to work in rubber miniskirts with razor
blades in her ears. She wore sexed-up stilettos even to print in,
which was quite an achievement. The Clash and the Sex Pistols
launched their debut albums in 1977; music at that time was furious and wild.

In art, my friend Duggie Fields had adopted a new approach:
his works took on an aggressive look, painting figures with
arms and legs missing, breasts exposed. I found myself trans-
fixed by the furniture sculptures of Pop artist Allen Jones, who
made models of pneumatic women in fetish costumes posing
as hatstands, tables and chairs. I was swept up in the punk aesthetic, and for the opening of Andrew Logan's Goldfield
installation at the Whitechapel Gallery in 1976, I wore an asymmetric dress with a breast exposed. I had designed it as part of
my 'Cactus Cowboy' collection a few months before but, the
prevailing mood being as rebellious as it was, I finally felt I
could wear it.

I was never interested in the sound of punk or even the anti-
establishment philosophy; I've always loved the monarchy. My
interest was an intellectualized idea of it – Dalí and Schiaparelli's
collaborations, for example. To me, it was an artistic expression,
and I recognized that what I had been doing – my floaty chiffon,
printed eveningwear – wasn't right for that new mood. It was too
delicate, too romantic. When Duggie suggested I explore a different, more severe direction, I agreed. For the first time, I didn't feel

like doing prints. I was being challenged by the confrontational vibrations that howled at me to try something new. Duggie came up with the phrase 'Conceptual Chic', which referenced punk as a form of high fashion rather than solely street level.

As usual, I started with my sketchbooks. I did some drawings in which I tore the paper by hand to make jagged holes, then took pieces of silken jersey and cut holes in them. These were passed round my design studio where we worked on creating the perfect Dalí–Schiaparelli tears. The edges were stitched, but we found that they lost their shape. I decided to use ordinary safety pins first as a functional way of creating the tear outline I wanted, but then I began covering them with tiny seed pearls and brilliant rhinestones and they took on an unexpectedly luxurious look, beautiful punk-inspired adornment. Simple dresses were cut up with a pair of scissors in a very considered way – strategically placed jagged holes that felt irreverent but seductive. These were fastened with my embellished safety pins and loops of silvery chains that I had used to secure coat-hangers to rails in my Harrods concession to prevent shoplifting.

Just as Schiaparelli had experimented with fabric, so did I. This collection called for a material that wasn't ethereal chiffon: I needed something more utilitarian. Instead I used a fine black rayon French jersey, which hugged the body beautifully. It looked good on everyone. I created glamorous sashes with jagged pieces of uneven jersey, pinning them to a satin band, to be worn either around the hips or around the bust. When we'd finished the collection, I was thrilled with it. I had pushed the boundaries of beauty – who says an item as commonplace as a safety pin or a bathroom chain can't be high fashion? We were doing something that had never been done before. People had had beaded dresses for hundreds of years, but they hadn't beaded safety pins and cut holes in dresses.

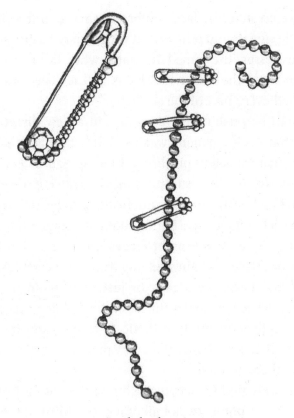

Beaded safety pins

When I look back, the craftsmanship involved was astounding – it took fifteen minutes to bead round each safety pin and there might be twenty to thirty on each dress. Just stitching the beading alone would take between five and seven and a half hours. The beads were all hand-dyed too, which was done by the team and me in the men's cloakroom behind the production office. We only ever had a few men working for us, so it seemed like the best use for it.

I also played with punk make-up and hair, which was new, too. With the help of the groundbreaking make-up artist Richard

Sharah, we created 'the face': eyebrows shaved and replaced by Morse code signals and punctuated with square beauty spots. My go-to hairdresser, the famed Leonard, who did all my shows, twisted and tied the hair with chains and jewelled safety pins. I considered every part of the aesthetic.

I knew I'd be pushing my customer in a new direction, so I ensured that each garment was as Zandrified as it could be. I made miniature safety-pin brooch kits to sell in my Grafton Street shop. To me, they summarized the collection – ordinary objects that had been elevated with beading to become a thing of beauty. In each, I included a handwritten note that offered styling suggestions: 'Wear them: as brooches on your collar, hanging from your necklace or chain, hanging from your earrings, pinned to one of my special necklaces, or just hook them together to make a bracelet. Have a lovely time. Zandra Rhodes.' I redecorated the store to follow my punk aesthetic, festooning our indoor tree with torn pink jersey, chains and safety pins, and installing ripped curtains in the windows.

When I presented Conceptual Chic in the autumn of 1977, it attracted a lot of publicity, not all of it good. Most of the fashion press thought it was too radical: it was simply inconceivable that safety pins and jersey could be luxury. Unfortunately, it didn't sell well in store either, and after a month we went back to chiffon dresses. Upon reflection, those dresses probably appealed to a younger audience than the typical Zandra Rhodes customer, and that younger audience perhaps had less money to spend. Regardless, I was christened the 'High Priestess of Punk', a title that Vivienne Westwood took great umbrage with. I only met Vivienne a handful of times and she was never overly polite, but I can appreciate her work. Vivienne felt I had co-opted the punk movement, but the reality is that all designers, artists, musicians take inspiration from everywhere. Ideas come from absorbing and reinterpreting the world, and my take on punk was completely unrelated to Vivienne's version. I gave London punk a feminine, glamorous polish, and I don't see why there can't be room for both viewpoints.

If Vivienne was dismissive of me then perhaps my work was of more value than she'd have liked to admit. Although we were British female designers whose careers might have blossomed around the same time, our approaches to design were very different. I draw objects and scenes that inspire me from wherever I am and from those I design a fabric. The garment is then created from the textile. Vivienne went back to the history books and reinterpreted what she found. I never claimed to be a punk. I have always been very clear about who I am: a Radio 4-listening, gardening-loving royalist, who also happens to have pink hair. I understand people will cast aspersions about me based on that, but it doesn't mean it's correct.

Despite the lack of commercial and press success for Conceptual Chic, I still had a strange inner belief that it was the right thing to do. A decade later, sexy black dresses held together with safety pins appeared on the Versace catwalk, one of which was famously worn by Elizabeth Hurley to the premiere of *Four Weddings and a Funeral* in 1994. When legendary fashion journalist Suzy Menkes pointed out the very obvious comparison in the *International Herald Tribune*, she was swiftly banned from the next Versace show. You can't get bitter about these things, but I do hope history remembers me as doing safety-pin dresses first.

In 2013, the Met Museum in New York hosted a major exhibition entitled *Punk: Chaos to Couture* and displayed two of my 1977 originals, the white slashed 'Wedding Dress' with a daring asymmetric thigh-high hemline and a chic black jersey gown with beaded safety pins and a metal-ball chain. Now those pieces, from the collection that didn't sell and was panned by most of the press, are seen as collector's items. The bridal look was given to the Met when former Costume Institute curator-in-charge Harold Koda retired in 2016, because it was, I understand, the one thing he wanted more than anything else.

I suppose the moral is we do things in life in the hope that the world will like them, and sometimes the world isn't always ready, but that doesn't mean you shouldn't do them.

35

Chinese Paintbrushes

I WASN'T ATTRACTED TO R. Couri Hay at first, but I was fascinated by him. I knew he was bisexual, but I didn't realize he was gay. I don't think either of us did. Not all relationships start with a thunderbolt moment, but there has to be some form of magnetism, a reason you want to see someone again.

When I first met Couri in the spring of 1978, he was a widely read gossip columnist for an American tabloid called the *National Enquirer*. He was friends with New York's art and style set, including Andy Warhol, Bianca Jagger and Halston, and he had more confidence than anyone I'd ever met. He boasted that his column was read by twenty-eight million people every week and how well paid he was almost as soon as we'd been introduced, which perhaps should have been a warning sign but, funnily enough, wasn't. He was the most exciting, interesting and intoxicating man I'd ever come across, and our romance was inevitable even if there wasn't immediate physical attraction.

It was either Divvy or Joan Quinn who introduced us, and we met at a party Couri was throwing for the British actress Hermione Gingold at the Plaza Hotel in New York. I was due to be in town then anyway, promoting my 'Conceptual Chic' collection, so came fresh from the airport, dragging my suitcase behind me. It was impossible not to notice Couri: he dressed very well, spoke very loudly and knew everyone. He schmoozed the room like nothing I'd ever seen and had a laugh that sounded ruthless. He had dark, lively eyes, frighteningly high cheekbones and a wide grin. His hair was a mess of tight curls. Above everything, he seemed so at home in this high-society environment that I had never felt entirely at ease with. Even aged thirty-eight, as I was then, I was still a girl from Chatham who found the hobnobbing side of my job a grim necessity. It didn't matter that I was famous myself: I was dazzled by him.

He was nearly ten years younger than me but was so sure of his standing in the world and of his own talent that it seemed the word 'self-doubt' had never existed for him. It probably still doesn't. He came from a wealthy American family and his first job had been as a writer at Warhol's *Interview* magazine. Couri loved my work and said my creativity was inspiring to him. He whisked me off my feet and took me to classical-music recitals at Carnegie Hall and for glamorous evenings in boxes at New York City Ballet. I'd often fall asleep exhausted midway, and he'd poke me to wake me up. In every way that I was an introvert, he was a glittering extrovert, who made new places come alive through spinning enthusiasm.

As the months wore on, Couri became almost a Svengali figure to me. He literally and metaphorically opened the doors to a shiny new world. I already knew Halston and Andy Warhol, but Couri made me feel I was one of them. We went to the elegant Met Gala together, which was then much less celebrity-focused than it is now. He threw me parties at his Manhattan townhouse, where I held court with Mrs Vreeland and Warhol. He was almost a hybrid between a publicist and a boyfriend. I still saw my original New York crowd whenever I could, but between my work commitments and Couri, I had time for only so much, and my new boyfriend was very good at telling me which events, parties and clubs I should be seen at. He would use my name to gain access to buzzy restaurants and nightspots, something that it had never dawned on me to do.

We would arrive at Studio 54 in a yellow cab and he'd give a cursory wave to the bitterly discerning doormen. The crowds would then make way for us, like a parting of the Red Sea. We spent evenings there with Divvy and Karl Lagerfeld, dancing to Donna Summer, who had worn my lily print white dress on the cover of her album *Once Upon A Time* the year before. It seemed to me that everyone at Studio 54 was Somebody: Andy Warhol, Liza Minnelli and Halston would hold court in one corner while Pat Cleveland, Debbie Harry and Manolo Blahnik would be laughing on the dance-floor. It was a room full of stars, but I never saw anyone ask for an autograph or a photo. To do so would have been as crass as it would have been at Max's. My dresses had gained a cult following and I'd often spot people wearing them there. The joy of seeing someone in one of my designs is a thrill that has never left me.

Everyone took drugs, but – other than cannabis, which was far too sleepy for Studio 54 – I stayed away from that scene because I was always aware that I had work in the morning. Couri worked to a different sort of schedule. Like Cinderella in a better dress, I'd always leave at midnight or not long after. I'd have to be up early whereas he'd sleep until noon, like a nocturnal animal. There is a photograph of Couri and me on the dance-floor, which was exhibited at the Brooklyn Museum as part of its Studio 54 show in 2020. I have my back to the lens and am holding my hair to stop it flying about. My printed chiffon dress is moving as I spin and Couri has his arms wrapped round my waist. When I look at it now, I can barely believe it was us.

During the course of our relationship, Couri also introduced me to people I could only have dreamt of spending time with, most unforgettably the great fashion couturier Charles James. Fashion experts all bow to Charles James, but wider audiences don't know much about him because his brand didn't survive beyond his death. He didn't advertise and there was no big conglomerate to buy his name so for many years he was forgotten. To me, he is one of the great fashion masters. His slender-waisted silhouettes inspired Christian Dior's iconic New Look – even Dior himself said so. James was a designer's designer – Balenciaga said his work was 'pure art' and Chanel and Schiaparelli, both discerning women, gave him the ultimate praise by wearing his pieces. I had seen some of his creations at the V&A Museum: they were that rare combination of brilliant originality, wearability and technical wizardry.

I admired his famed perfectionism: James once spent five years on a sleeve to create the perfect armhole. He wasn't one of those designers or artists whom inspiration struck out of the blue: he worked to find inspiration, then laboured at his craft with meticulous dedication until something was perfect. I related to that sensibility and found it somehow reassuring, the idea that inspiration and the consequent beautiful creation don't magically materialize: they are born through the work we put in, through the rigorous and sustained application of workmanship through high times and low. To meet this man, whose work I had gazed at in awe back in London, was hugely surreal.

He and Couri were long-time friends, having met at Max's a decade before, so we went to visit him at the legendary Chelsea Hotel in Manhattan, where James was then living. He was down on his luck, and his glamorous looks were no longer as fashionable as they had once been. Halston, who also admired and was inspired by James, was paying for his suite at the Chelsea because his finances were in such bad condition. I must have been nervous about meeting him, but Couri's brazen confidence bolstered me. He wanted to film the whole interaction, although I forget what for.

In person, Charles James wasn't at all intimidating: he was only a few inches taller than me at five foot six with bushy eyebrows that framed genial eyes. The room smelt of a musky fragrance he had made. We spent an hour together in his three-room suite where I tried on some of his designs, one of which was the original of the style I'd seen at the V&A – a fabulous, floor-length cloak created using ribboned silk. The construction of the garments was staggering. It was truly one of the most wonderful experiences of my life to hear a real-life genius explain his inspirations and method. Couri kept interrupting our conversation, but it didn't seem to matter: my ears and eyes were so alive to everything Charles was saying that Couri almost fell away. Charles James died only a few months later, on 23 September 1978, of pneumonia, which made our meeting seem all the more special. I'll never forget it.

When we weren't flitting around New York's social scene, Couri and I did a lot of travelling. Perhaps six months into our relationship, Couri suggested we go to China, and on New Year's Day 1979 we became two of the first Westerners to travel there that year. Diplomatic relations between America and China had been restored in December 1978 only weeks before our adventure, which made our trip all the more incredible. There were no flights from America to China back then, so we flew first to Hong Kong and from there we travelled by train to Canton. My first impressions were that it was freezing. I had to keep my camera in my bra because otherwise the battery would have been too cold for it to work. Gloves were essential for me to sketch, which I did furiously.

Everywhere we went, people stared at us because they were so unfamiliar with Westerners – we must have looked like aliens to them. Despite the chill, the locals would stand and watch us as we went about our trip. I have never felt so conspicuous, and I even hid my green hair under my hat so as not to attract even more attention. It was one of the only times I have played down my appearance. The Chinese all wore washed-out navy blue or army uniforms. Everyone was clothed in the same thing, which was very strange to me as someone who experiments with the way she looks on a daily basis. No one wore dresses or make-up. There was no embellishment or adornment; a tiny wristwatch was as decorative as it got. The only colour came from the children who wore floral padded coats to keep warm.

We visited Shanghai, and I was struck by the absence of cars, just bikes as far as the eye could see. It's unimaginable to be in a city as big as London without any traffic other than push bikes. The department stores sold basics; there were no lifts or escalators, only stairs, and in the corner of every staircase stood spittoons for people to spit into. While in Shanghai, I met with the uncle of my friend and mentor Michael Chow, who introduced me to the majesty of the Peking Opera with its elongated beards, headdresses and dramatic make-up. Off stage, there was still so much to look at – the intricate fretwork and trellises that appeared on buildings, the carved stones of water and clouds in so many of the palaces, and the dragons that decorated walls. We also travelled north to the Great Wall of China, the greatest wiggle I'd ever seen.

I was astounded by the purity of design, and eventually what I saw made its way into my work via my 1980 'China Collection'. Michael Chow said to me at the time, 'China will rule the world.' I couldn't see it then, but how right he was. Its immense and irrepressible growth is a testament to its strength of character.

Couri and I did a spectacular trip to Kenya in 1980, which

resulted in another collection. The colours, prints and landscape are still imprinted in my mind. Couri was a great travel companion because he didn't mind me spending hours sketching, always happy to busy himself.

Our relationship was odd in that it was transatlantic, which – in the absence of the internet – was much harder then than it would be now. I was always between cities, flying back and forth from London to New York for work most months. It was a strange dual life: in the US, I was a huge star always in demand at parties and events, wooed by celebrities and magazine editors. In the UK, I was holed up in my studio working all hours like a flamboyantly dressed hermit.

Couri might have come to London once, but he certainly never met my British best friends, like Andrew, Duggie or fellow designer David Sassoon. He existed for me only in New York; out of context he would have been all wrong. I was often exhausted and unfocused. Couri would stay with me wherever I was staying, sometimes at hotels, sometimes at friends' places. I never stayed with him, which I didn't question at the time, or maybe I simply didn't want to know why I hadn't been invited. Although I was aware that he'd had boyfriends before me, I didn't realize he was still dating a man. I found out when we broke up that he was living with his lover, but oddly it didn't hurt me as much as perhaps it should have. My indifference is telling of how over it I was.

Couri proposed before we broke up. It was one of the few occasions that I had been to his home when it wasn't filled with others. The fire was roaring and an Andy Warhol flowers painting hung over the mantelpiece. When I came back from the bathroom he had lit candles and there was a bottle of champagne on ice (Couri was, as ever, feeling confident). I don't remember whether he got down on one knee or not, but he presented me with a ten-carat diamond ring and asked me to marry him. He then held out a matching diamond band. For some mad reason, I said yes. Marriage proposals are always exciting, even if you're not sure about the person doing the proposing. We drank the champagne and talked about buying houses in New York and London.

After I left his house the next day, I started to feel the hideous, scratching dread that so often comes before the end of the relationship. The excitement of the wedding was replaced by the potential reality of being married to Couri. I felt overwhelmed by the sense that something wasn't right. Over the next few weeks, I tried to work, but felt riddled with angst. I tried to lean into wedding planning, and even designed the invitation, but I felt trapped and alone. So much of Couri wasn't anchored in reality: he was fun, and being with him had been a pleasure-seeking ride, but something inside me knew that wasn't enough to sustain a long-term relationship. Perhaps I knew, on some level, that he was gay. Time does such a good job of clouding one's memory.

As always when I feel lost, I turned to one of my close friends. I called David Sassoon, who was in New York for a celebration of his work at Saks. 'I don't know what to do, David,' I remember crying down the phone. 'I don't know what to do.'

David said, 'Zandra, I think you know exactly what to do, and it says a lot that you feel unsure.' He didn't moan about Couri or tell me one way or the other what to do, and I felt a little better. He was right. I did know what to do. I knew I had to call it off. This was a New York affair that fitted New York. In the context of parties, glitter and schmoozing, it worked, but would he have fitted in with everything else? No. I met Couri and told him it was over. He looked surprised, but not devastated. There was no real anger on either side. I think our relationship had served a purpose for both of us. We opened doors for each other in a way I couldn't see clearly at the time: I felt he was the portal to Oz, when really I held the ticket all along.

I have heard since that Couri blames our break-up on my unwillingness to have children, which isn't true. He says I dropped this news on him after our engagement, a deal-breaker for him. By the time I met Couri, I had already thought that having children was something I probably wouldn't pursue. My career had taken off in such a way that it didn't seem viable. I didn't feel I could do the two things as well as I'd have wanted at the same time. My sister's life is devoted to her children and grandchildren, which I admire tremendously. My mother managed to work and have children, but I never felt I'd be able to do both. I didn't consciously decide I didn't want to have them, but time went by and it didn't happen. I was never with the right person at a time when it would have felt right. I never felt I could take a break from my career, and I enjoyed my work too much to stop. My life could not be carved up. There was always so much to do professionally, and I was always travelling – I wouldn't have had the time to spend with children.

It is interesting to me how often child-free women are asked about not having children. I very much doubt male designers of my age are ever questioned about it. I hope I'm proof that one doesn't need children to live a fulfilled, loving life. There are many ways to skin a cat.

But back to Couri, who now runs a successful PR company and is wonderfully gay. At the time, he made me feel like a star. I couldn't see then that I didn't need his fairy-dust to belong in these places, that my hard work and persistence had already earned me the right to be there. Couri astutely figured out how to harness my success and talent long before I did. I loved meeting so many different people and being encouraged to explore the New York high life in a way I might not have felt confident enough to do otherwise. He introduced me to so many things, from travels to people to parties. It was fun and sometimes, for a while, that's enough.

It was one long party, but I'm not a big party person really. I like having friends for dinner but I don't need glitz. For all the glamour and razzmatazz of that time, the object that calls him to mind is a set of five Chinese paintbrushes. I bought them during our China trip in a specialist art shop in Shanghai. They were the only purchase I made during our adventure there. I've never used them because they're too beautiful. They look like artefacts more than functional objects and hang from a porcelain frame painted with traditional Chinese dragons.

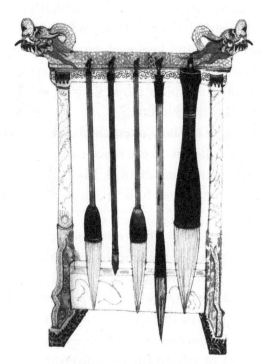

Chinese paintbrushes

36

Pinkissimo by Crazy Color

BEFORE MY HAIR WAS PINK it was green and before that it was brown. Now I can't imagine not having pink hair; I find it very uplifting and it sets the tone for the day. I accidentally stumbled on my own look, not through calculation but through luck and intuition. I didn't dye it for its usefulness, but it's turned out to be a very convenient form of recognition.

I never have a bad-hair day because my hair always looks the same, although I do have pink wigs if I feel my bob isn't up to scratch. You must always have the courage to do what makes you feel good. If you feel good you're halfway there. You have a choice in life – you can either be the sort of person who worries about what people think, or you can be lucky enough to have the reserves inside you to decide that, even if they don't like it now, maybe they'll grow to like it. I don't think all my looks were perfect: some were dreadful, but at the time they made me feel good, and that's really what matters. It's like putting on a suit of armour.

My hair is naturally dark brown. When I was young, I wasn't allowed to wear make-up or nail varnish at school or at home so I never dabbled with it. There had been a bit of toying with the way I looked at the Medway College of Art in the late fifties – I outlined my eyes with black and wore a long overall, which I dyed purple and trimmed with lace, then layered over trousers. I looked like a funny Victorian person. When I got to the Royal College of Art in 1961, I really started experimenting with my appearance and learning what I wanted to say to the world. I graduated to large false eyelashes and wearing colourful tights, but the hair stayed brown. After I left college in 1964, Vidal Sassoon launched these wonderful coloured wigs, but I found they pinched my head. They didn't feel comfortable and gave me a headache, so dyeing my hair was the next step. I went to Vidal – a hugely enthusiastic, engaging man with a Cockney accent – and asked him to bleach it, but he said no because it was so dark. I ended up going to Leonard, who agreed. At the time *Vogue* would work with one of two hairstylists, Leonard or Vidal, which was where I think we first met a few years after I'd left the Royal College, on a *Vogue* photoshoot, and Leonard became a big part of my life, doing the hair for my catwalk shows. Leonard had trained with Vidal, but they couldn't have been more different. Vidal saw hair as a commodity to be turned into avant-garde sculptures but Leonard understood how interlinked our hair is with our emotions and who we want to be. He was into wild experimentation, but he also wanted to tailor each hairstyle to the individual in a way that made them feel good. It was a groundbreaking approach at the time – the idea that hair shouldn't look uniform and stiff. He would ask you what you wanted and then he'd help you achieve it. He always said, 'The only way hair works is between two people.' Once you'd talked about what you were going to do, Leonard preferred to work in silence. He came from a working-class family in West London and his father used to mix with gangsters. I imagine hairdressing was not a natural career choice, but after he'd watched a French film, *Coiffeur Pour Dames*, about a sheep-shearer who remakes himself into a stylist adored by

Parisian society, he was hooked. Leonard, I think, always wanted to be adored by the Mayfair set – and he certainly was.

It was Leonard who convinced Twiggy to get rid of her long hair, cutting it into that bleached crop, which – as everyone knows – catapulted her to stardom. He was always totally elegant and a natural performer – he gesticulated as much as an Italian. In the end, everyone went to Leonard, from Elizabeth Taylor and the Beatles to Jerry Hall and David Bowie during his Ziggy Stardust period. A bit later, Leonard took on a young assistant called John Frieda. He was charming, always busy sweeping up hair. Later in his career, John did my hair and worked on my shows.

Anyway, Leonard and I came up at the same time. He started to bleach my hair with green streaks. I took in my own fabric dye and thought, 'Well, if you can dye sheep's wool, you can dye human hair.' It never crossed my mind to worry about whether it might be harmful, but I suppose I'm lucky it wasn't. It was cut in a deliberately raggedy style, again by Leonard. There was something in the air at that time – a real thirst for experimentation and creativity. I liked having my hair a different colour, and I enjoyed doing bold things with it, like sticking feathers to the ends with eyelash glue. I removed my eyebrows and replaced them with two blue glitter dots. Back in the sixties, eyebrows were of great interest. People like Donna Jordan, one of Andy Warhol's muses, used to bleach them. I treated myself as a design and drifted into face experimentation. Now my eyebrows don't grow back at all, which I find quite useful because I can draw them in all different places to create different looks.

Over the next decade, I continued to experiment with my hair. When I was running the Fulham Road Clothes Shop in 1967, I shaved my hairline back so I had more space to play with my make-up. It seemed perfectly logical to me. I was so close to

Leonard that I'd be in and out of his salon every few weeks, trying new shades and cuts, many of which would end up appearing as ideas on my catwalks.

From the mid-sixties, I began to realize that my entire physical entity and my work were tools to communicate my vision and beliefs, that I could be a vehicle for my sales. I can't begin to imagine how many different hairstyles I've had, but it wasn't until 1980 that I landed on pink. I had visited China for the first time, where there was a complete lack of colour, so when I got back I reached for the brightest shade I could think of – red, which was synonymous with China and Chairman Mao – and created a collection largely in that colour. Red hair dye didn't exist at the time, so I went with the next best thing: hot, shocking pink. I liked it immediately; it felt so cheering. It was also very easy to maintain – even today, pink just keeps. Every two months or so, if it goes pale, I just whack a bit more on. Back then, dyeing your hair was still uncommon, but I always thought it would take off. In the seventies, when I was a relatively big name, I approached one of the big American beauty companies about doing a Zandra Rhodes hair dye. The representative said, 'Excuse me for saying so, but in my day women who dyed their hair were of dubious virtue.' Maybe I should have pursued it for longer.

Leonard's then colourist, Daniel Galvin, now a famous hairdresser in his own right, worked carefully on my hair, experimenting with various dyes, and eventually introduced me to the specific one I still use today, Pinkissimo by Crazy Color. Pink is a complicated colour. At some point it became deeply embedded with traditional notions of femininity, but the shocking acid versions have a more punk, irreverent feel. I'm not irreverent: for me it's as simple as pink making me feel more presentable to the world. I didn't dye my hair initially for PR purposes: I did it because I liked the way it looked, but I'm happy that it's been useful. It's always made me distinctive.

Pink aside, Leonard and I continued to work together for many years. I loved his flair and all the incredible hairstyles we pioneered together, but his lack of attention to detail eventually clashed with my perfectionism. Whenever a show began, he would always run out to the front to watch the action, rather than be backstage, leaving his assistants to do the finishing touches. He wouldn't stay to see that everything had gone out correctly, which eventually led me to a trainee of his called Trevor Sorbie.

In the eighties, after I met my life partner Salah Hassanein, I

Pinkissimo hair dye by Crazy Color

dyed my hair brown again. A high-powered Warner Bros. executive, Salah was conservative so I thought I'd give it a go. I barely lasted a week. Nobody recognized me, and I felt too ordinary, not like myself at all. It made me feel terribly flat. Having pink hair has always made it easier to be Zandra Rhodes. My hair says that I'm a designer, someone creative, someone with a personality that you can either embrace or reject.

Relying entirely on appearance to feel good about yourself or empowered can be a bit empty. I strongly believe that beauty comes from within; it's about being at ease with yourself. If you radiate happiness, smile and see yourself in the best light, you will convey that to the world. As I've become older, I've watched the people around me inject their faces with all sorts of things. Botox and cosmetic surgery change the face but they don't make someone look younger. They look different, distorted. Having worked in America for so long, I can spot it a mile off – and I suppose it works over there because people accept that distortion. Eventually, though, the fish lips and padded cheeks go wrong and you end up looking like the Bride of Wildenstein. I want to look real, not lose my character. It seems to matter to some people that they look younger, rather than being who they are. To my mind, personality overrides age – what's important to me is how interesting or curious you are and how you approach the world. Beyond that, my one beauty rule is, contrary to what the experts tell me, I never take off my make-up at night.

37

Cannabis Plants

RECOLLECTIONS OF MY FORMER CANNABIS usage may vary among my friends and ex-colleagues, but it's fair to say that my enjoyment of the odd joint has landed me in trouble over the years. Although I don't smoke any more, it is technically true that I am an octogenarian criminal who was once charged and convicted of possessing illegal drugs.

I started smoking cannabis back in the seventies. I have dabbled with edibles too, but never alone and always strictly in social settings. I found that the drug freed up my mind and gave me the scope to think creatively. It took me away from the pressures of running a business, which would often leave my brain feeling too full. I was almost constantly worrying about money and where the next idea would come from, and I needed something to loosen me up a bit, which cannabis did very well. In fact, my former agent Reggie Morton always said I did my best work when I was stoned.

To maintain my supply, I had a rather beautiful plant (possibly three) growing at my home in St Stephen's Gardens. And although it was hardly a drug den, in the early eighties we also had a few plants growing in my Bayswater studio – some on the staircase and landings and another on the windowsill, all of which our

Cannabis plant

accountants did a wonderful job of ignoring as they walked upstairs to the tiny office.

One day in 1982 when I was out with clients, the studio doorbell rang. Gill, my right-hand woman at the time, opened it to find two plain-clothes police officers wanting to search the place. Gill, rather astutely, told them they couldn't come in without a warrant and shut the door in their faces. She called me and asked what to do. 'Oh, darling,' I said, 'just hang some tomatoes on them. They'll never know the difference.' Gill paused, and then diplomatically suggested we move the weed away from the windowsill to the staircase, which we promptly did.

Nonetheless, the police had clearly clocked that there was some suspicious activity going on. They returned a few weeks later, this time to my home in Notting Hill. That evening, it just so happened that I had with me my friend Rajeev Sethi, who had recently introduced me to the wonders of India. Rajeev was and is a terribly elegant and grand sort of person, always beautifully decked out in flowing white or beige Indian traditional dress. We had just collaborated on the exhibition celebrating Indian craftsmanship at the Barbican and intended to celebrate the success of opening night at home with a cup of tea. Resplendent in our finery, we were still buzzing when I heard a knock at the door. I opened it to find two police officers, this time in uniform and with a warrant.

After conducting their raid of the house, they found the cannabis plants. 'Zandra Rhodes, we are arresting you for the possession of illegal drugs,' one chimed, and proceeded to read me my rights. I was mortified! Rajeev, ever the gentleman, offered to help and come with me but in those days the Indian community was treated with great suspicion, so I had no wish for him to be involved. 'I'll be back shortly,' I called cheerfully, as I was marched off to a Black Maria with my pots of cannabis.

My brush with the law resulted in a court appearance, which I attended in a purple dress with silver Lurex detailing, a suede jacket, maroon cowboy boots and hair streaked with pink and blue. I may have been the most unusual thing Blackfriars Crown Court had ever seen. After a brief hearing, I was let off with a fine, which was annoying enough – I had to pay it by selling one of my artworks – but what I found really galling was that my misdemeanour went on my record. As a result, every time I go to the States – which I did frequently in the eighties and nineties when Salah and I lived in California – I have to apply for a new visa and queue at the American Embassy with a police report stating that I no longer cultivate or possess cannabis. Do you think Keith Richards or Mick Jagger has to do that when they travel to America? I'd bet good money they don't. I'm always hauled back into a Customs office and grilled before I'm allowed to proceed. I imagine it's a funny sight to behold, a pink-haired woman in her eighties sitting patiently awaiting interrogation. I have to remain incredibly polite because Customs officials don't have much of a sense of humour in my experience.

Needless to say, I haven't smoked since, although it has fostered an interest in gardening. I love tending the plants on my roof terrace, but you'll find nothing except camellias, hydrangeas and tomatoes up there. Once bitten, twice shy.

38

Princess Diana's Watercolour Sketch

ONE WET DAY IN THE early spring of 1981, two twenty-something women walked into my Mayfair shop and changed the profile of my brand for ever. Lady Diana Spencer and Sarah Ferguson were firm friends, and the former had recently become engaged to Prince Charles in February that year. Their wedding – fated to be one of the biggest events in royal history – was scheduled for 29 July. There was enormous buzz surrounding Diana, a timid-looking nursery-school teacher who had won the heart of a prince.

As a royalist, I was very keen to see Diana, the future queen, in my designs. By this point, I had already started dressing the Royal Family, having created Princess Anne's engagement gown nearly a decade before and fitting Princess Margaret at Kensington Palace. Despite my reputation among the royals, I still wasn't considered a traditional choice. My designs, for all their feminine romance, were still bold, unique and attention-grabbing. I had bright pink hair and could hardly be considered the typically genteel sort of designer normally found working with princesses. There was a strong chance that the demure-looking Diana would find me a bit much. What I hadn't recognized was her quietly determined sense of daring, which was exactly what led her to me. She might have been bound by tradition for a large part of her life, but Diana found small ways to be nonconforming.

Anne Knight, who was running my store then, came up with the canny idea of sending an engagement gift to Diana in the hope that she might wear it, or at the very least that it might put me on her radar. I never got round to asking Diana if she ever received my note and present, but she found her way to my boutique. No one had any clue they were coming – their visit was entirely impromptu – so I wasn't at the shop when they arrived. Anne, frantic with excitement, called me in my studio as soon as they'd left. There had been no entourage or fanfare. They had, to Anne at least, come across like any other well-heeled friends out for a day of shopping: giggly but very polite. Diana bought Sarah a dress – my Manhattan style, made in flowing white chiffon printed with a shocking pink New York skyline. I have no idea if Sarah ever wore it, but that was the start of my relationship with Diana.

At around the same time that spring, I received a phone call from British *Vogue* asking if I would submit a design for the royal wedding. The magazine was running a feature on bridal ideas for the princess and had asked six other designers of that period to do the same. The last time I'd been asked by *Vogue* to create a dress for a VIP, it had ended up as the gown Princess Anne wore in her engagement portrait, so I did wonder if my sketch might be presented to Lady Diana as an actual wedding-dress option. Securing the job of designing this royal wedding dress would have been a huge honour and would have boosted my brand beyond my wildest dreams. I thought long and hard about what an Elizabethan bride might wear and decided only gold lamé and theatrical pleated panniers would do. Was it bold? Yes, but there's no point dialling down who you are for the purposes of others. My royal-wedding look eventually took the form of separate garments that could be worn together or individually – a black satin lace corset with gold pleated sleeves and matching collar, a full skirt supported with boned panniers topped with circular pleated swirls either side to emphasize the dramatic shape.

Apparently, by this point, married design duo Elizabeth and David Emanuel had already been chosen for the job. I knew the Emanuels, having designed Elizabeth's wedding dress five years before in 1976, and was aware that they had been dressing Diana before she was engaged. I'd be lying if I said I wasn't disappointed not to be chosen, but I was honoured to have been in the running. Either way, I'm glad I remained true to my design aesthetic. In the end, my Elizabethan-bride look formed part of my 1981 'Renaissance/Gold Collection' and is now owned by the Victoria & Albert Museum. Diana Ross wore the gold-sleeved bodice and matching panniers with black leggings for a 1981 *Vogue* shoot with the great photographer Richard Avedon. She looked dazzling, so my work certainly didn't go to waste.

What I didn't know then was that I would build a relationship with Diana much later at a very different point in her life and over the space of years, which was just as important. It created a continued interest in my business rather than a one-off boom that perhaps, even at my peak, I might not have been able to sustain. In 1986, five years after the royal wedding, Diana visited my shop unannounced again, this time with a security guard. She couldn't travel anywhere at that time without being trailed by the paparazzi, so the protection was very necessary. There were rumours that her marriage was under strain – it was the year that Charles rekindled his relationship with Camilla, or so his official biographer Jonathan Dimbleby wrote in his authorized biography *Prince of Wales*. Whether or not Diana came to me – the flamboyantly dressed, pink-haired 'princess of punk' as I was then known – as a form of rebellion is, of course, conjecture. We can never truly know the truth about these things, but it was certainly a left-field choice for a princess whose wardrobe had previously been filled with the work of beautiful yet traditional designers such as Catherine Walker, David Sassoon and Bruce Oldfield.

During her second visit to my shop, she tried on an off-the-shoulder dress from my 1985 'India Revisited' collection. It was black with red beading, cinched with a quilted satin waistband and fell to mid-calf. Royals are discouraged from wearing black except for funerals so, following her trip to the store, I received a request from Kensington Palace on behalf of Diana to remake it in pink and to her specific measurements, which were shared with me. I would be required to visit Diana at her apartment to fit the dress in person, and to submit a sketch of what the design would look like in the new colour. It was a huge honour to be asked, and I instinctively kept the sketch as a record. It's buried in a drawer now, filed away for a rainy day.

Despite my previous experience of working with Princess Anne and Princess Margaret, I turned to David Sassoon for advice. I knew I had to get this right. David was a favourite among the Royal Family, who understandably loved his sophisticated, beautifully made looks. As one half of the British fashion label Bellville Sassoon, he had been working with Diana since before her engagement. He understood the protocol and how to behave when dealing with royalty. He told me how to respond correctly in writing to a royal – I had no idea that there was a set way of doing so, that correspondence always begins with 'Dear Sir' or 'Dear Madam' and always ends with 'I have the honour to remain your obedient servant'. He pointed out that working with Diana was very different from working with other royals. 'She is more relaxed,' he said, noting that she – unlike other royals – didn't mind if you turned your back in her presence.

When the day of the fitting arrived, I drove to Kensington Palace through the trade entrance, as I had for Princess Margaret seven years before. I managed to stifle any nerves by focusing on the task at hand. The pink dress lay on the back seat of the car, wrapped in tissue paper, and I gingerly carried it to the door where a liveried member of staff whisked me up to the apartment where Charles and Diana were living. She was just as beautiful in real life, but shy. Her fingernails were bitten and her shoulders were hunched. Happy wasn't a word I would have associated with her, but she was very warm. I curtsied and told her it was a pleasure to meet her. 'After you, Zandra.' She smiled and gestured for me to come inside.

As I entered the first room, I noticed the ugliest fanged toy I've ever seen. 'What's that?' I asked.

'Oh, it's William's favourite doll,' she replied. I was glad not to have imparted more comment. William and Harry were tucked away and I never saw them during any of my visits to fit Diana.

The fitting took place in Diana's dressing room. It wasn't huge – a dressing-table covered with printed cloth to one side and a deep mahogany chest of drawers on the other. Pictures of her with the boys hung on the walls. The dress looked gorgeous and so very feminine in the soft pink. The diamonds and pearls embroidered on the pointed tips of the hem glittered without being too ostentatious. The neckline could be worn off the shoulder or on, depending on how formal the occasion. It fitted her perfectly, and Diana seemed happy. She told me she was going on a royal tour to Japan next month and hoped to take it with her. I was excited, but decided not to get my hopes up in case it stayed in her luggage and wasn't worn. A few weeks later, I was in the studio when one of my design assistants came over to my desk with a newspaper. She was quite giddy. There on the front page was a photograph of Princess Diana in my pink dress at a state banquet in Kyoto. I was delighted. I couldn't have asked for a better ambassador and knew it could only have a positive impact on my business. At that point, I didn't get involved in sales, but I'm fairly sure they were even busier at the shop after that. Diana electrified people with what she wore – like two of my other clients, Jackie Kennedy and Lauren Bacall, she made clothes come alive.

Over the next few years, I dressed Diana a further four times. Each time it worked in a similar way, although she started arranging her visits in advance rather than turning up as she had done before. We would close the shop while she browsed the rails, she'd try a few dresses on and then I'd usually receive a letter from the Palace the week after, asking for small changes – alterations or a different colour. I would submit sketches of the desired amendment and then I'd fit her at the Palace. As I've said before, you can never really know a member of the Royal Family. Even with Diana, as friendly as she was, there was an inevitable formality that was very hard to penetrate. Dressing her gave me a glimpse of the pressure she was under from the press. In 1987, I made her a white wrap dress edged with pearl beads and sequins, which she wanted to wear to a charity gala at the Palladium. She said she needed to know that it wouldn't fall open and show her legs if she got out of a car. 'You can be sure that when I get out of that car, there'll be photographers waiting at just the wrong angle to get me.'

Three of the five dresses I made for Diana were sold as part of a high-profile Christie's sale in 1997 in New York to raise money for her various charities. That evening, 23 June, was the last time I saw her. She had been divorced for nine months and was in a relationship with the heart surgeon Hasnat Khan. A few years had passed since our last meeting, and she was different – more confident somehow. She had always been charming, but she had

Watercolour sketch of my 'India Revisited' dress worn by Diana, Princess of Wales

blossomed. I must have stood out at that grand event – there were a lot of classically elegant outfits in those rooms, whereas I'd gone for a more daring baby-blue off-the-shoulder dress, accessorized with Andrew Logan's mirrored brooches and dangling earrings. My dyed red hair was scraped up in a high ponytail and I'd tied matching blue bows throughout. Diana saw me across the room and walked across with a glass of champagne in her hand. 'Fancy seeing you here,' she said, and laughed. I don't remember what else we talked about, but I do remember how happy she seemed. She was on the edge of entering the world stage on her own terms. She finally had her freedom.

Two months later, she was dead. I was in San Diego when I heard and I couldn't believe it. I don't think anyone could. It felt like a giant's foot had come down and stamped on a butterfly who had only recently found her wings. I was appalled by how the paparazzi had chased her to death and devastated that her life had been snatched away just when it felt as if she was coming into her own.

David Sassoon and I were lucky enough to be invited to her funeral on 6 September 1997, a day I will never forget. It was a strange, deeply moving afternoon. David's nephew drove us to Westminster Abbey and we were talking so much we ended up in the wrong queue at the wrong door, and were sent to another. It was such sombre occasion, and it felt odd to be rushing. When we reached the right door, there were barely any seats left in our allocated area so we ended up right at the back. In the pews in front sat Karl Lagerfeld, Donatella Versace and Victor Edelstein, other designers who had also dressed her. We saw the family file down the aisle, William and Harry bowing their heads, and then the service began. I'll never forget the way Earl Spencer's voice cracked as he spat out the last words in his speech, or the applause that followed, beginning at first with the public outside then swirling onwards through the congregation to the Royal Family. It was like the world's saddest Mexican wave. The same thing happened when Elton John finished playing 'Candle In The Wind'. The crowds outside erupted; the sound was deafening. Even through the ancient stone walls of the Abbey, the collective grief was overwhelming. Like so many others, I cried a lot that day.

Diana got a raw deal. You can have all the riches in the world, but it doesn't mean much if the person who has promised to love you loves someone else. If you don't have love, or don't feel loved, you have very little. I can't claim to have known Diana well, but I liked her tremendously and I'm glad to have been of service at a time when she was growing into the woman she would become. I hope my clothes gave her confidence and helped her see herself the way I did at our last meeting – resilient, clever and fabulously luminous.

39

Gladys Palmer's Oscars Illustration

IF I COULD CHANGE ONE THING about myself it's my tendency to fall asleep in public. One minute I'm there and the next I'm gone. My eyelids close like shutters and that's it, I'm out. It's a habit that's followed me my whole life, I suppose as a result of working too hard. I've always been terrible at relaxing. Even as a child, I never really rested – we were the sort of family that was always doing things, drawing, walking or solving jigsaws. It wasn't acceptable to sit on the sofa and do nothing, so I learnt from an early age to be busy. As I grew older and my career took off, I didn't have to find ways of being busy – there was just a never-ending list of things to do, and I enjoyed doing them.

For most of my life I've slept for no longer than five hours a night, although more likely just four. I don't recollect a single dream: I have a theory that you must sleep for at least seven hours in order to dream, and that has simply never happened. Until the last few years, I would get up at 6.30 a.m. and be in the studio for 7.30 a.m., often working until midnight. What this means is that, as soon as I feel relaxed, I fall asleep. The situations in which I have conked out range from press interviews, nightclubs and awards ceremonies to after-parties, shows and dinners. My drowsiness doesn't discriminate – it isn't personal,

I'm just tired. Each of my friends has at least one story about somewhere unexpected that I've fallen asleep. In a way, it's a blessing – how fortunate to be able to doze absolutely anywhere.

There have been times in my life when I've had less sleep than at others. In the nineties, when I was living between the UK and America with Salah, I would typically work all night to feel prepared enough for the trip. I flew back and forth every two to three weeks to manage my two offices. The jetlag was insane, and I must have been exhausted, but it was necessary to maintain my relationship and my business. Everything has its price. Like Alice in Wonderland, I looked at the jar that said 'famous fashion designer' and swallowed the pill. If that meant I had to work long hours to get the job done, so be it. That said, being in one place, as I am now in London, makes life much easier.

Since the pandemic, I have learnt to appreciate rest. I have a TV for the very first time in my life. I sit up in my bed, which is piled with cushions, and watch it before I fall asleep – but I always have my sketchbook to hand to make drawings and notes on what I'm supposed to do the next day. I'm not sure if I'd call it a bedtime routine, but it's my relaxation time. Today, I start work slightly later at 8 a.m. and finish at 6.30 p.m., and I do a lot more sitting than I used to. I still find myself nodding off at dinner parties or grand events, but my friends don't mind. If I was to be sanguine about it, you could say it's a compliment – if I'm asleep in your company, it means I've finally relaxed.

The inappropriate moments I've fallen asleep over the years are endless and range from dinners with friends, memorably with my head nearly falling into the soup at Sandie Shaw's place in the sixties, to the after-party David Bailey kindly threw for me following my Roundhouse show or watching Divvy at his *Women Behind Bars* show at the Whitehall Theatre in the seventies, to nights out in the eighties at Studio 54, where I was famously

Me asleep at the Oscars, 1997

snapped snoozing next to Tina Chow at its reopening, or on a train en route to John Waters's home in Baltimore when I ended up in Washington DC instead. Perhaps the most conspicuous occasion was the Oscars in the nineties with Salah. Because of his role at Warner Bros., he was invited every year and had become very uninterested in it. I, however, loved every moment of the Oscars. I adored getting dressed up, seeing the stars and the glamour. I hid a camera down my knickers to avoid security just so I could steal a few surreptitious snaps. Salah wouldn't even let me go to the bar on my own because he knew I was just making excuses to gawp at the big Hollywood stars.

In 1997, we invited the great fashion illustrator Gladys Palmer and her husband to join us. It was the year *The English Patient* won Best Picture, and we'd had a fabulous evening. I had flown in that day from London, so was a little jetlagged. The excitement of the night kept me going, but eventually it was time to head back to our hotel. There was a wait for our limo to arrive and I was wearing very high heels, so I briefly sat on the ground, with my back against some railings, to rest my feet. Before I knew it, I was in the Land of Nod. Gladys took a picture of me slumped in all my finery, red hair tied up in a striking bun decorated with purple orchids. She then did an illustration of it, which appears in her book, *Fashion People*. The photo her drawing was based on adorns my studio bathroom wall, among my many treasured photos of Salah.

40

Hobo Box

IN MY LIBRARY AT HOME, the walls are lined with shelves filled with books and curiosities. Sandwiched between a Venetian travel guide and a recipe book on Scandinavian cooking, a distinctive box is hand-carved from cigar cases. It's rectangular and covered with layers of geometric triangles that grow smaller until they form a point. On top there is a small transparent plastic handle. This unusual box is an example of 'tramp or hobo art', a form of American folk art that emerged in the nineteenth century: untrained artisans used recycled or scraps of wood to create objects, some functional, some purely decorative. The wood is whittled, notched and stacked to create small trinket boxes, photo frames, candlesticks and big chests. It involves a lot of precision, patience and skill. The derogatory name comes from the belief that the originators of this rare woodwork technique were homeless or at least wanderers.

No one knows the roots of the art form, but it is certainly true that the makers were incredibly ahead of their time – taking society's detritus and turning it into objects of beauty. The box I have in my library was bought by my great friend Joe Lombardo, whom I met during my first trip to New York in 1969. He found it in the Manhattan shop of a mutual friend of ours, Michael

Malce. Joe was an incredibly talented graphic artist and the closest of my many friends to die during the AIDS epidemic. It was typical of him to find beauty somewhere it doesn't usually exist.

My funny, opinionated friend was only forty-five when he died on 15 August 1985. He had won awards for his clever packaging designs and ran his own Manhattan-based firm. He had one of the best apartments I've ever visited, a large glamorous space in New York's Upper East Side, where he'd painted the floor with the names of his friends, including mine. I often stayed there when

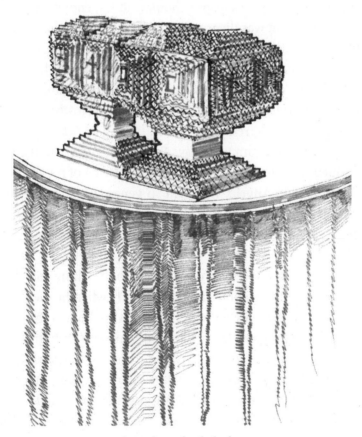

Carved wooden hobo box

I was in town. *House & Garden* devoted a spread to his home, which was so original and interesting. He was half Sicilian, half American, and – like many Italians I know – he took up space. Not physically, he was always slim, but he was loud, warm and didn't shy away from expressing his views and emotions. I try not to think about moments that make me sad, but I miss Joe tremendously.

Within my circle, AIDS arrived, like a shadowy storm, in the early eighties, the kind that gives you goose-pimples before it reaches you. It began, of course, in New York, where it became the topic that every newspaper shouted about, endless reports of a new disease that was disproportionately targeting the gay community. The city shifted gear dramatically – what had been a glorious, glittering party destination became a slaughterhouse. The sound of disco was replaced by an awful stillness. AIDS gripped a generation of artists and killed them slowly.

Strangely, I can't remember ever talking about it with my friends, many of whom were gay. As the years went on, the crisis intensified. Angelo Donghia was among the first of my friends to go. Dear genteel Angelo, who had so generously loaned me his townhouse to present my first catwalk show in 1971 and always lit up the room at parties in Fire Island. I didn't have a chance to say goodbye because I didn't know he was sick – Angelo kept his condition a secret for nearly two years, only telling his closest friends right at the terrible end. He was fifty when he died.

There was a time when it felt as if everyone who was gay was ill. The American designer Perry Ellis, who came up with the idea of elevated classics, died in 1986. We had travelled to Japan together for a catwalk event only a few years before, in 1982. Again, he didn't want anyone to know what was causing him to fade away – there was such a stigma. That was one of the other miserable aspects of AIDS: the sixties and seventies had been a wonderful period of sexual freedom for everyone, yet the LGBTQ+ community was hit harder than others by this epidemic. In 1986, Andrew was forced to change the venue of his Alternative Miss World from Chislehurst Caves just days before the event: a local newspaper had run a homophobic article suggesting that the pageant would lead to an AIDS outbreak. The journalist assumed that people would go to the toilets in the Caves, and that AIDS would spread down the pipes and up into people's houses. The ignorance was astounding.

The fashion illustrator Antonio Lopez, with whom I'd enjoyed many a dinner, went next in 1986. I still have one of his gorgeous drawings on my bedroom wall. Often, AIDS victims would up sticks and leave to be with family without telling anyone why, which was what Halston did when he moved to San Francisco in the late eighties before his death in 1990. There was no chance to say goodbye. People simply disappeared.

AIDS was never explicitly mentioned within my group, but it was so obviously with us. People grew thinner and thinner until it became clear that they were visibly dying. I buried myself in work because it was the only way I found I could cope. There were so many funerals. I never went to any. Sometimes I felt great shame at not attending, but I couldn't bring myself to go and I blamed work. There was a lot of denial at that time, not just from me but from those who had contracted the disease and wanted to enjoy the time they had left. None of us wanted to acknowledge what was happening. If you don't face the awfulness you can somehow carry on. I was surrounded by death but I just got on with it, which isn't the same as dealing with it. Work was the only way I knew how to process the loss.

Joe didn't tell me he had AIDS, but I knew. I wasn't frightened of the idea of the disease, but seeing friends grow weak and gaunt was different. A low-level, unshakeable fear peaked in me every time I saw a friend who looked thinner than when I had last seen them. That was the moment I knew they were starting to die. Joe became thinner and thinner, withered and skeletal. His cheeks were still framed by his long dark hair but they were sunken and grey. There was no desire in either of us to discuss symptoms because it made us feel so powerless. I visited Joe in hospital. American hospitals always feel so vast compared to British ones, and I remember snaking my way through that labyrinthine place, trying to find my way to him. He was still making the nurses laugh by lying about his age even in his final days: he was trying to pass himself off as twenty-five rather than forty-five. He had pneumonia caused by AIDS and breathing was increasingly hard. By then he was always between sleep, and I held his hand in that sad hospital room. Darling Joe slipped away like a gladiator not long afterwards.

As time went on, the epidemic killed more and more people I knew and loved. Freddie Mercury died the following year, 1991, then the luminescent model Tina Chow in 1992, the first woman to say publicly she had contracted the disease via heterosexual sex. Derek Jarman, who had choreographed my 1983 'Medieval Collection' catwalk show, was taken in 1994. Another incredible talent obliterated. Five men who had worked in my London studio died. They weren't working with me when they fell ill, but it was very tough all the same. Loss was so frequent that it became normal to call someone at home, and if they didn't answer, you knew that they were probably gone.

AIDS deprived us as a society of so much collective greatness. Think of the music, the designs, the wonderful art we would have been gifted if the disease had been brought under control sooner than 1996 when the number of new AIDS cases diagnosed in the US declined for the first time since the start of the epidemic in 1981. On a personal level, it deprived me of a great many friends but what can you do other than continue living? As I have grown older, and many of my peers and friends have passed, I think the only thing you can do when it comes to loss is support the people left behind, those who were closest to the deceased. Remember to call in the months after the funeral, and answer the phone if they ring you during inconvenient hours. All that's left is to carry on and live as enthusiastically and fully as possible on behalf of those who couldn't.

41

Buckingham Palace Christmas Tree Fairy

BY THE MID-NINETIES, MY BUSINESS was struggling. The one thing you can be sure of in fashion is change, and the landscape had moved on from the flamboyance that had characterized the eighties. Clothes took on a new simplicity, with Calvin Klein and Ralph Lauren leading the charge. Grunge arrived in all its scruffy glory, led by Kurt Cobain and Courtney Love. Rave culture flooded dark nightclubs with Day-Glo fluorescent colours; glamour and excess were replaced by baggy jeans and smiley-face T-shirts. As a result, there was less demand for what I was doing.

The impact of this shift was difficult. Up until the mid-nineties, I was still very famous in America and my collections remained popular there. I hosted intimate fashion shows at big department stores such as Neiman Marcus and Saks where they sold my clothes, but when these in-store outlets started drying up, I was forced to reduce production. I still had American customers, but not enough to sustain a business of the same scale.

There was no rock-bottom moment: I simply started running out of options until there was only one very thin and pothole-ridden path ahead. I wasn't running the sort of fashion label that could easily be adapted. It was too singular and strong – what I do isn't neutral, which means the road will always be challenging.

My concession in Harrods was gone, my shop had shut and interest in my work was low. I decreased the printing space at my Shepherd's Bush factory, first bought in the mid-eighties and employing around seventy people, to rent out part of the building. My printing was again being done in my poky studio in Porchester Road where I had started out two decades before, a miserable step back.

I stopped paying myself, choosing instead to live off a small amount of savings. Taking myself off the payroll was a blow, but the real agony was in scaling back the team. The business had become smaller, so I had no choice but to make redundancies and stripped back my workforce by dozens. I found that very difficult. When you have a work ethos like mine and have required the same level of dedication from your team, the people you work with become so much more than colleagues. They end up being much-relied-on family members, who have weathered my moods and demands. My staff were and are the people who make my ideas come alive. It was heart-wrenching to let them go – I knew the impact it would have on their lives. I felt disloyal and that I was letting them down. I have never forgotten it.

Just when I thought things couldn't get much worse, in December 1995 a storage unit containing thousands of my precious historic garments flooded due to frozen, burst pipes. I have always kept the original of every design I've created because, one day, they will enable the world to see and remember my work. At the time of the flood, I was in America but I flew home immediately. The damage was huge and I stood no chance of dealing with it by myself. I called Frances Diplock, who had run my hand-finishing workroom, because she was one of the most capable and reliable people I knew. Despite having been made redundant as part of the cuts about six weeks earlier, she agreed to come back and help me. I have never felt more grateful for anything than when Frances arrived that January at the huge freezing warehouse with a Thermos flask in hand. Together, we went through five thousand sodden garments, drying, repacking and cataloguing them. A few of the prints had run into each other, but we managed to save the majority.

Sometimes life hits you full force but it makes you realize how much strength you have. I found the money to hire Frances and she still works for me today, an ever-dependable, quiet talent who has disentangled the workings of my mind more times than I can count. In January 1996, as I sat sifting through wet, icy clothes with shivering fingers, I felt as if I had nothing left to say and no one in the industry who would listen anyway.

The reality is that if you have a long career as a designer, you will fall out of fashion at some point. If you've got something original to say it will fit in again at the right time. The fashion world is exciting, creative and sometimes glamorous, but there is a price to pay and that price is keeping up or withstanding the lows. So many great talents have fallen by the wayside after an initial flurry: a designer will come up with a great idea and the fashion press goes wild for it but the next minute they're out in the cold and support is withdrawn.

Handbags and fragrance are the categories that generate money, not ready-to-wear. I had embarked on several perfume projects but they'd never fully taken off, and somehow I never managed to design the perfect It bag. If I had been bought by one of the big fashion conglomerates, such as LVMH and Kering, no doubt I'd have had an easier time financially, but I would have had less control over my business, which would have been too high a price for me to pay. I could have lost my name, like Halston and Lacroix, but I chose not to.

When I look back, although there were a few difficult years – and who doesn't have those? – there was also an odd relief in the quiet. When I was riding high, I often felt like a prisoner – there was such an immense pressure to create more and more. The churn of coming up with new, better and more dazzling ideas was often paralysing. The industry is much faster now than it was in the nineties and the expectation to innovate is even greater. We have to be very careful not to push every designer to the brink just because we want a new outfit. As much as the lack of interest in my work stung initially, it gave me more room to draw and reflect. When everyone wants a piece of you, it's much harder to slip away.

During the late nineties, I learnt to accept that no big brand will be buzzy for ever and it's a case of riding out the lulls with integrity. Different things will be fashionable at different times, but there is no point in transforming who you are to appeal to everyone. I think that's a mantra to live by in general, not just in fashion. There's no sincerity or authenticity in doing so, and the results will inevitably be shoddy. Stand by your work if you believe in it and eventually the world will return to you. It's one thing to adapt and respond to what is happening around you, but it's another to hide or completely remodel who you are.

I made small adjustments to meet the more relaxed fashion landscape by introducing daywear, which I'd never done before. I entered the world of licensing, which is where one company gives another permission to manufacture duplicates of its products for an agreed payment. I enjoyed collaborations with the Japanese department store Seibu where I designed a range of printed bedding, then later with another Japanese brand, YA, on a line of tights, and a small British label, Nimi Singh, on Italian silk scarves. Over the years, I've worked with a number of companies to create one-off or ongoing lines, from fashion names such as Topshop, Marks & Spencer and Free People to lifestyle brands including Ikea, Millets and Fuli Carpets. Some of the businesses I've paired up with might seem remote from my brand, but I've always viewed them as another way to display my designs on a new type of product. The ability to turn my hand to different mediums of design outside fashion has always been important to me – after all, I'm a textile designer trained to bring pattern to different mediums.

Beyond that, though, it's sensible to have a Plan B. Not only do I enjoy the creative challenge of Zandrifying everyday objects, like bed linen or even tents, as I did for Millets, licensing projects have provided an invaluable revenue stream when I needed it. Longevity in the fashion business involves getting over yourself, and going where the work is. Today I duck and dive between various projects and often they take me places, both literally and metaphorically, where I wouldn't otherwise have been.

Falling from a great height in fashion taught me how to think laterally – it also freed me up to pursue other projects I would never have had time to do, including the Fashion and Textile Museum in 2003, and designing opera sets and costumes. My career took a different course, but self-belief and the love and support of my friends kept me going when I thought I couldn't carry on. Within a few years, my life had shifted, and in 1998 I found myself with Queen Elizabeth II at Buckingham Palace having been commissioned to create the family Christmas-tree angel. I'd been asked alongside milliner extraordinaire David Shilling and five hundred amateur embroiderers to create an ornament to decorate the tree. Each one was to be displayed at the V&A before it was auctioned for charity afterwards. I designed a pink printed outfit for my fairy with a full chiffon tulle skirt and a demure boat neckline. I'd dyed her hair the same colour as mine – Pinkissimo pink – and given her statement eyebrows: one was more traditionally shaped and the other was one of my signature wiggles. Her wand was an Andrew Logan mirrored star.

My Christmas fairy for the Buckingham Palace tree, 1998

I had met the Queen before, when I received my CBE in 1997, but it wasn't something I ever took for granted, even on later occasions when we met again. She liked my bright festive fairy, smiled broadly at it and asked me to talk her through the fairy's look. The Queen was less grandiose than her sister Margaret. Of course I always curtsied and remembered protocol, but she had a calming, gracious way about her. I remember thinking back to that ghastly Christmas only three years before and how I couldn't have imagined then my situation now: laughing with Her Majesty over my fuchsia-haired fairy, or the new life I was beginning to create for myself. I had entered a new phase, both professionally and romantically.

42

Photo of Salah and Me

EVERY ROMANTIC RELATIONSHIP I'VE EVER had has ended because I put my work before the man. The exception was Salah Hassanein, the love of my life, whom I was with for twenty-five years until his death in 2019. The difference with Salah was that we were both workaholics, and therefore understood each other. He wasn't threatened by my success, and didn't use it for his own ends. He was assertive, driven, and made me feel special. When Salah talked to you, he made you feel like the most important person in the world.

We met in 1994 when work was quietening for me. I had dated various people since my relationship with Couri ended, but no one I considered a big love. I was fifty-four and resigned to single life. I had vowed to dedicate myself to work and my friends, but the world operates in unexpected ways and a new chapter began for me. I have learnt that you should never worry about hitting those big milestones when society tells you to: there are so many ways to live a life, and you never know what might be around the corner. Defying convention makes you interesting, standing apart from, not behind, the crowd. Perhaps it was because my professional life was less all-consuming that I had space to meet someone and nurture the relationship.

He came along at a time when I had more room for love, and ultimately there was a strong physical attraction between us, which initially bound us together. Meeting your big love later in life is different from any first love. The older we become, the better we hope to know ourselves, to know what we need and want in a partner, and maybe have a better chance of contentment. With age comes more metaphorical baggage, and the important thing is working out whether your respective suitcases are compatible. You can have the greatest sex in the world, but if your design flaws and histories don't complement one another, it won't work. I always thought my mother found Salah for me – he was exactly the sort of man she'd have picked. Not only was he successful and driven, but he accepted me for who I was.

It's best to be honest about how Salah and I first met, which was through his then wife, who was a client. She invited me to a charity dinner in New York at which Salah strode up to me, in that confident, friendly way of his, and asked, 'Why is your hair pink?' As a businessman, he wasn't used to people looking so unconventional, but I think he was attracted to me because I was different. I remember thinking he was handsome, but he was much older than me: there was a nineteen-year age difference. He would have been seventy-three when we met. That was it for a while and I didn't think much more about it. Maybe a year later, Salah changed his job from president of Warner Bros. International Theatres, a job which had involved him expanding Warner Bros. theatres across the rest of the world, to becoming President of the Todd-AO Corporation. During a work trip to London, he invited me to lunch. I said, 'I'm terribly sorry, I don't do lunch (it's a waste of time and takes too much of the working day) but I'd love to hear about your work. Maybe we could meet for a cocktail instead.' He said yes, and we started meeting regularly. His story astounded me.

Salah was born into poverty on 31 May 1921, in Alexandria, Egypt. He was illegitimate, which was quite a scandal back then, after his Italian mother refused to marry his father because she wouldn't trade in her Catholicism to become a Muslim. The decision plunged her into financial hardship. Despite their socioeconomic disadvantage, his mother encouraged him to attend an English-speaking school. He soon discovered he was a natural mathematician, and while he was still studying, he got a part-time job balancing the books for a local hotel.

After he finished school, he moved to Edfu where he began working in a bank. It was there that his talent for numbers was spotted by the head of the Cairo branch, who offered him a job which also enabled him to attend the London School of Economics' Cairo campus. Ultimately, Salah knew that if he was to make something of himself, he needed to leave Egypt for the US. In 1945 he arrived alone in America, aged twenty-four, on an American troop ship at Ellis Island, with just sixty dollars in his pocket. Upon arrival, a Customs officer told him, 'You either become a US citizen and join the army or go back to Egypt.' Salah chose the former option and served in the US armed forces from 1945 to 1947 during which he was sent to Germany.

Through Greek–Egyptian contacts in Cairo, he was taken under the wing of a Greek immigrant called George P. Skouras, who was president of United Artists Theatres and Skouras Theatres Inc. Skouras gave him a job as an usher at one of his cinemas, and Salah worked relentlessly hard, eventually becoming president of Skouras Theatres Corporation in just under fifteen years. By 1987, he was appointed president of Warner Bros. International Theatres where his job was to build a network of multiplex theatres in Europe, Japan and Australia. He read more than anyone I've ever met, and spoke four different languages, French, English, Italian and Arabic. Salah just wanted to learn as much as he could about the world in whichever way he could. Philanthropy was very important to him, and he donated regularly to various charities. By the time I met him in the early nineties, he had divorced his first wife, with whom he had five children, and was in his second marriage.

You can't always account for what you do when you fall in love with someone. I couldn't believe that someone loved me and wasn't put off by my theatrical appearance or my commitment to my career. Those two things combined put everyone else off, but Salah seemed to respect and admire the entirety of who I was. We were often in the same country at the same time: I'd be in Japan doing a show and he'd also be there expanding Warner Bros. I did a huge event in Berlin, and coincidentally his business had taken him there too. I remember meeting him in Canada when I was working there on something or other and he was doing some work for the charity Variety. He fitted in with my lifestyle and work so easily, I couldn't believe my luck. During the early stages, we hid our relationship from our friends and family, and I suppose the illicit nature made it more exciting. I would go out with him wearing wigs to disguise myself from public and press. Even then, I knew I loved him. He was simply so brilliant – interesting, clever and charming. Eventually, his wife found out and divorce proceedings began.

Ever since my childhood, and my mother's constant reminders that she paid for everything, I was raised to believe that success was very important in a partner. My mother resented my father for not bettering himself, and as a result I have always been drawn to high achievers. When I read *Lady Chatterley's Lover* aged twenty, it was obvious to me that the central relationship wouldn't work: she was a lady and he was a gamekeeper, so he would never have been accepted in her life. I never wanted an unhappy relationship, like my parents had had, so I sought what my mother looked for and never found in my father: a more level playing field. I've always been attracted to powerful men, and Salah was certainly powerful.

He was always working and led a glamorous life. When he re-opened the new Warner Bros. Vue theatre in the West End in 1993, he did so with Harrison Ford and Princess Diana. He regu-larly mingled with the rich and famous but remained completed unaffected by it. On one occasion, when we attended the Oscars together, he in his capacity as a Warner Bros. executive, he decided to skip the red carpet and we entered the theatre via the somewhat unglamorous car park. I was in floods of tears – I loved the idea of a red-carpet moment – but for Salah it was just business, pure and simple. He had an amazing brain and was as keen to absorb know-ledge as to excel in business.

I wasn't just attracted to his power and status. We were kindred spirits who liked doing the same things. Salah and I travelled to some of the world's most glamorous destinations together, from the Italian Riviera to Mexico, but one of the things we always did when we were together in those amazing places was go for long walks. We liked sunrises as we were both early risers. We'd then return to the hotel and do some work: he'd be taking business calls and sending faxes while I'd be sketching. I was never made to feel bad for working. If anything, he admired it. He believed in me implicitly.

When I received my CBE in 1997, he threw me a huge party. He was over the moon for me and understood what it meant for me to be recognized after so many years of feeling forgotten in fashion backwaters. We both loved socializing, and he was a great fan of my cooking. I introduced him to different sorts of people he perhaps wouldn't have come across otherwise: Salah's friends were serious business people; mine were fabu-lous bohemian creatives from all different walks of life, ages and sexualities. He welcomed all of them and enjoyed their company.

Salah always wanted to retire in Del Mar, an affluent, sleepy seaside resort in California, and in 1995 he asked me to move there with him. We chose the house together, a beautiful place on the beach. Outside, I designed – with renowned Australian terrazzo artist, David Humphries – an expansive terrace made using mosaic inserts of onyx mirror-backed glass and semi-precious stones all in my designs. It seated up to two hundred people, and we hosted fabulous catered dinners there while watching the sun go down. I would be in charge of making everything look wonderful, from the tables to the crockery I commissioned from my friend, the great ceramicist Carol McNicoll. I loved entertaining for him, and we both enjoyed those evenings. I think we found Heaven in creating a joyful life together. The transformation of our lives was a happy surprise for us both.

Knowing that my career was still crucial to me, Salah also paid for me to have a satellite studio in the neighbouring city of Solana Beach and hired two people to work for me. Over the course of our relationship, he opened doors for me (it was Salah who came up with the plans and loan for the conversion of the Fashion and Textile Museum building in 2003) and perhaps my profile enabled him to be a better-known philanthropist. We were a good team. We never married, initially because I didn't want to lose my name. In the end, I don't think it made much difference. You don't have to marry someone to show you're committed to them.

For a time, I tried to make the break and move permanently to Del Mar, but I realized I needed to be in London too. I still had my small studio in Porchester Road and my Shepherd's Bush factory, which couldn't be run entirely remotely. I know you have to nurture love, and I regularly reprimanded myself because I didn't give it the time it deserved. I would travel back and forth every two to three weeks, despite the gruelling twelve-hour flights, often changing at the airport to go on to an important dinner. As used to travelling as I was, sometimes it felt relentless. It was a strange double life, but for the most part we managed the distance well. I would have found it stifling to spend every moment with my partner, and I value my independence. There were times when I felt cripplingly exhausted, but everything has its price.

A decade or so into our relationship, when he was around eighty-four, he found it harder to let me go. When I would leave for London, he would ask, 'How do you know I will be alive when you get back?' It was awful, but I could not and would not abandon my business. Salah was a large man and his health started to deteriorate when he was in his mid-nineties. Despite his age, it was still a shock to see the strong, great man grow increasingly immobile. In his final two years, he was bedridden and if it wasn't for modern medicine he wouldn't have lived for as long as he did. He hated hospitals so had two at-home carers to ensure that he was as comfortable as possible. I found it very, very difficult to face his demise. It was frightening and ugly to imagine a world without him. As his illness grew, so too did his ill-temper, probably out of frustration. The intellectual and physical humiliation was awful to watch, to see someone who was previously so commanding and dazzling slowly wither away. As usual, I buried myself in my work, which made it somewhat bearable. I don't think he'd have responded in the same way.

I was in India filming *The Real Marigold Hotel* when I received the call that he might die. I flew home to find him semi-comatose. Even in his final week, he always wanted to look out at the sea and watch the sun setting. I stayed for a few days, and when it seemed his condition was stable, I flew to Barcelona for a scheduled appearance. It might sound callous to have left his side when he was so unwell, but I did what I needed to do to cope: work. When I landed, I was told Salah was dead. It might sound strange, but part of me was still surprised. When someone's been ill for that long, it's impossible to know when the time might come.

Memories of Salah are dispersed all over my home, a place I wouldn't have if it weren't for his encouragement and belief in me. He has contributed to my legacy. I have photos of him in my living room and bedroom, of us at parties in California smiling into the camera. My downstairs loo is filled with pictures of him: Salah with Princess Diana, Salah with President Reagan at our home in San Diego, Salah with Cary Grant. I always thought it was a funny and unexpected place to celebrate him but the location really commands your attention. You can't miss him when you're using the facilities. I did the same with our bathroom in San Diego – it made it a popular place to spend time: guests used to love looking at the pictures.

The photo I have chosen for this book was taken by a brilliant photographic printer called Gene Nocon, whom I knew through his work with the legendary photographer Norman Parkinson. Gene moved to San Diego after he met his American wife and he was a regular at our place. During one visit sometime in 2006, Salah and I were sitting on our sofa and he asked if he could take our picture. We never usually posed for photos, but I suppose we felt comfortable enough to say yes to Gene. I think we look very content – Salah is tanned with a hint of a smile, and I am giving a big toothy grin. I rather love my black turban too, which is pinned by an Andrew Logan 'New Moon' brooch. We'd been together just over a decade: he would have been in his eighties. Despite or perhaps because of our long-distance arrangement and our age difference, we were very happy together.

Me and Salah from a photograph by Gene Nocon

Life goes on, and of course I miss Salah when I think about it, but I try not to. It was a happy part of my life that I was privileged to have. In a strange way, I don't wish I had met him sooner. Starting our relationship when we did meant my career had been given the chance to flower and develop. Salah arrived when my professional problems felt insurmountable and changed the direction of my story. Love is not something that can be turned on or off, and he is with me through every part of the world he altered.

43

Absolutely Fabulous Quilted Caftan

BURIED IN A CHEST IN my London studio is a colourful quilted satin caftan. It is made using two different prints – the 'Button Flower' and the 'Frilly Flower' in vivid pink, yellow and blue. Its scalloped edge is trimmed in red, and bright buttons are used as the key fastening. The button florals were inspired by finds at a Soho button shop and the button flower shapes influenced by Henri Matisse's artworks. They were a focal point of my 1971 'Paris, Frills and Button Flowers' collection. The look was photographed by Clive Arrowsmith for British *Vogue* in October that year, in what the magazine described as my most important collection to date. Little did I know then that my quilted caftan would be worn again over twenty years later by Joanna Lumley's Patsy on the TV show *Absolutely Fabulous*.

I was invited by the makers of *Ab Fab* to appear as myself in an episode in 1994. The TV show was still in its infancy, and my PA received a call asking if I'd like to feature in the second series as a guest. I hadn't watched *Ab Fab*, but I had heard of it. Back then, there were still few channels and if a TV show was truly funny or interesting it became big very quickly. All my friends were watching it, so I said yes. It was a huge compliment to be asked. I often agree to feature in certain TV shows because you don't know where they might lead – you may experience something new or meet someone interesting. Without them, I'm just my boring self, getting on with work, never coming up for air. They're also very useful for raising one's profile. TV appearances enable me, and therefore my business, to reach an audience that goes much further than the fashion industry, which is crucial if you want to survive long-term. In 1994, that was becoming increasingly important to me – fashion's mood was switching from maximalism towards minimalism. Designers like Calvin Klein and Donna Karan were on the rise, and with them their understated, more casual looks. My bold, colourful clothes were never going to be low-key, and there's no point in doing a second-rate version of something other people do well. I was very much aware that change was in the air, a shift that was incompatible with my designs, so I was keen to make sure I remained in the public eye.

Something I have noticed over the course of my long career is how, although you might sense a change is coming, it often takes a few years for it to materialize in earnest. The look that defines an era usually arrives in a big way mid-decade. There might be a strange feeling of discontent with the status quo earlier, but it's difficult to grasp until much later. For example, punk sounds arrived in the early seventies in New York, with the Stooges and New York Dolls, but only reached the international masses in the mid-seventies when the Sex Pistols formed and Vivienne Westwood and Malcolm McLaren opened their famous King's Road store Sex. Shoulder pads are widely associated with the eighties, but Thierry Mugler launched them in the seventies. Sometimes it takes a while for a look to percolate before it makes the big-time. The same happened with the nineties. Everyone thinks it was ten years of minimalism and grunge when, in fact, the early years of the decade were still very much centred on flamboyance, glamour and excess. The theatrical looks of Christian Lacroix ran alongside low-key Calvin Klein and relaxed Ralph Lauren. *Ab Fab* was first launched in 1992 and the two lead characters, Patsy and Eddie, adored his bold designs. 'It's Lacroix, sweetie,' became one of Eddie's most famous mantras.

As a renowned queen of maximalism, I was brought on board for an episode. I wasn't required to do much prep for my appearance, which was lucky. There were very few lines to learn but I didn't need to get into character because I was playing myself. The episode was about Patsy and Eddie making each other jealous by befriending famous people. There were two other celebrity cameos, both friends of mine: Lulu, whom I had met through her ex-husband, the hairdresser John Frieda, and model Britt Ekland, who used to hang out at my Porchester Road studio with her ex-husband Peter Sellers in the sixties. In my first scene, Patsy and Eddie see each other in a Kensington restaurant and try to induce envy in the other by attempting to make new best friends. Patsy invites herself to have lunch with Britt and me, and Eddie forces her client Lulu to eat with her. Patsy tries to convince me that we're great friends by reminding me of an awkward photo shoot I did with her in the sixties when she was a budding model. In my next and final scene, it flashes back to the shoot in which she wears a pink wig and my quilted button-flower dress and reveals herself to be a terrible model.

I was needed for two days, and it was set at an elegant café called Joe's in West London. Britt, Lulu and I spent most of the time talking and drinking coffee while Jennifer Saunders and Joanna Lumley did all the hard work. We were brought in for the fun parts and spent most of the day laughing – it was a wonderful break from work. I had met Joanna a few times before, but only got to know her better during the filming. She's a really charming person and very good company. When the episode came out a

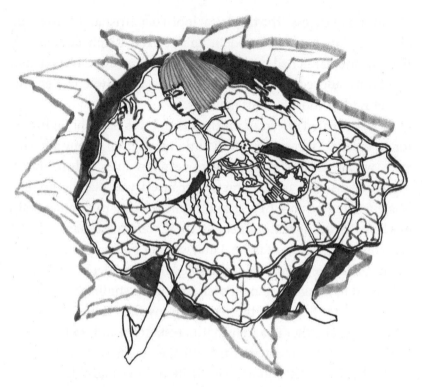

Joanna Lumley's Patsy in Absolutely Fabulous in my quilted caftan

few months later, I thought it was a success – it made me laugh at least. Fashion takes itself so seriously sometimes that it's good to see the ridiculousness in it.

More recently, I competed in *Celebrity Masterchef 2019* and appeared in *The Real Marigold Hotel*. I chose to do both shows because they were good exposure for the business. Whenever I am asked to do a television programme, most of the time I haven't watched it so I talk to my team to see if it would be a good fit and something I'd enjoy. I'd never do *Big Brother* – it seems far too exposing. *Masterchef*, on the other hand, seemed well suited because I like cooking, although it wasn't as much fun as I'd anticipated. I'm glad I did it, but it was hard work to make dishes in very little time – you try making a fully cooked bread-and-butter pudding in forty-five minutes. I had to do practice runs the evenings before to work out that my recipe was possible within the time constraints. I reached the semi-finals of the show, but not the final, which turned out to be a good thing because I'd been offered a place on *The Real Marigold Hotel*, where a group of celebrities find out if they would have a better retirement in India than the in UK. I wouldn't have had time to do both shows, and I'd have hated to turn down a trip to my beloved India. I hadn't been there for six years, and it felt like a fabulous reason to visit.

It was probably a bit of a culture shock for some of the eight other celebrities on the show, but I loved it. We travelled by night train to the ancient city of Madurai, where we saw its famous temple, made up of fourteen towers of beautifully painted stone statues. Perfectly carved deities look down at you from heights of up to one hundred and seventy feet. Everyone raves about the Taj Mahal, and understandably so, but I was blown away by the vivid majesty of Madurai Temple. We then stayed up all night for the Chithirai Festival, based in the same place, which celebrates the coronation of Meenakshi as the divine ruler of Madurai and her marriage to Sundareshwa. I doubt I would ever have witnessed it were it not for *The Real Marigold Hotel*. It was also a pleasure to visit my wonderful old embroidery studios in Chennai, co-founded and run by a talented woman called Annie Titus, where all of my beaded dresses were made. We needed to be available for filming from 8 a.m. each day, so I'd get up at 6 a.m. and head out to the streets to draw whatever inspired me, always making the most of every opportunity.

Doing TV shows enabled me to reconnect with people I had lost touch with – it was wonderful to be reunited with Britt Ekland and Lulu on *Absolutely Fabulous* and with Britt again on

The Real Marigold Hotel – and to meet new people I might not otherwise have encountered. One of my highlights from *The Real Marigold Hotel* was spending time with the cricket commentator Henry Blofeld and his golden voice, with which I was so familiar from listening to him on BBC Radio 4. He also knew India very well and was as enthusiastic about it as I was. As one grows older, there is a tendency to stop expanding friendship circles and to become insular. I refuse to do that. Making new friends is one of the most energizing things we can all do.

44

Cristal Champagne

A BOTTLE OF CRISTAL CHAMPAGNE may seem an unlikely item to associate with this quieter period in my design career, but it reminds me of one of my best and most loyal clients, the outrageous American socialite and philanthropist Mickey Easterling, who was as unconventional in life as she was in death. It was women like Mickey who enabled me to keep my business going when I was no longer flavour of the month. Her flamboyant style was never dictated by trends: she knew what she liked and wasn't about to drop me for Helmut Lang. Not that we ever discussed it, but Mickey would have found understatement quite awful. I never compromised on colour, drama or glamour so my collections still appealed to people who didn't gravitate towards minimalism or grunge. Stick to your guns and you will find your tribe, who will stick by you when times get tough. Mickey stuck by me until her extraordinary end.

Since the early seventies, I had acquired a number of wealthy individual clients whom I got to know personally. As a designer, selling your clothes to big department stores is fantastic exposure to new audiences, but there is something wonderful about creating something, one to one, with the women who wear your clothes. There are multiple benefits – profit margins, of course – but also you stand more chance of brand loyalty if you have worked with and met the client personally. It was also an opportunity to find out which pieces women in general loved, and what was working well in the marketplace.

I met the majority of my private clients through trunk shows – intimate fashion events usually held in stores where high-spending customers are presented with a new collection and, sometimes, meet the designer. The idea is that the more emotionally invested a client is in a label, the more likely they are to buy more. I would travel across the US to big department stores like Neiman Marcus and Saks to meet the customers, talking them through the collection and conducting fittings. The customer is important and it's vital to look after them. Every now and again, I would start working with a client I'd met at a trunk show on a private commission. I first met Mickey at one such event in the mid-eighties at a Houston-based department store called Sakowitz. She was based in New Orleans, the jazz-obsessed city in America's Deep South, which later became home to a multi-floor Saks where I hosted a number of trunk shows.

Mickey was a small woman at five feet, even more petite than me, but she was larger than life in every other regard. Her clothes were outlandish and she was never without a dramatic hat. She never left the house without her rhinestone diamond brooch, proclaiming 'Bitch', or without a loaded cigarette holder in her mouth. She had a wicked laugh, swore like a trooper and wintered in Morocco. She drove a black Lincoln Town Car, complete with a blue flashing light mounted on the dashboard, which she used when she was running late or needed to park somewhere she shouldn't. When at dinner in restaurants, on being gently asked to stop smoking inside, she would stop and apologize only to light up again a few minutes later. She was one of the most widely recognized figures in New Orleans, having married and divorced a rich local investor called Vern Easterling.

We all knew Mickey was a shrewd businesswoman who ran an import–export business, but she always remained mysterious about work, and I thought it rude to pry. Apparently, she invested in the Broadway comeback of singer and actress Lena Horne, which turned out to be very lucrative. Whatever she did to make her money, she was generous with her wealth, donating to many worthy charities.

Mickey's dinner parties, held at her palatial New Orleans lakefront house, were magnificent. My assistant Bouke and I would arrive in the beautiful two-storey foyer and watch Mickey float down the stately curved staircase to greet us, always in one of my dresses. We'd then be treated to endless supplies of Cristal champagne (she referred to it as medicine) and course after course, all cooked by Mickey but served by her butler. After dinner, we'd waddle into the French-themed living room or huge balcony to drink late into the evening. She was a wonderful host and great fun.

Every time my assistant and I visited the city, usually once a year, Mickey would order five or six dresses at a time. It was terrific business, but also a wonderful experience. Bouke and I would stay for a few nights and Mickey would take us to fabulous restaurants, plays and shows. She carried a Waterford crystal champagne flute in her handbag because she said you never knew when you might need one. On one occasion, at the Michelin-starred restaurant Commander's Palace, while we waited for our table, Mickey ordered a bottle of Cristal champagne, one of the most expensive kinds you can buy. When it was time to go to the table, the waiter asked if he could bring over the half-finished bottle. She looked at him in a sympathetically withering way and said, 'God, no, darling, I never drink already-opened champagne.'

Bottle of Cristal champagne

On another night, we arrived accidentally late to a concert with Irma Thomas, known as the soul queen of New Orleans. Mickey was so important to the city that the show had been held up until we'd been seated. I was stunned and mortified to find an orchestra, bigger even than the audience, patiently waiting for us. We sat down and were given a waiter each, who stood behind our chairs with individual bottles of champagne, which they poured for us all evening. Mickey didn't look remotely fazed by any of this: it was as normal to her as brushing her teeth.

Over the course of fifteen years, Mickey continued to be a loyal patron and I understand that her wardrobe was largely dedicated to my work. Her long-term support helped me stay afloat. When she died on 14 April 2014, aged eighty-three, after years of ailing health, she had a very specific, yet unusual wish: to attend her own funeral. She wanted to be embalmed and asked her daughter to stage an event at which she would be propped up wearing her best clothes and hat, with a champagne glass in one hand and her cigarette holder in the other. I wasn't invited to the funeral, but I do know that her wishes were obeyed.

A week after her death, a memorial took place in New Orleans's Saenger Theatre, where Mickey's embalmed body was positioned sitting on a wrought-iron bench, eyes closed, and dressed in her finery. On her head perched a statement black net hat, and a hot pink feather boa was wrapped round her shoulders. Her signature 'Bitch' brooch glittered against her bold printed outfit, and she held a flute of champagne in her cold hand. The space was designed to resemble Mickey's garden, filled with orchids and greenery. It really did look as if she'd simply thrown one of her famous parties, meandered into her backyard and fallen asleep. I heard that more than a thousand people came to pay their respects, drinking champagne and eating canapés at Mickey's final soirée. A jazz band played and New Orleans dining institution Galatoire's did the food. CNN broadcast it on TV; it was quite the happening. Aside from the corpse, it sounds like a rather nice party, which was exactly what Mickey would have wanted. I didn't design her final look, but I can't fault her originality. To you, Mickey, may we all be as irreverent, loyal and flamboyant.

45

Fashion and Textile Museum

CAN YOU CALL A MUSEUM an object? I'm not entirely sure, but for the purposes of this book I'm going to pretend you can. In 1996, I was still pedalling hard to keep the business going. There was still demand from America and I continued doing in-store trunk shows and appearances, but the mainstream fashion industry was looking in the other direction. It wasn't long after my storage unit had flooded and my precious garments had been soaked in water that I received a call from my great friend Andrew Logan that changed everything. 'Zandra, there's a large warehouse up for sale near me and you've always wanted to create a museum,' he said.

'Do you think I'm made of money?' I replied automatically, but I sat down and gave it some thought.

Andrew wasn't wrong. I had saved the original of every design I had ever made for posterity purposes. I had amassed thousands of garments that needed a better home than a storage unit prone to flooding, but my desire for a museum went way beyond myself. I'd always felt that textile designers never received fair representation for what they do. The Cinderellas of the fashion industry, they are never given credit for their role in making a garment look spectacular – the recognition always goes to the fashion designer. People don't realize that it's not just the shape or the cut of a piece that makes it special, but also the print or the weave. A textile designer's work is described as 'decorative' arts, whereas a painter's output is seen as fine art, when the two require exactly the same level of workmanship and creativity. I wanted to highlight and celebrate the talent and skill of the person designing the print or textile. Also, it had always seemed strange to me that there was no dedicated fashion and textile museum in London. The UK is terribly good at producing great fashion and textiles, but so many designers are forgotten because no one thought to preserve their work. The V&A has an excellent fashion collection and a wonderful textiles study room, but there was no standalone institution solely devoted to both industries. Textile designers get the worst deal of all. I wanted to change that and to give them the respect and recognition they deserved.

In short, I had big ideas, but my career was in such a precarious position that I didn't have the funds to go ahead. I decided to park my financial concerns temporarily and look at the property with Andrew's architect partner, Michael Davis. The building was a rundown former cash-and-carry warehouse in a forgotten, clapped-out area near London Bridge. It was situated on Bermondsey Street, which was lined with dilapidated buildings that had been boarded up since wartime bombings. There was only one shop, a café and a pub, none of which looked particularly appealing. It wasn't a district where anyone wanted to live then, except Andrew and Michael, who had been enticed by the relatively low prices and lived in a magical glass building five minutes' walk from the warehouse. Fellow Royal College alumnus printmaker and artist Norman Ackroyd had taken a punt on Bermondsey the decade before and was working from a disused industrial building there. Bermondsey Street now is full of galleries, restaurants and pubs, but back then it was a wasteland. None of the attractions that bring visitors to the area today existed – neither the Shard nor the Tate Modern had been created. To say it was an unfashionable area of London would be an understatement.

The building – a 1950s concrete-framed warehouse – was huge and needed a lot of work, but it had so much potential that I couldn't get it out of my head. I didn't want to become someone destined to spend the rest of my life moaning that the world had passed me by. The industry might have forgotten about me, but I still wanted to move forward with my life and do something worthwhile. At the very least it would give me something to do in my old age. Slowly, I began to formulate a plan. The warehouse could be a perfect way of consolidating my life: it had space for a museum, but it could also be where I lived, worked and stored my garments. There was a long area on the side of the building I could make into my print room and a studio for textile design and manufacturing. I decided to sell my Notting Hill home, which, since I'd bought it in 1973, had increased in value, and get rid of my Bayswater studio and Shepherd's Bush factory to buy the Bermondsey warehouse. That paid for the building, but I still needed to find the money for the renovation. I heard that the National Lottery was issuing grants to construct or renovate noteworthy buildings so I began investigating that option.

The next step was designing the museum's exterior. It had to be attention-grabbing but not so extreme that it wouldn't have mass appeal or pass UK building regulations. I didn't want to give the Lottery any reason to turn us down. I knew we needed a notable architect if we wanted to attract media publicity, so I met Zaha Hadid to discuss the project. But her designs were so bold that I worried they might hinder our chances of Lottery funding.

By that time, Salah and I had been together for a few years, and he introduced me to Ricardo Legorreta, a highly influential

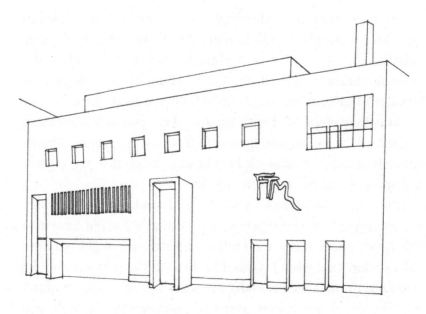

The Fashion and Textile Museum which I founded in 2003

Mexican architect. I was familiar with his work; he represented colour and purity. His designs were boldly modern, but without being alienating. He favoured geometric shapes, which were often drenched with blocks of orange, ochre, yellow and – best of all – hot pink. If Legorreta was to come on board, the museum would be his first building in Europe, an added bonus for us. I flew him from Mexico to London first class on my air miles and convinced him that we were a match made in Heaven, which, in terms of vision, we were. Both he and I were hell bent on bringing a splash of colour to London – the museum would be flamboyant and vivid, with simplicity of line. Ricardo never usually took on existing buildings, preferring to work on new builds, but, to my amazement, he agreed and created a scale model of his proposed design.

The shocking pink and orange exterior looked like a bird of paradise on our grey South London street. The interior would be equally colourful with a pink entrance hall, yellow walls and a neon-lit staircase. We enlisted David Humphries, following his wonderful work on our Californian home, to create a spectacular mosaic floor embedded with marble, semi-precious stones and glass. It all felt so exciting; momentum was truly growing. Unfortunately, another roadblock lay ahead. I submitted my Lottery bid and was rejected a few months later.

It was devastating news and I never found out why we were turned down. For a brief period, it looked as if I might have hit a dead end, which was when I talked to Salah. He might not have fully understood what I wanted to do with the museum, but he had faith in me. One of Salah's strengths was his ability to think round a problem – when your back was against the wall, you could always rely on him to devise a lateral solution. He suggested building apartments above the museum – we created nine in total – which we would pre-sell to finance the conversion of the property. I was to live in the top-floor penthouse (a happy perk of the job). Salah lent me the money for the construction work and found the labour through contacts he had made when rebuilding the Warner Bros. cinemas in the West End. I couldn't have done it without him. He also helped me form a fundraising arm in the US called the American Friends of the Zandra Rhodes Museum. So many of my Californian friends became key members, including Joan Quinn, Pat O'Connor, Judi Sanzo and Mindy Aisen. I have not forgotten their generosity.

The transformation took around seven years to complete, but it was worth it. On 8 May 2003, the Fashion and Textile Museum opened. My friend David Sassoon talked one of his clients, Princess Michael of Kent, whose wedding dress he'd designed, into becoming its patron and she cut the ceremonial ribbon at the entrance. She has been a wonderful supporter of the museum ever since, opening retrospectives for myself and David Sassoon. I was sixty-three at the time, and fresh from a hip replacement, not that I let that slow me down. Age is what you make of it. I was very keen that the space wasn't seen as 'The Zandra Rhodes Museum', so for the inaugural exhibition I invited seventy international designers to showcase their favourite dress. Thomas Heatherwick, who has since gone on to become one of the world's foremost designers, from architecture to the new Routemaster bus, was hired to create the look of the show.

The response was phenomenal: the most talented names in fashion, from John Galliano and Karl Lagerfeld to Alexander McQueen and Diane von Fürstenberg, nominated the dress they most wanted to be remembered by, along with a written explanation as to why. Diane understandably chose her iconic wrap dress, a radically breezy, flattering style that became a symbol of the seventies' Women's Liberation movement. Some of the other choices were more surprising, and proof of the emotional attachment designers have to their creations. One's favourite dress has as much emotion for the person who made it as it does for the person who wears it. John Galliano, for example, picked a demure fuchsia satin dress from his autumn/winter 1995 collection. Roses tumbled over the shoulder to give way to a plunging back. For all the visual drama and showmanship with which his name is associated, John is a designer who loves the romance and beauty of fashion most of all, and his choice reflected that. Alexander McQueen selected an unexpectedly feminine lace and chiffon cocktail dress with dragonfly detailing from his autumn/winter 2002 collection. It wasn't wildly avant-garde, which he was known for, but instead had a quiet fragility. Each dress displayed in the exhibition demonstrated technical skill and impressive workmanship, but really it was about the emotion our favourite clothes carry – how they become living objects once they have been instilled with memories and individuality. It was a huge success, in terms of media attention and turnout. There were some who said it was a vanity project, but I hope time has proven that untrue – the Fashion and Textile Museum was always bigger than me.

Over the years, we have staged countless exhibitions. Two have focused on my work, but mostly they have celebrated the contribution of unsung British designers, such as Bill Gibb and Thea Porter, and unrecognized textiles greats, including Lucienne Day and Pat Albeck. It takes an enquiring mind to run a successful museum – one must work out what people might be interested in and where there might be a gap in their knowledge. Next comes the necessary pragmatism: the costs, commercial appeal and the potential of an exhibition to travel to other museums. Every time a museum rents an exhibition from us, the Fashion and Textile Museum receives a fee – Anna Sui's 2017 retrospective started with us and has travelled around the world since.

In late 2006, we reached an agreement with East London-based Newham College, one of Europe's largest further-education colleges, to take over the day-to-day running of the Fashion and Textile Museum. The idea came about after FTM board member David Reeson brought Newham College principal and chief executive Martin Tolhurst to the board. Together, they saw a great opportunity for college students in linking the East End to central London. The FTM is now run by curator Dennis Nothdruft, who has worked closely with me in California and London. Today, it is still a museum, but also a hub of learning, ideas and networking for the fashion and clothing industry. Running the museum was a fabulous experience, and ultimately led to my being made a dame in 2014.

As my work underwent a revival in the late noughties, it became too difficult to juggle everything. There are also fundamental differences in the running of a fashion brand from running a fashion museum. If you're a dress designer like me, you make a garment and create a textile design, and if people like it they buy it; if you run a museum, you have to envisage and curate exhibitions that you then need to fund to stage. Both jobs require commitment to succeed, and I was glad to hand over the reins of the museum to Newham College. I have close ties to the museum as an adviser and my studio is still in the same building. I continue to live on the top floor in my rainbow-coloured penthouse, which is my very favourite place to be. I love sitting on my plant-filled roof terrace (nothing untoward, these days) with a cup of tea, looking at the new buildings going up around the city.

What I didn't realize when Salah and I set about creating the museum was that we would also be creating my dream home. My apartment, spread over two floors, is a kaleidoscopic homage to the mood-boosting properties of colour. It is filled with objects – many of which I have described in this book – from my past and present that bring me joy, like the artwork of friends such as Duggie Fields and Andrew Logan, photographs of people I love (there are a great many of Salah and me) or ceramics by Kate Malone and Carol McNicoll. Everything is tinged with an eye-popping flash of something – fuchsia, lime green, electric blue, turmeric orange. I don't believe in the idea that you can have too much of a good thing.

The Fashion and Textile Museum is my little colourful hub among a whole lot of rain and grey. It is an institution that will go on after I've gone, and I can't help but feel tremendously proud of it.

46

Damehood Medal

MY PINK HAIR HAS OFTEN caused people to mistake me for being wild or anti-establishment, but I am quite the opposite. When I was thirteen, my family and I walked four miles to a friend's house to watch Queen Elizabeth II's Coronation as we didn't have our own television, a moment that marked the start of my love of the Royal Family. To be appointed Commander of the Order of the British Empire (CBE) by Her Majesty in 1997 was an unquestionably huge honour for me. Then to be made a dame for services to British fashion and textiles in 2014 remains the greatest achievement of my life. After fighting so long for my work to be valued, particularly in my own country following success in America, Australia and Asia, it felt fabulous to be appreciated and to receive the ultimate recognition for having contributed something useful and, importantly, meaningful. To this day, I still have no idea who nominated me for either award. If anyone who did so is reading this, thank you very much. Please make yourself known to me and I'd love to have you round for one of my salmon dinners.

Salah, my sister Beverley and one of the museum's investors, Priscilla Kauff, joined me at Buckingham Palace for that first investiture in 1997. In the weeks running up to the event, I agonized about what to wear. The brief was very specific – occasionwear – and whatever I chose had to represent me as an individual while also being appropriate. In the end, I went for a bold black and pink Stephen Jones hat, which looked rather like a Zaha Hadid-designed building, and a purple velvet devoré coat with a big shaggy fur collar. Purple has been associated with royalty since ancient times, so it felt like an apt shade and was colourful enough for me to feel true to myself. To finish the look, I painted my nails deep burgundy and outlined my eyes in black kohl. My hair was, of course, pink.

Despite feeling comfortable in my outfit, the whole day was overwhelming. When we arrived at Buckingham Palace, all the recipients and guests were separated. My three guests were taken into a grand ballroom while I was taken to another room. A man with spurs dangling from the back of his shoes clomped in and boomed at us that when our time came we were to move three paces forward, then curtsy or bow. The Queen would ask us two questions, at which point we were to retreat. I wish I could remember what the Queen said to me, or what I said to her, but my mind just went foggy and it's all a bit of a blur. I do recall, though, that she had a blue handbag, which she popped onto the throne before she turned around to greet everyone.

By comparison, everything from the day I received my damehood on 13 February 2015 remains crystal clear. I was dressed in head-to-toe blue with one of my fabulous prints. I accessorized with a lovely Piers Atkinson hat shaped like a rhinestone egg, a chunky silver necklace and blue mirrored brooches, both by Andrew Logan. I was once again accompanied by Beverley, Joan

Quinn and also by my dear friend David Sassoon, who had arranged for us to arrive in a chauffeur-driven car. I felt wonderfully grand.

As the only person to receive a damehood that day, I was called up first. From their beautiful velvet seats, David, Joan and Beverley watched Princess Anne present me with my medal in the Throne Room. As I dutifully answered Anne's questions, the woman next to my sister turned to her, looked at me and whispered, 'I wouldn't have worn *that* outfit, would you?' My sister, ever my chief defender, replied coolly, 'No, but that's my sister and she has.' The poor woman was mortified. Beverley, of course, found it very funny, consoled her and said that people were often taken aback by what I wore. I didn't mind one bit: I was used to standing out from the crowd.

It's not every day that you're made a dame and I celebrated by throwing a party at the Fashion and Textile Museum. Everyone wore crowns (mine was a mirrored silver style, another artwork from Andrew) and I greeted my guests on a makeshift throne that I covered with red velvet. I have a lovely picture of David Sassoon pinning my damehood onto my silver swirl dress just before the party got going. All sorts of friends from over the years passed through that evening, from revered fashion journalist Hilary Alexander and ballet dancer Wayne Sleep to Duggie Fields and Betty Jackson.

It was an evening I'll never forget, which is good because, unfortunately, I don't know where my damehood medal is. I feel terrible about misplacing it. I thought I'd given it to Beverley for safe keeping, but she assures me she's only ever stored my CBE, which – in the absence of my damehood – is what I've drawn to accompany this chapter. You'll have to take my word that a DBE looks very similar to a CBE, and just has an additional cut-steel

My CBE medal

cross with an engraved gold portrait of King George V in the centre; it is rather beautiful.

Receiving this accolade made me feel I'd really made an impact. I'd like to be remembered not just for my contribution to fashion and textiles, but for doing things differently, of which my DBE is a sparkly, shiny affirmation. I'm sure it'll turn up.

47

Lion Shield

OUT ON MY ROOF TERRACE, screwed into an orange wall, stands a rather imposing golden shield around a metre and half tall. Made from fibreglass, it is carved in the shape of a roaring, rather angry-looking lion. The eyes and teeth are painted a glittery silver and its mane splays out in squiggly rings until they hit the floor. This object was one of the costumes for *The Magic Flute*, the first opera I worked on in 2001. As if building a museum wasn't enough to keep me busy, in the late nineties I branched out into opera.

The relationship between fashion and the stage is well established. Coco Chanel did it first when she created ballet costumes for Ballets Russes' *Le Train Bleu* in 1924, and a great number of fashion designers have followed her lead, including Christian Dior, Halston, Christian Lacroix and Alexander McQueen. Opera is one of the most theatrical artforms, so it's the perfect medium for a designer with an eye for drama to sink their teeth into. There are different requirements for making costumes, but it fundamentally needs a heightened sense of imagination. The world of costume design makes me feel like a fairy with a magic wand. There's no need to worry about commercialism, whether or not a garment might sell. Instead a designer is free to create

The Lion Shield I designed for Mozart's opera, The Magic Flute

fantastical pieces that can be wildly outlandish. The costumes need to be bold enough for the audience to see them from a distance, which suits me very well.

My entrée to opera took place in San Diego, where I was living with Salah. During one trip there in 1998, he and I hosted a dinner party attended by Ian Campbell, then the director of the San Diego Opera. He wasn't a fashion follower but was so taken by my work that not long after he asked if I might consider designing costumes for an upcoming production of *The Magic Flute*. It was wonderful to be asked, especially as I knew very little about opera and certainly had no experience in designing operatic costumes. I had created costumes for *Romeo and Juliet on Ice* in 1983, which, of course, had won me an Emmy, but I had never conceived anything specifically for the stage. I was nervous, but Ian was persuasive. He told me he had been bowled over by the design of my home in San Diego. The colours, furnishings and fabrics had convinced him I'd do a good job of operatic costume design. What sealed the deal was his argument that the stage presented a larger canvas than even a catwalk to project my vision. Opera was so dramatic and over the top that my imagination would have very few limits. I accepted his offer and got to work.

I was open about my lack of opera knowledge and asked the team to teach me as much as they could. David Hockney had been doing stage designs for decades, and I'd seen how he'd immersed himself in the narrative and music. I decided to do the same. All I knew about *The Magic Flute* was that it was by Mozart, but I soon found out that it's ultimately a love story in which a prince rescues a princess using magical musical instruments. The director Michael Hampe explained the meaning of each scene and gave me a better understanding of each character and what they stood for. From there, I would develop an appropriate costume.

In the main, Michael and I got on very well. We had only one real creative disagreement, which was when he asked that I dress some of the characters in black T-shirts. *Black*. I had never worked with black or grey and wasn't about to start for the opera. It's an explosion of colour or nothing. I called Ian and told him there was no point in me working on the production unless the costumes looked recognizably mine. He spoke to Michael and I was given *carte blanche*.

My imagination was freer than ever before. Unlike with ready-to-wear, there was no focus on aesthetic detail. Practical detail, yes, the singers had to be able to sing, but artistically, I focused on creating broad-brush statements that had strong visual appeal. Every seat in the house needed to be able to see clearly. The biggest difference between opera and catwalk shows is the size of those wearing the clothes. Opera singers tend to be larger, so it's a case of creating spectacular costumes that also fit wonderfully. The construction of a garment needs to be different – it's not just about scaling up but considering the details – for example, the positioning of buttons to prevent gaping. It can't be so tight that the performer can't breathe. I wanted to make a size-eighteen singer feel as princess-like as anyone else in the cast. Only a shoddy or inexperienced designer would be unable to do that.

I learnt how to cater to the specific needs of singers. For instance, you have to make sure their ears aren't covered. You might think it would be deafening to be on stage while someone sings opera next to you, but it's important that the singer is able to hear the orchestral accompaniment. It's a very delicate balance. And – no matter how curious the costume – they must always be able to see the conductor, whether he is in the pit or on a tiny screen. Fabrics can't be too heavy or warming as the act of singing produces terrific body heat. Indian silk worked very well because it's so breathable. We developed man-made feathers – fabric on the bias backed by a tough plastic strip, which meant that even when the performers were moving on stage the feathers didn't break and still held their form. It was perhaps one of the only times in my life where I was forced to go bigger with my designs. One print I designed to be worn by the dragon character wasn't bold enough when we tried it out on stage.

I learnt so much over the course of the two years I worked on *The Magic Flute*. The team were magicians who knew how to construct a garment in a way that truly popped on stage. My drawings were interpreted in the most fabulous ways – it was a completely new form of storytelling for me and I was utterly absorbed by it. For some costumes, I drew on previous designs from my ready-to-wear, then adapted them. One key character, the Queen of the Night, wore blue swirling panniers, an iteration of a gold piece from my 1980 'Elizabethan Collection'. When the Queen made her stage entrance, she floated earthward from the ceiling in a huge cradle of crescent moon and cascading purple gossamer. I designed it to look as if the sky was attached to her back with a cloak that filled the whole set. That costume inspired me to create a 'Queen of the Night' collection for my own line back in London, but for the opera it was a case of creating drama on top of the natural fantasy of my designs.

The object I've chosen for this chapter, the lion shield, came about as an alternative costume for performers dressed as lions pulling the king's chariot. I wasn't keen on the silly body suits that were usually worn by performers playing the lions, so instead I conceived the roaring shields, which the performers held in front of themselves as the chariot arrived on stage. They have a much more imperious air as grand lions.

Ahead of the 2001 opening, there was a buzz around the show – in part due to my involvement. Some of the costumes were previewed at the Athenaeum Library in the nearby town of La Jolla, which attracted further attention. When it came to opening night, I looked out from behind the stage curtain to see an audience of three thousand, all wearing pink feather boas in recognition of my hair. I was completely overwhelmed and I don't think my feet touched the ground for weeks afterwards. The production went on to win an award for Best Live Theatrical Styling in the annual Hollywood Make-up Artists and Hair Stylist Guild Awards in 2002.

In 2004, after the success of *The Magic Flute*, I was invited to create the costumes *and* the sets for the San Diego production of Georges Bizet's *The Pearl Fishers*. The less famous cousin of Bizet's *Carmen*, it wasn't an opera I was familiar with, but I did the initial reading and agreed. It was a huge challenge to do both costume and set design, but I couldn't wait to get started. *The Pearl Fishers*, set in Ceylon, now Sri Lanka, tells the story of Zurga, a leader of a fishing village, and his friend Nadir, and the love triangle that ensues when the priestess Leïla shows up to bless the pearl harvest. I decided to travel to Sri Lanka on my way back from a planned trip to India for research purposes, sketching everything I saw. I was told the sky was the limit when it came to design because Bizet had never been to Ceylon so I was free to use my imagination as much as I liked.

The villagers were dressed in varied shades of blue, all of which were printed in my London studio, and the religious characters were decked in shocking pink and orange. I think that colours make people happy, and *The Pearl Fishers* isn't a tragedy, so I Zandrified the palm trees to be fuchsia and turquoise. I created the set to look like a fantasy land by the sea. The fabrics looked rich and detailed, but some were originally inexpensive Indian bedspreads and others were mass-market polyester saris bought at a warehouse outside LA. I decorated them with Zandra Rhodes prints – shells, ferns and waves – in my London print studio. People don't come to me for realism, they want fantasy. For this particular job, originality was essential if my Bizet production was to be bought and rented by other theatres outside San Diego. It ended up as perhaps the most colourful opera production in history and travelled to eighteen other cities around America, including San Francisco, Miami and New York.

In 2007, I was enlisted by Houston Opera to work on Verdi's intense opera *Aida*, once again designing both costumes and set. I was thrilled to find out that the production was being planned around me, which is very unusual. It transpired that Verdi and I had very similar ideas about vibrant, eye-catching colour, which laid a strong foundation for the production. The story was set in Egypt, a country I had been lucky enough to visit more than twenty years before when it had inspired my 'Secrets of the Nile' collection. I looked back at my sketchbooks from that trip, which helped to develop stage concepts based around an evil eye and pyramids. I chose colours that had stood out to me during my stay – metallic gold, brilliant turquoise, scorching orange, yellow sand and lapis-lazuli blue. I created a modern take on historic Egyptian costume with pleating, headdresses that resembled birds, hand-printed cloaks and beaded detailing. One of the unique properties of my work, aside from the colour, is that I trained as a textile designer – I make and love pattern. In my own collections, they're usually hand-printed on silk chiffons. For the stage, they're hand-printed on existing fabrics so that the eye is overwhelmed with the pattern and the ear is bowled over by music. I want my operas to be a complete sensory overload.

We had one small glitch with *Aida* – the conservative crowds of Houston, where the production was opening. I had envisaged all the Egyptian women authentically bare-breasted (as seen in the hieroglyphics), planning to clothe the singers in skin-tight body stockings with breasts painted on top. The performers' modesty would have been protected, but it would have looked realistically nude. There was no way I'd have them go stark naked, but the director Anthony Freud put his foot down. 'This is the Bible Belt!' he cried. As a compromise, the bodysuits had to be raised to cover the breasts so that you couldn't see anything at all, which kept everyone happy.

Aida first opened in Houston in 2007, travelling to San Francisco in 2010 and London with the English National Opera in 2011. Someone said it looked as though I'd taken Egyptian tomb paintings and turned up the colour – something like restoring an old film, bringing back the original richness.

My favourite part of opera design is seeing the whole thing come to life on stage – the magical combinations of music and colour. It's impossible to see that in the costume sketches and the preliminary set designs, and it usually takes around three years from inception to production. The workload is immense, but the pay-off is huge. Every now and again one of the productions will be rented by another theatre and I'm invited to oversee the set and costume design again – in 2022 *The Pearl Fishers* opened in Dallas, Texas, but I sadly couldn't travel because of Covid.

My stage career has also turned me into an opera fan – I can hum along to it just as happily as I do to Abba. I'd happily do another so I hope a director somewhere will think of me and my colourful stage spectacles, and give me a call.

48

Valentino Loveblade Collaboration

IN THE EARLY NOUGHTIES, Christian Dior's new star designer – a talented South Londoner named John Galliano – started filling his collections with beautiful, floating printed chiffon dresses. It was the start of a number of homages to my work that formed a Zandra Rhodes renaissance. Over the next decade and at the start of the 2010s my influence began appearing on catwalks once more, from Marc Jacobs to Max Mara, from Alberta Ferretti to Stella McCartney right through to Kate Moss's sellout Topshop line – swirling surreal prints that formed the silhouette of the garment, uneven handkerchief hemlines, billowing floaty shapes, bejewelled safety pins, and pleated lamé. The renewed interest in my design vocabulary was acknowledged in *Vogue* in 2010, although for the most part wasn't explicitly acknowledged by the brands themselves. I chose to take it as a compliment.

Some of the homages were strikingly similar to my original designs to the extent that some of the prints almost looked as if they had been traced from my sketchbooks, but knock-offs are a reality in fashion. They appear not just on market stalls, but also on the runways of one's peers. You can either become obsessed and eaten up by the injustice, or you can choose to see it another way. I choose to see it as evidence that I have had long-term influence in an industry I love. Whether credited or not, those tributes proved that my work had lasting value and that was vindicating. If I became angry over every copycat design, I'd be too bogged down to see them as a positive or to continue with new work. I'm no multi-millionaire, but my business still exists, and I have seen that my approach to design has influenced countless others. There's no point in becoming sour about what is essentially proof of my worth.

As the years went on, I continued working on the museum and the operas, and also on numerous collaborations. I did make-up with MAC in 2006, then ready-to-wear with Topshop in 2007 and Marks & Spencer in 2008. My print room was busy again, and my work was being discovered by a new audience. The American designer Anna Sui, who had been inspired by me after attending the Circle in the Square show in New York as a young student, invited me to work on a line of prints for her spring/summer 2016 collection. I revived some of my most iconic designs, returning to my archives for collections with British label Three Graces London in 2019, and another exclusive line for luxury online store Matches Fashion in 2016.

The biggest collaboration in recent years arrived in summer 2016 when I was approached by Valentino designer Pierpaolo Piccioli to work on a line of prints. He was working on his first solo collection for the Italian brand after his former design partner Maria Grazia Chiuri had left to become creative director at Christian Dior. I had been a fan of their work at Valentino from afar – I found the use of colour and simplicity to create feminine but strong-looking clothes very compelling. The collections expressed fantasy differently from how I did it, but in a way that I could very much appreciate and admire. Both of us have the same objective of wanting to make women look and feel beautiful.

Pierpaolo called me from his office in Italy to ask if I would design something new for him. He wanted to create a new version of the Hieronymus Bosch painting *The Garden of Earthly Delights*, which depicts the Garden of Eden on the left, Hell on the right, and human depravity in the centre. It's an unsettling, almost surrealist image that I was already familiar with, and the opportunity to reinterpret it through a fashion lens was an exciting proposition. The detailed landscape and the fantastical imagery were ripe for Zandrifying. Pierpaolo said he wanted to work with artistic personalities who had lived through transformations, and although Bosch and I came from very different time periods, he saw synergy in the way we approached the world. We both, he said, had been strongly connected to the epochs we had lived through, but looked at them with originality of thought. It's not every day one is compared to a Renaissance Flemish painter, and I took it as a compliment. I was thrilled to be asked, especially to be on a project as important as his first solo collection. He was writing a new chapter in his career and I was thrilled that he wanted me to play a key role.

Within weeks of our initial call, Pierpaolo and his team visited my studio in London. I gave them free rein in the archives. We looked through my previous work, including my 1974 Uluru print and my sixties lipstick designs. I wanted to bring colour and a Pop sensibility – Heaven and Hell portrayed through acidic and pungent shades of pink and violet. I picked out different motifs from the painting and expanded on them. My lipstick prints were turned into blades that sliced through hearts, which was the object I chose to mark this significant collaboration.

These were embroidered with beading onto swooshing dresses. I took my hand-drawn wiggle signatures along with the cacti from my Uluru design, then drew and printed magical palm trees, animals and birds for added whimsy. Once I'd created the artworks, they were sent to Italy where they were developed by Pierpaolo's highly skilled team. The scenes appeared on jackets and gorgeous georgette dresses, some floor-length and others shorter and more playful. Flying flocks of swallows on diaphanous silk and intarsia pieces were woven on a loom warping machine designed by Leonardo da Vinci. The whole process from start to finish took perhaps a month. It was fast, but well executed. I was very pleased with the results, which looked as if I'd drawn them straight onto the garments. They looked like Zandra Rhodes prints using Valentino's feminine silhouettes as a canvas. It was all so delicate and light, juxtaposed with highly saturated punk pink.

I was invited to the Paris Fashion Week show in October 2016. It was one of the only times in my life when I've worn black as Pierpaolo gave me a beautiful Valentino black dress to wear on the day, which was then tailored to fit me perfectly. If I must wear black, it might as well be bespoke Valentino. I felt no nerves on the day of the show. It was the first time my work had seen a catwalk for more than a decade, but I was bolstered by Pierpaolo's confidence in me. Watching the designs float by as I sat on the front row was very moving. Fashion is an industry that craves new ideas, and sometimes I have worried, especially as I have grown older, that I'll finally run out of creative steam. That show confirmed not only to me but to everyone else in the industry that I certainly hadn't.

I went on to work with Valentino on his 2018 resort show, which was unveiled in New York in May 2017. It was a sportier

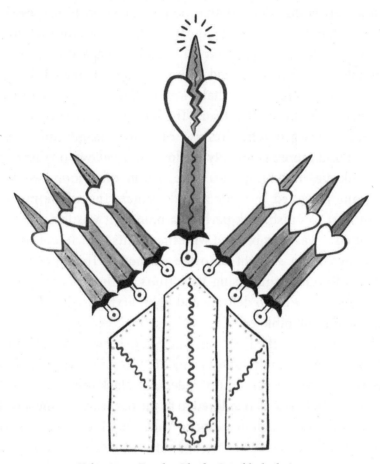

Valentino x Zandra Rhodes Loveblade design

collection, but no less pretty. My Pop Art-inspired lipstick and lip motifs were embroidered on youthful mini dresses and varsity jackets. Again, it was a pleasure to see my designs re-imagined in a different, more relaxed context.

My collaboration with Pierpaolo, who has since become a friend, was reinforcement that ideas *will* come with the right stimulus. The trick is in knowing who you are while remaining open to the world around you and remembering that great design will always come round again. It's not easy to become a successful fashion designer, but retaining your place within a business that thrives on the next big thing is even harder. My mantra has always been never to give up. Through my work with the museum and opera design, I diversified. Rather than get sucked in by trends that wouldn't have suited me, I stuck to my guns and weathered the storm. As my work gained new relevance and traction, I was hit by another near-fatal challenge – this time to my health.

49

Yoga Mat

I WAS LYING ON MY lilac yoga mat in early spring 2020 when I first felt the cancer. My bile duct was stuffed full of a rare, aggressive form of the disease called cholangiocarcinoma, which has one of the worst prognoses of any cancer. A determined, inconvenient tumour was edging its way towards my stomach and pancreas. Of course, I didn't know what it was back then, but it was the initial indication that all was not well.

My friend Andrew used to hold yoga classes for friends in my penthouse because the light's good and it's a wide-open space. He's been a practising yogi since he was fifty and is now a trained teacher. I never usually went to his classes – they used to start at 6 p.m. when I was still working. I certainly didn't have time to be lying around on my back in the early evenings, but it turned out doing exactly that was what saved my life. In February 2020, I found myself at home in London after a period of extensive travel. Salah had died eight months before and I'd been trying to con-solidate my life in the UK following decades spent living half the year in San Diego together. Although I was still adapting to a world without him, it felt good to be in one place for the first time in years.

One evening that February, Andrew persuaded me to join him

for one of his yoga sessions. We were all lying on our backs on lilac mats when he told us, in that calming voice of his, to breathe deeply. I inhaled slowly, and found my stomach felt full. It seemed strange because I hadn't eaten all day. I very rarely ate three meals a day because I was working and didn't bother. There was always something more important that needed doing. It struck me as unusual – to feel full on an empty stomach – and something told me I should get myself checked out, so I phoned my doctor, who arranged for me to have a scan. I honestly didn't give it much thought – in fact, I felt pleased I'd taken the time out of work to organize the initial appointment. Job done.

Around a week later, my doctor Michael Harding called and said he had done some research and found an oncologist who had examined my X-rays. The results were in and a specialist, Dr Khurum Khan, would be looking after me from here, and wanted to see me in person. His voice was neutral, using the very specific tone that medical professionals have honed over years of giving bad news and advised that I bring a relation. Of course, I knew then that there was trouble ahead. I suspected there was some sort of growth, but I wasn't worried. I called my sister Beverley and her husband David to come with me. We had taken each other for granted until that point, only speaking every few months. Our lives had always been so different – she had dedicated her life to her family, and I had dedicated mine to work. Still, she and her husband agreed instantly to accompany me to my Harley Street appointment.

As soon as I saw Dr Khan and he gazed at me with the professional tragedy face I knew it was time to stiffen my resolve. 'The test results were not quite what we hoped,' he began, before telling me I had cancer in the bile duct. 'You have probably six months.' It was too advanced to be treated surgically, and our best chance of treating it would be a mixture of chemotherapy and immunotherapy. Even so, the odds weren't good, he said. My immediate response was that I had far too much work to do. My planned Ikea homeware collaboration wasn't due out for another eighteen months and I simply had to keep going. If Dr Khan was surprised by my reaction, he didn't show it.

It was at this point that Dr Harding, who had joined the meeting on Zoom, said, 'Zandra, there's a question you haven't yet asked.' I couldn't think what it might be. 'You haven't asked if you'll lose your hair.' I replied, 'Well, that's because I can wear one of my wigs if I need to. I have a blue wig, and a great pink wig.' My sister didn't see my diagnosis in quite the same way and burst into tears. I didn't know what to say or how to make her feel better. I was glad her husband was there.

I don't understand why I wasn't scared. Cancer is frightening – we all know people who have had it. It's a condition that instantly provokes sad memories. My mother had lung cancer and it killed her within months. She handled it with similar pragmatism; she was bent on making the most of the time she had left by not letting emotion overcome her. For me, I don't think I even thought about it in that much depth. All I knew was that I had to get organized: if I was about to die, I needed to put my affairs in order.

The diagnosis was a godsend in the sense that it pulled me together. I had a legacy worth preserving – my seven-man team and I set about going through the six thousand garments and lengths of printed chiffon I had saved and squirrelled away since I'd begun my career more than sixty years before. I needed to work out what would go to which museum and what should be sold at auction. Each garment needed to be catalogued. I had to decide what should happen to my apartment and how I would live what was left of my life.

When I arrived home after my diagnosis, my head was filled only with business. Morbid thoughts of mortality didn't come into it. I've never felt as if I have enough time to do what I need to do, but if the doctor was right, the clock was really ticking and I needed to get moving. I decided to embark on the recommended treatment but made sure I had a 'Do Not Resuscitate' order in place. I formed the Zandra Rhodes Foundation, a charity that ensures future generations of designers, artists, researchers, students and educators are able to study my life and designs, with an emphasis on my methods and techniques. Beginning in the mid-1960s and continuing to the current day, the Foundation is cataloguing my six thousand garments, printed textiles, drawings, accessories, fashion films, Kodatraces (special photographic papers used in the process of exposing an image onto silk screen), silk screens, press cuttings, personal memorabilia and collected artworks. A central collection will stay with the Foundation and the remaining material will be donated to permanent collections of major museums across the world. I am incredibly proud that my Foundation has formed partnerships with leading universities, especially De Montfort University in Leicester, which now holds my working archive of press cuttings, fashion films, licences and opera designs, and the University for the Creative Arts, which is continuing to expand its digital library of over 500 of my original garments. It was and is so important to me that my work be remembered and I sincerely wish it to be used for the purposes of learning, creativity and imagination.

Since the swinging sixties, I've adapted to incorporate digital methods into my design process, but I strongly believe in the benefits of hands-on research and the beauty of handcrafted techniques. I love meeting people full of enthusiasm and new ideas and it is exciting to think how my work may live on through them. I made Piers Atkinson, my former intern and now a hugely talented milliner and university lecturer, the head of the

Foundation. He not only understands my work inside out, but who I am and how I want my legacy to be used for the inspiration of generations to come. We hope that my rainbow penthouse will form the hub of the Foundation's activity and that it will be kept as it is so that researchers will be able to see how I worked and lived.

I realized very quickly that I couldn't go public with my news. A terminal-cancer diagnosis would be bad for business – I wouldn't have been given any new commissions and risked losing those I had already agreed to. I also had a head count of seven people to consider; I couldn't let them or my company down. I told only a few people: Beverley and her husband David, David Sassoon, Duggie Fields and Kelly, my then PA who now runs my press. That March, I began three months of chemotherapy, and while my pink hair thinned, it didn't fall out. Not that I worried about that as I had my wigs to fall back on should I have gone totally bald.

Not long after my diagnosis, Covid-19 arrived and the world entered an enforced lockdown. The pandemic was monstrous in so many ways, but for me there was a silver lining in that it allowed me the space to deal with my disease privately. It enabled me to hide it from the public. No one needed to know how ill I was, that I had to lie down between treatments, because no one was seeing anyone. If I had to do an interview, I could do it via Zoom in full make-up and take a break afterwards. No one knew that I was struggling to walk and that I was increasingly breathless. For me, Covid came at the right time. I would not and could not lose my work. It has become clearer to me than ever over the course of writing this book that diving into my work is the only way I know of dealing with a crisis, and it's no surprise that it's also how I managed cancer. It pulled me through.

After the chemotherapy came the immunotherapy, which is a

relatively new cancer treatment. Cancer is a malign but devilishly clever thing. These drugs disguise themselves as chemical markers that tell your body's natural immune system to recognize and attack the cancerous cells. I had to travel to the clinic on Harley Street every three weeks to be pumped full of these magical drugs through an IV drip. London was a ghost town. Without its people it felt hollow, a frustrated concrete desert. I couldn't bring friends or family with me to the appointments, which was hard. At one point, I was asked to self-administer the drugs with injections, which eliminated the need to make as many in-office visits for each dose. I didn't like the idea of that one bit. Two artist friends with cancer, Duggie Fields and Janet Nathan, had both been asked to do the same during Covid, but had refused.

Dr Harding laughed at my protests. 'Zandra, you'll soon learn to do it if you want to avoid coming to a clinic more than you need to in the middle of a pandemic.'

Well, that set me straight.

Everyone always wants to know when you've had a life-threatening disease whether it has changed your perspective on the world. Perhaps it sounds trite to talk about the upside of cancer, but rather than shifting my outlook on the universe, my illness brought me closer to my sister. From the day of my diagnosis, Beverley and I were talking once, sometimes twice a day. She became a tower of strength for me. Her career has been raising a family and supporting them. I don't think I ever really appreciated that for the huge achievement it is until cancer arrived and she wrapped me up in support and care. I'm not sure that I realized what her job involved, the dedication, energy, labour and skill required to run a family. I admire her hugely. When I was finding it hard to walk, she would collect me from the clinic and help me back to my bedroom at home. It was lockdown and the rules were so strict that we felt we couldn't and shouldn't break them. She and my brother-in-law would Zoom me every day from their house and make sure I tried to walk so that I never lost the impetus to do so.

When it came to self-administering the immunotherapy medication, I would video call my brother-in-law, who was conveniently a GP, and he'd tell me where to aim. I always asked him to look as I injected myself, which somehow made it feel less difficult. Beverley and I still talk every day. I used to think if I got very ill, I'd take myself to Switzerland where voluntary euthanasia is legal. I thought it would be a simple solution but I don't know any more. My sister has said she'd look after me if it came to that.

I still have immunotherapy every three weeks, when I take myself to Harley Street before returning to the studio to work. The treatment has been a success and I've been in remission for around eighteen months. For the most part, I've been left relatively unscathed – I am more breathless than I was before and I avoid stairs now. I start work a little later at around 8.30 a.m. rather than 7 a.m. and I tend to finish at 6 p.m. If Andrew hosts one of his early evening yoga classes, these days I can usually make it. I am still probably more active than most eighty-three-year-olds at the time of writing this.

The thing is, immunotherapy isn't a cure, it just buys you time in whatever way you choose to spend it. Cancer will probably be the thing that kills me, but maybe not. Maybe I'll be crushed by an avalanche of my archived garments with my sparkly pink trainers sticking out from underneath, like a colourful version of the Wicked Witch of the East from *The Wizard of Oz*. We can't really know, but I refuse to wallow in self-pity. I have had a fabulous life and I've already outlived my initial prognosis six times over. I have started working with the Alan Morement Memorial Fund (AMMF), a cholangiocarcinoma charity, because I was horrified to find out that more than half of those who receive the same diagnosis are not given any treatment.

No doctor can concretely tell me how long I've extended the show by, but I think I've got another few years in me. That gives me an opportunity to get myself together and get things done. I don't have time to worry about how long I have left: each day passes so quickly. I live for the present and I urge you all to do the same.

50

Piers Atkinson Hat

THE YEAR 2022 WAS A great time to be a dame. That spring, Buckingham Palace called and asked if I wanted to be part of the Queen's Platinum Jubilee Pageant to mark the seventieth year of her reign. Of course I said yes immediately – what an honour to travel through cheering crowds in London to pay tribute to Queen and country. It was right up my alley.

I was to ride through the city along a three-kilometre route from Horse Guards Parade to Buckingham Palace in a vintage open-topped Jaguar. I was one of seven dames to be chosen, alongside Twiggy, an old friend from the sixties, Joan Collins, whom I've known for decades through her late sister Jackie, as well as the dancer Darcey Bussell, House of Lords peer Floella Benjamin, choreographer Arlene Phillips and celebrity chef Prue Leith. It meant an awful lot to be asked – there were many dames, but only seven Jags. I was chuffed to be chosen.

We were each allowed to invite a partner to travel with us in the car, so I invited darling David Sassoon, who has a long history in dressing the Royal Family. I knew he'd be as delighted to be there as I was. There was no dress code, so I decided to wear the colours of the Union flag, red, white and blue. It was an occasion when only the most jubilant of outfits would do, so

I chose my red lipstick-printed trouser suit, an Andrew Logan bracelet and asked Piers Atkinson to make me a suitable hat. He makes such joyful, dramatic creations, and he didn't disappoint, coming up with a fittingly royal blue pill-box-style

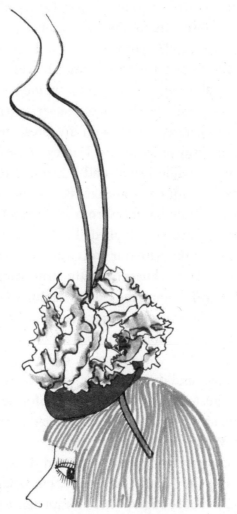

Me in my Piers Atkinson hat at the Platinum Jubilee of Her Majesty Queen Elizabeth II

topped with a cluster of white peonies from which rise two wandering red tendrils.

On the day, we were all asked to find our way to a government building near St James's Park for 9.30 a.m. sharp. What a riotous crowd it was – models Kate Moss, Naomi Campbell and Erin O'Connor were nestled in one corner; Joan Collins and her husband Percy Gibson in another. A Union-flag-jacketed Cliff Richard sat at a table, and Olympians Mo Farah and Kelly Holmes stood nearby. The gardener Alan Titchmarsh, wearing a blue suit, red tie and white shirt, was talking to *Coronation Street* star William Roache and Basil Brush. Nicole Scherzinger, the former Pussycat Dolls singer, was there with TV presenter Holly Willoughby. Dancers Wayne Sleep and Darcey Bussell appeared in deep conversation, while David and I made good use of the breakfast buffet (Continental and above average in standard). There were so many familiar faces from all different media that it felt quite trippy, and everyone looked like they were having a ball, all of us hanging around with our croissants and jam.

We were whisked off in buses (only the Brits would stuff celebrities into buses) to Trooping the Colour at Horse Guards Parade where we were taken to our respective vehicles. Some of the guests were piled into double-deckers, each of which represented different decades of the Queen's reign, while David and I, with the six other dames and their partners, were escorted to our Jaguars. We were greeted by our charming, uniformed driver who gestured to a picnic basket and a bottle of champagne on the leather back seat. With that we were off.

I've been lucky enough to have seen and done a great many magical things in my eighty-three years, but being part of the Queen's Platinum Jubilee Pageant was an experience of a lifetime – better than any night at Studio 54. The morning's drizzle stopped and the rain graciously held off for the rest of the day. We travelled through Parliament Square, past Whitehall and up the Mall, which was lined with fluttering Union flags. It was spectacular. Our car followed Joan Collins's. By then she wore an elegant pale pink ensemble. As we rode along the Mall, the crowd yelled my name and waved. I waved back, thinking now I knew how the Queen felt when she made her way through London. Poor Prue Leith suffered the indignity of her Jag breaking down, so a gaggle of stewards had to push it for the remaining distance. She didn't let it get her down and continued waving to the crowds. Before I knew it, we arrived at Buckingham Palace where we watched the rest of the procession from stands on either side of the building. Two rows in front of us sat the then Prince of Wales, now King Charles III, and the Duchess of Cornwall, now Queen Camilla, beaming, joined by Princess Anne, the Duke and Duchess of Cambridge, William and Catherine, and their children, Prince George, Princess Charlotte and Prince Louis. None of them would sit still and poor Catherine spent a large part of the procession desperately telling them to be still. At one point, David returned from the loo to say that he'd seen Catherine with little Louis in a tight grasp under her arm as he kicked his legs out behind him. Royalty or not, you can always rely on children to play up when you need them to behave the most.

Our view of the procession was fantastic, and it made me feel incredibly proud to be British. We do eccentricity and pageantry very well in the UK, and there was so much of it that day. The procession started with the pomp of military marching bands, but then out came nuns playing tambourines, and tuba players wearing pith helmets. The world's largest human-operated puppet – a dragon called the Hatchling – sauntered along telling the story of a young princess meeting her destiny. A group of toy Corgis, the Queen's most beloved pets, walked in tandem, followed by a number of African wildlife puppets. I saw the Teletubbies and

Paddington Bear in the stands. I don't know if it's what the Queen had in mind for her big celebration, but I had a wonderful time – it was bright, bonkers and tremendously charming. The pageant featured a six-thousand-strong cast of volunteers, key workers and performers from the arts, and what a show they staged for us all – more of a joyful carnival rather than a stuffy procession.

After an hour or so, we noticed the Royal Family slip off and reappear on the famous Buckingham Palace balcony with the star of the show, the Queen herself, in a gorgeous apple-green outfit and matching hat. She gave us all a little smile and the crowds went bananas. As she went back inside, the proceedings came to a close. Feeling festively full of cheer, David and I said our good-byes, and I hopped on the heaving Underground and went home, beaming all the way.

In the same way that the Platinum Jubilee Pageant celebrated the Queen's seventy years on the throne, this object wraps up the end of my book, although not the end of my story. It is fitting that my final item is a wonderful hat by Piers Atkinson, who has already done so much in securing the legacy of my oeuvre through the Foundation's extensive cataloguing of my vast arch-ive going back to the mid-sixties. I have loved working with him and looking back through all of my archival treasures. I trust him completely to oversee the future of my work when I am gone. I don't know what lies ahead, but I don't plan on going anywhere soon. Like the Queen, I will work until I drop.

If I were to retire, I don't know what I'd do with my time – I think I'd rot.

Before writing this book, I never looked back. My ethos has always been to move forward, not dwell on the past or on difficult or painful periods. I have since emerged with an understanding that sometimes unpacking what's gone before can shift your per-spective in a positive way. This book has made me think of my family, and particularly my parents. Although I never wanted to know about my father's background, finding out about it has left me with a greater sympathy for him and a better grasp of why he led the quiet life he did. In a sense, he was a survivor. As for my mother, her influence on me has always been clear, and I know that if she were here she'd be helping me organize my work, cigarette in hand.

For now, I'd better get back to work. I always seem to have so much to do that sometimes it feels endless, but rather that than have nothing. What I have learnt about life is this: try to do everything to the best of your ability, and don't waste your life because it won't come back. Friends are important: they are life's double cream. When it comes to love, find an equal and don't settle until you do. You don't always know what you need in a partner until they arrive. Part of finding the right person is luck, but for God's sake, follow it when it falls at your door. If it's right, you won't need to sacrifice any part of who you are for it to blossom.

I hope I've proven that age is whatever you make of it. Darlings, you are never too old or wrinkly for a second or third act. Run at life head-on. Go to bed in your make-up, eat too much bread-and-butter pudding and always, *always* fill your world with colour.

Acknowledgements

There are so many people who have helped bring my memoir to life. Like all ambitious creative endeavours, it has involved a lot of collaboration and hard graft, and I am very grateful to everyone who has played a part. A special thank you to Ella Alexander, who conceived this book and has worked tirelessly with me on it for two years. Composing my story has been the most wonderful experience and I could not wish for anyone better to have written it with.

I am lucky to have such a fantastic team, all of whom have been instrumental in bringing *Iconic* to fruition. Thank you to my ever-patient co-workers Lottie McCrindell, Kelly Robinson and Hayley Cowling, as well as Director of the Zandra Rhodes Foundation and dear friend Piers Atkinson for your continued support and trusted ear. Thank you also to Lorna Glenister, who has been integral in forming the Zandra Rhodes Foundation.

I owe a great deal to my family, particularly my sister Beverley Haydon, who has always been there for me, and also to Harriet Nash, my wonderful grand-niece, who thoroughly researched the Rhodes family tree.

Thank you to my friends, former colleagues and contemporaries who generously gave up their time to be interviewed for this book, reliving past adventures we shared together: Andrew Logan, Alex McIntyre, Anne Babb, Barbara Brown, David Sassoon, Kevin Arpino, Gill Griffiths, Frances Diplock, Karen Bowen, Tim

Street-Porter, Celia Birtwell, Lynda Peck, Anna Sui, Bouke de Vries, Suzy Menkes, Sylvia Ayton, R. Couri Haye, Piers Gough, Maxine Smith, Manolo Blahnik, Richard Holley, Joan Quinn, John Waters and Pat Cleveland.

I want to acknowledge former staff members who were crucial to the growth and success of my business. Some have been named above, but you cannot be too grateful for people who have contributed so significantly to your life's work: Anne, Gill, Frances, Bouke, and, of course, Ben Scholten, who was with me through thick and thin, helping me design collections for over thirty-five years. Thank you to Ronnie Stirling, who invested in my boutique that made me internationally visible. Thank you to Richard, who started my American adventure, and also to Alex for putting up with me for thirteen years! I must expressly credit my former teacher Barbara Brown for putting me on the first rung of my career journey.

This book would not have been possible without the Transworld team, who have devoted so much of their time and expertise to making my memoir the best possible version of itself and getting it to you: Zoe Berville, Steph Duncan, Hazel Orme, Katrina Whone, Phil Lord, Vivien Thompson, Tom McWhirter, Isabella Ghaffari-Parker, Rosie Ainsworth, Irene Martinez Costa, Phil Evans, and the sales team. Thank you also to the incredible Rankin, who took my portrait for the cover of this book.

Throughout this process, my dearest friends have been endlessly supportive. I have already mentioned darling Andrew and David, but I would also like to give thanks to David Reeson and Rajeev Sethi. I am so grateful to all of you for sharing so much of your daily lives with me.

Finally, thank you to Salah, the love of my life.

Index